As a Catholic, I found it fasci̇̇̇̇ on a conversation about natuṛaḷ ḷaw ċọṇḍụċẹḍ ḅẏ aṇ ọụṭṣṭaṇḍ̇ịṇg gṛọụp of Lutheran scholars. The authors consider such topics as whether there really is a natural human capacity to identify and affirm valid moral norms, and whether belief in a moral law accessible to unaided reason is compatible with an acknowledgment of the devastating impact of sin on the human intellect as well as the human will. Lutherans will benefit from reading these essays, but so will everybody else.

Robert P. George
McCormick Professor of Jurisprudence
Princeton University

Natural law was a common idea among the Reformers and their heirs. There has been some fledgling reconsideration of this heritage in recent years in my own Reformed tradition, and it is very encouraging to see similar discussions taking place among Lutherans. *Natural Law: A Lutheran Reappraisal* helpfully wrestles with natural law from various historical and theological angles and also explores its relevance for several important social and ecclesiastical controversies of the present day. These essays on natural law—some enthusiastic, some cautious, others skeptical—are a wonderful contribution to the literature and should help to stimulate important conversations about this perennial issue for years to come.

David VanDrunen
Robert B. Strimple Professor of Systematic Theology and Christian Ethics
Westminster Seminary California

God's law is written in two ways and two places: not only in the words of revelation, but in our being, for we are made in God's image. For a long time, many Christians neglected or even denied this insight because of the mistaken idea that if the image of God can be obscured by sin, then for all practical purposes there is no natural law. How ironic, and how deadly to our common witness, that this common ground among all human beings, this universal prologue to the Gospel, should have become a battleground among Christians themselves. Catholic myself, I rejoice to see the rekindling of reflection on natural law among Lutherans, and I look forward to many interesting conversations.

J. Budziszewski
Professor of Government and Philosophy
University of Texas at Austin

Natural Law
A Lutheran
Reappraisal

About This Painting

In Europe, it is still not uncommon to see portraits of Martin Luther and Philip Melanchthon together, as in this 1543 double portrait by Lucas Cranach the Elder (1472–1553). Formerly, such portraits were frequently displayed in churches and homes.

After Luther's death, and no doubt due to the loss of his strong, persuasive influence, Melanchthon's willingness to compromise became even more apparent. Nevertheless, without the collaboration of Luther, Melanchthon, and many others, including countless faithful lay men and women, the Reformation as we know it today would not have been achieved.

It should be no surprise, then, that both Luther and Melanchthon are depicted together beneath the saving cross of Jesus Christ, above the Wittenberg Castle Church doors where in 1517 Luther had nailed his Ninety-five Theses. And we should also not forget that Luther and Melanchthon are buried not far from each other at the entrance to the choir of the same church, both waiting for that joyful day when Christ will return and bring all believers—both living and dead—into eternal life.

Natural Law
A Lutheran
Reappraisal

General Editor
Robert C. Baker

Editor
Roland Cap Ehlke

CONCORDIA PUBLISHING HOUSE • SAINT LOUIS

Copyright © 2011 Concordia Publishing House
3558 S. Jefferson Ave., St. Louis, MO 63118-3968
1-800-325-3040 • www.cph.org

Unless otherwise noted, Scripture quotations are from the ESV Bible® (The Holy Bible, English Standard Version®), copyright © 2001 by Crossway Bibles, a publishing ministry of Good News Publishers. Used by permission. All rights reserved.

Quotations marked KJV are from the King James or Authorized Version of the Bible.

Unless otherwise indicated, the quotations from the Lutheran Confessions are from *Concordia: The Lutheran Confessions*, second edition; edited by Paul McCain, et al., copyright © 2006 Concordia Publishing House. All rights reserved.

Unless otherwise indicated, the quotations from Luther's Works in this publication marked AE are from *Luther's Works*, American Edition (56 vols. St. Louis: Concordia, and Philadelphia: Fortress Press, 1955–1986).

Glossary adapted from *Lutheran Cyclopedia: A Concise In-Home Reference for the Christian Family.* Copyright © 1954 by Concordia Publishing House. All rights reserved.

Selections from the "Foreword" are from J. Daryl Charles, *Retrieving the Natural Law* © 2008 Wm. B. Eerdmans Publishing Company, Grand Rapids, Michigan. Reprinted by permission of the publisher, all rights reserved.

The HebraicaII font used to print this work is available from Linguist's Software, Inc., PO Box 580, Edmonds, WA 98020-0580, USA; telephone (425) 775-1130; www.linguistsoftware.com.

Cover painting: akg-images
Cover photos: ©iStockphoto.com

Manufactured in the United States of America

Library of Congress Cataloging-in-Publication Data
Natural law : a Lutheran reappraisal / general editor, Robert C. Baker editor, Roland Cap Ehlke.
    p. cm.
  ISBN 978-0-7586-2733-9
  1. Natural law. 2. Natural law—Religious aspects—Lutheran Church. I. Baker, Robert C. II. Ehlke, Roland Cap.
  K460.N3465 2011
  241'.2—dc22
                        2010046558

1 2 3 4 5 6 7 8 9 10   20 19 18 17 16 15 14 13 12 11

CONTENTS

NATURAL LAW AND EARLY LUTHERAN TRADITION

NATURAL LAW AND LATER LUTHERAN TRADITION

CONTRIBUTORS

Rev. Robert C. Baker (LCMS) received his MDiv at Concordia Seminary, Saint Louis, Missouri, and is pursuing an MS degree in health care ethics at Creighton University, Omaha, Nebraska.

Rev. Dr. Carl E. Braaten (ELCA) is professor emeritus of systematic theology at the Lutheran School of Theology in Chicago, Illinois, and is the former director of the Center for Catholic and Evangelical Theology.

Mr. Matthew E. Cochran (LCMS) received his MA at Concordia Theological Seminary, Fort Wayne, Indiana.

Rev. Dr. Albert B. Collver III (LCMS) is director of church relations and assistant to the president of The Lutheran Church—Missouri Synod.

Mr. Jacob Corzine (LCMS) received his MDiv at Concordia Theological Seminary, Fort Wayne, Indiana, and is a PhD candidate at Humboldt University, Berlin, Germany.

Dr. Adam S. Francisco (LCMS) is associate professor of history at Concordia University, Irvine, California.

Rev. Gifford A. Grobien (LCMS) is assistant pastor of Emmaus Lutheran Church in South Bend, Indiana, and is a PhD candidate at the University of Notre Dame, Notre Dame, Indiana.

Rev. Dr. Korey D. Maas (LCMS) is associate professor of theology and church history at Concordia University, Irvine, California.

Dr. Ryan C. MacPherson (ELS) teaches courses in American history, the history of science, and bioethics at Bethany Lutheran College, Mankato, Minnesota.

Dr. Thomas D. Pearson (ELCA) is associate professor of philosophy at the University of Texas—Pan American, Edinburg, Texas.

Rev. Prof. John T. Pless (LCMS) is assistant professor of pastoral ministry and missions at Concordia Theological Seminary, Fort Wayne, Indiana.

Rev. Dr. Carl E. Rockrohr (LCMS) is assistant professor of religion at Concordia University, Ann Arbor, Michigan.

Rev. Dr. Armin Wenz (SELK) is pastor at St. John's Lutheran Church and serves as guest professor at Lutherische Theologische Hochschule, Oberursel, Germany.

Rev. Dr. J. Larry Yoder, STS (NALC) is professor of religion at Lenoir-Rhyne University, Hickory, North Carolina, and pastor of Grace Evangelical Lutheran Church, Newton, North Carolina.

Prof. Marianne Howard Yoder (NALC) is adjunct professor of philosophy at Lenoir-Rhyne University, Hickory, North Carolina.

Rev. Prof. Roland Ziegler (LCMS) is assistant professor of systematic theology at Concordia Theological Seminary, Fort Wayne, Indiana.

Abbreviations for Documents in the Book of Concord

AC   Augsburg Confession

Ap   Apology of the Augsburg Confession

Ep   Epitome of the Formula of Concord

FC   Formula of Concord

LC   Large Catechism of Martin Luther

SA   Smalcald Articles

SC   Small Catechism of Martin Luther

SD   Solid Declaration of the Formula of Concord

Tr   Treatise on the Power and Primacy of the Pope

Citation Examples

AC XX 4 (Augsburg Confession, Article XX, paragraph 4)

Ap IV 229 (Apology of the AC, Article IV, paragraph 229)

FC SC X 24 (Solid Declaration of the Formula of Concord, Article X, paragraph 24)

FC Ep V 8 (Epitome of the Formula of Concord, Article V, paragraph 8)

LC V 32, 37 (Large Catechism, Part 5, paragraphs 32 and 37)

SA III I 6 (Smalcald Articles, Part III, Article I, paragraph 6)

SC III 5 (Small Catechism, Part III, paragraph 5)

Tr 5 (Treatise, paragraph 5)

FOREWORD

J. Daryl Charles

Director and Senior Fellow of the Bryan Institute for Critical Thought and Practice
Professor of Theology and Christian Thought, Bryan College

At the heart of the historic Christian tradition that spans two
millennia lies the baseline conviction of a shared nature in all human
beings, regardless of culture or location. It is a conviction shared by the
Early Church Fathers, the medieval fathers, the Reformation fathers, as
well as early-modern fathers. And it is one assumed by the apostle to the
Gentiles himself who, writing to Christians in the Imperial seat, assures
them that even pagan unbelievers who "do not have the law" nevertheless
"*by nature* do what the law requires." Thereby, Paul observes, with their
consciences bearing witness, they confirm the law to be "written on their
hearts" (Romans 2:14–15).

What is conspicuous to the theologian and moral philosopher is the
disappearance of this conviction in modern Protestant thought—a disappearance that surely requires an accounting. For this reason it is enor-
mously gratifying to witness renewed interest in the natural law, particu-

larly within a Lutheran context, where historically natural-law thinking has been at home and anchored in a sturdy theology of creation orders.

Different people and different cultures, of course, have used different means to describe what we call "the natural moral law." What the Chinese wisdom tradition calls the *Tao*, what has been depicted in Plato and Jesus as the "Golden Rule," what is embodied in the Ten Commandments as well as in the wisdom literature of the Old Testament, what St. Paul described as the "law written on the heart," and what the founders of the American republic referred to as the "laws of nature" (mirroring "nature's God") and "self-evident truths"—one could identify (at least, until recently) a *consensus* among human beings as to what constitutes good and evil, right and wrong, just and unjust. And this, notwithstanding our seemingly eternal propensity for excuse-making.

In theological terms, historic Christian belief distinguishes between special or particular revelation and that which is general in character. As distinct from divine revelation mediated through salvation-history, that which is common to all of human creation bears witness to "necessary truths"[1] and moral law. Deep within the human consciousness is found a "law" that we did not create, yet which we are constrained to obey. Because this "law" is rooted in human "nature"—which is to say, the *imago Dei*—nonreligious peoples' "conscience also bears witness" to moral reality, with their thoughts accusing (or excusing) them. This is none other than the language of the natural law. It is "nature" because it describes human *design* and *the way things are*; the fact that not everyone gives assent to the natural law does not assail its universal reality. It is a "law" because *nothing can change our essential nature*. The potential in humans for moral depravity, devastating as it may be, neither eliminates our ability to choose to do good (freedom) nor releases us from the sense of moral obligation (culpability) before the Creator (righteousness) or other human beings (the common good).

To the surprise of many, the notion of the natural law is resolutely affirmed in the writings of the Protestant reformers, who thought deeply about issues of legitimate authority, civil society, and the common good, and not merely matters of faith and ecclesiastical culture. However deeply entrenched a present-day bias against natural-law thinking would

---

1.   See in this regard Hadley Arkes, *First Things: An Inquiry into the First Principles of Morals and Justice* (Princeton: Princeton University Press, 1986).

seem to be among Protestant thinkers,[2] it cannot be attributed to the sixteenth-century reformers themselves. While it is undeniable that they sought to champion a particular understanding of grace and faith that in their estimation was tragically lacking,[3] their emphasis was *not* to the exclusion of modes of moral reasoning that were rooted in natural-law thinking. And as such, it is accurate to insist that the Reformation controversies with the Catholic Church were foremost *theological and not ethical* insofar as the reformers assumed the natural law as a moral-theological bedrock in their system and therein maintained continuity with their Catholic counterparts.

Both Luther and Calvin believed that the "Golden Rule," as expressed in both Plato and Jesus' teaching, was simply the restatement of a higher inviolable law or norm, rooted in a moral universe, by which human deeds are judged. Natural-law thinking is firmly embedded in the thought of Luther, who adopts the basic definition of natural law that had been set forth in Philip Melanchthon's commentary on Romans 2:15: the natural law is "a common judgment to which all men alike assent, and therefore one which God has inscribed upon the soul of each man."[4] In his 1525 treatise *How Christians Should Regard Moses*, the reformer distinguishes between the law of Moses, with its historically conditioned components, stipulations, and illustrations for theocratic Israel, and the natural law. "If the Ten Commandments are to be regarded as Moses' law, then Moses came too late,"[5] Luther can quip somewhat wryly, for "Moses agrees exactly with nature" and "what Moses commands is nothing new."[6] The law that stands behind the Ten Commandments, he notes emphatically, was in force prior to Moses from the beginning of the world and also among all the Gentiles. Luther's position is unambiguous: the moral norms that apply to all people, Christians and non-Christians, are the same; no two ethical standards can be thought to exist within the realm

---

2. On the Protestant neglect of the natural law, reasons for this neglect, and the ramifications for moral discourse, see Stephen J. Grabill, *Rediscovering the Natural Law in Reformed Theological Ethics,* Emory University Studies in Law and Religion (Grand Rapids: Eerdmans, 2006), and J. Daryl Charles, *Retrieving the Natural Law: A Return to Moral First Things,* Critical Issues in Bioethics (Grand Rapids: Eerdmans, 2008).

3. See, in this regard, Alister E. McGrath, *Iustitia Dei: A History of the Christian Doctrine of Justification* (Cambridge: Cambridge University Press, 1998).

4. *The "Loci Communes" of Philip Melanchthon*, ed and trans. Charles L. Hill (Boston: Meader, 1944), 112.

5. AE 47:89.

6. AE 35:168.

of divine revelation. Everyone, he observes, must acknowledge that what the natural law dictates in the human heart is right and true. There is no one, he insists, who does not sense the effects of the natural law. "Nature provides that we should call upon God. The Gentiles attest to this fact . . . [who] have it [the natural law] written on their heart. . . ."[7]

Luther's own position stands in radical opposition to leading voices in twentieth-century Protestant thought.[8] Unlike many of his spiritual offspring, Luther was perfectly content to allow the natural law and righteousness that comes by faith to stand side by side. In no way did he perceive general revelation as canceling out or undermining faith; as any good Thomist, Luther understood that grace perfects (rather than eliminates) nature. The natural law, hence, was presumed to be at work within all people and to be lodged *at the core of Christian social ethics*. Were this not the case, Luther observes, "one would have to teach and practice the law for a long time before it became the concern of conscience. The heart must also find and feel the law in itself."[9] Otherwise, it would not become a matter of conscience for anyone.

Surely Luther would have commended C. S. Lewis's argument regarding the *Tao* in *Mere Christianity* and *The Abolition of Man*. Not only does the natural law not contravene the ethics of Christ, Lewis insisted, but as an ethical standard it simply cannot be circumvented insofar as it is the source from which all moral judgments spring. Basic virtues such as reliability, faithfulness, justice, mercy, and generosity form the backbone of all "civilized" societies and are intuited as true, independent of human or religious experience. There is, then, common moral ground on which *all* people stand and by which we may engage in moral persuasion with *all*.

Lewis, of course, was well aware that Christians—and Protestants in particular—object to the natural law precisely because they believe it to detract from Christianity and the need for grace. But Lewis rejected this view. Far from contradicting Christian social ethics, the natural law is

---

7. AE 35:168. In his treatise *On Temporal Authority*, Luther urges Christians to participate intelligibly with unbelievers in the public square. Two such situations that potentially involve believer and unbeliever are the unlawful seizure of private property and resolving financial debts. Luther exhorts his readers to use both "the law of love" and "the natural law."

8. For example, Karl Barth, Paul Lehmann, Jacques Ellul, Helmut Thielecke, John Howard Yoder, and Stanley Hauerwas have been vehement in their rejection of natural-law thinking.

9. AE 40:97.

presupposed by it. And Lewis himself leaves little room for misunderstanding, offering the reader further rationale in *Christian Reflections*:

> The idea . . . that Christianity brought an entirely new ethical code into the world is a grave error. If it had done so, then we should have to conclude that all who first preached it wholly misunderstood their own message: for all of them, its Founder, His precursor, His apostles, came demanding repentance and offering forgiveness, a demand and an offer both meaningless except on the assumption of a moral law *already known* and *already broken*.[10]

The conclusion, for Lewis, is patent: "It is no more possible to invent a new ethics than to place a new sun in the sky. Some precept from traditional morality always has to be presumed. We never start from a *tabula rasa*: if we did, we should end, ethically speaking, with a *tabula rasa*."[11] There is wisdom, I think, in what Lewis is insisting—wisdom that counters some of the autonomy and false dichotomy lodged at the heart of contemporary Protestant ethics.

Already a generation ago the prevailing disjunctive mood of the Western cultural moment was captured by Richard John Neuhaus, who observed: "Whether in melancholia, in panic or in religious-revolutionary ecstasy, many experience our time as a sense of ending."[12] For Joseph Cardinal Ratzinger (Benedict XVI), and for his predecessor,[13] the sense of mental and spiritual dislocation characterizing contemporary culture is the by-product of "the darkening of truth."[14]

---

10. C. S. Lewis, "On Ethics," in *Christian Reflections*, ed. Walter Hooper (Grand Rapids: Eermans, 1967), 46 (emphasis added).

11. Notably in *The Abolition of Man*, Lewis presses the argument of objective moral truths: "This thing which I have called for convenience the Tao, and which others may called Natural Law . . . is not one among a series of possible systems of value. It is the sole source of all value judgment. If it is rejected, all value is rejected. If any value is retained, it is retained. The effort to refute it and raise a new system of value in its place is self-contradictory." C.S. Lewis, *The Abolition of Man* (New York: Macmillan, 1947), 56.

12. Richard John Neuhaus, *Time toward Home: The American Experiment as Revelation* (New York: Seabury, 1975), 1.

13. See especially John Paul II's encyclical *Veritatis Splendor* ("The Splendor of Truth"), published in 1993.

14. Joseph Cardinal Ratzinger, *Truth and Tolerance* (San Francisco: Ignatius, 2004), 66, 72.

It is by no means incidental that during the last century a renewal of natural-law thinking has often followed periods of totalitarian cruelty and intense societal upheaval. Thus, with the social and metaphysical disorientation that distinguishes the present cultural moment, we may rejoice in ecumenical dialogue on moral first things and the natural law—and particularly that which arises in a Lutheran context. Let the dialogue begin.

PREFACE

In many respects, *Natural Law: A Lutheran Reappraisal* was conceived during the creation of *Concordia: The Lutheran Confessions* (CPH, 2005, 2006), a contemporary update of the English translations of the Lutheran Confessions found in *Triglot Concordia: The Symbolical Books of the Ev. Lutheran Church* (CPH, 1921). That project was initiated by the Rev. Paul T. McCain, and was ably assisted by the Rev. Edward Engelbrecht as an effort to disseminate the cherished Book of Concord to a wider audience of Lutheran laypeople—a truly noble goal.

During that process, having been assigned as an editor to the daunting and imposing task of making Professor Dau's Oxbridge-sounding, collegiate-English translation of Melanchthon speak with a twenty-first century voice, I became particularly drawn to Melanchthon's line of argumentation in Ap XXIII, in which he contends against mandatory priestly celibacy on the basis of natural law and natural rights. As I had not studied natural law to any great depth in seminary, and because my own ignorance was exposed by this text that binds Lutheran pastors upon ordination, I began to look for reasons why arguments such as Melanchthon's are rarely made by Lutherans today.

This volume is partially the result of multiple conversations over the years about natural law, how it was interpreted by Luther and Melanchthon, the role it played in the theology of Lutheran orthodoxy, and possible applications of the doctrine for our own time. Yet this volume also represents an ongoing conversation of sometimes similar, sometimes divergent, but always thoughtful views about natural law in the Lutheran tradition. For those who are new to this conversation, a helpful study guide, as well as indices to the Scriptures and the Lutheran Confessions cited in this volume, can be found at the end of the book. In short, what you are about to read was borne out of a study of those Christian resources. Would that all of our conversations—about natural law and all Christian teachings—began and end there.

Robert C. Baker
General Editor

Natural Law
and Early Lutheran Tradition

A Lutheran Affirmation
of the Natural Law

Carl E. Braaten

Introduction

This essay deals with the law from the perspective of Lutheran theology. Other disciplines deal with dimensions of law from their own specialized perspectives, such as physics, sociology, jurisprudence, and the history of religions. Theology is concerned primarily with the biblical concept of the law of God the Creator and the various ways in which His law is revealed through the structures of creation and the history of redemption recorded in the Holy Scriptures. Lutheran theology understands that there are two sources of God's revelation: (1) through the way things are made (the law of creation) and (2) through the biblical history of salvation (the written Word of God).

THE BIBLICAL UNDERSTANDING
OF THE LAW

Christian theology gets its understanding of the law of God primarily from the Bible. *Torah* is the Hebrew word for law. In Judaism, the term came to refer specifically to the Pentateuch, the first five books of the Old Testament. Torah reveals the will of God; it stipulates the attitudes and actions necessary to sustain the covenant that God made with His people Israel. In the New Testament, the law is understood in new ways. Jesus showed great respect for the law, emphasizing the permanent validity of every "iota and dot" of the law (Matthew 5:18). He chastised the scribes and Pharisees for neglecting "the weightier matters of the law" (Matthew 23:23). Yet, Jesus was criticized for placing Himself above the law, even being willing to break the Sabbath laws and the rules of cleanliness, declaring all foods clean (Mark 7:19).

Some biblical scholars interpret Paul as setting aside the Law in favor of the Gospel. Such a misinterpretation led to the Antinomian heresy, held by Marcion and the Gnostic theologians in the ancient Church (Valentinus and Basilides), as well as by some of Luther's followers (e.g., Johannes Agricola) at the time of the Reformation. For the apostle Paul, the law was "holy" and "good" (Romans 7:12–16), showing sin to be sin and the need for Christ to save His people.

The question of whether Christians ought still to obey the law became highly controversial in the Early Church. Jewish Christians could not accept Paul's teaching that contrasted the righteousness of faith with the righteousness of works. James 2:24 expressed the feeling of many Jewish Christians, "You see that a person is justified by works and not by faith alone." An underlying issue was whether Gentile Christians were obligated to observe the Jewish law of circumcision. The Apostolic Council at Jerusalem ruled that what was required of Jews—to keep the law of circumcision—did not apply to Gentiles. Thus began two millennia of disputes concerning the right relationship between the Law and the Gospel. This relationship still continues to be a central issue of Christian belief and moral practice.

The Law in the Christian Tradition

The first Christian theologians had no doubt that the law of God was given to Moses in the form of the Ten Commandments. When the first theologians preached the Gospel of salvation to non-Jewish people, to Greeks and Romans, the nonbelievers asked what God had revealed of Himself. Some Church Fathers of the first five centuries of Christianity (e.g., Tertullian, Cyprian, Origen, and Augustine) acknowledged that the ancient Greek philosophers (Plato and Aristotle) had received some general knowledge of God "through the things He has made," as the apostle Paul wrote in Romans 1:19. This idea gave rise to the concept of natural law. Both Christian theologians and Greek philosophers taught that the universe is governed by law inscribed into the nature of things, which bears the imprint of their divine origin. Humans are endowed with reason and therefore can know what is in accord with the law of nature. We also have the capacity to choose between good and evil, that is, to obey or disobey the law of God written on our hearts to which our conscience bears witness (Romans 2:15).

This view of natural law was the common conviction of philosophers and theologians for some twenty-five hundred years, from Plato and Aristotle to Aquinas and Bonaventura, as well as from Luther and Calvin to Kant and Hegel. The bare bones of this common tradition entail the belief that the natural law is grounded in the eternal mind of God and knowable by human beings through reason and conscience. The unwritten natural law is universal, the same for everyone and everywhere. The universal natural law is the norm and standard of all laws enacted in society. This belief in natural law is the bedrock of the Constitution of the United States and the Universal Declaration of Human Rights adopted by the General Assembly of the United Nations in 1948. Thomas Jefferson's triad of inalienable rights—life, liberty, and the pursuit of happiness—is founded on the theory of natural law.

The Demise of Natural Law in Protestant Theology

One of the most surprising developments in the twentieth century was the nearly wholesale rejection of the natural law tradition in modern

Protestantism. It is a well-known historical fact that both Martin Luther and John Calvin (1509–1564) believed in natural law. The great Reformation historian, John T. McNeill, offered this conclusion from his studies: "There is no real discontinuity between the teaching of the reformers and that of their predecessors with respect to natural law. Not one of the leaders of the Reformation assails the principle."[1] Yet some theologians who claim to be followers of Martin Luther (1483–1546) and John Calvin regard the natural law as contrary to Scripture and inimical to evangelical theology. We will say more about this later.

We will leave it to historians to explain why the tradition of natural law has virtually collapsed in modern Protestant theology. Let me give one example. When the Task Force of the Evangelical Lutheran Church in America released *A Social Statement on Human Sexuality: Gift and Trust*,[2] in addition to relativizing the force of the passages in the Bible that condemn homosexual behavior, it made no reference to the natural law, which traditionally has been one of the strong pillars undergirding traditional Christian morality. Once the social statement succeeded in muting Scripture, which in our view clearly and forcefully regards homosexual activity as contrary to the revealed will of God, there was nothing left to stem the rising tide of the rampant Antinomianism endemic in contemporary culture. Theologians are doing the Church no favor when they reject the classical Christian endorsement of natural law.

The pressure to abandon the teaching of natural law does not arise from faithful biblical interpretation or from arguments internal to the logic of Christian theology; rather, it derives from developments in modern philosophy, especially utilitarianism[3] and positivism.[4] Combined with the loss of confidence in the truthfulness of Scripture and the competence of the Church to interpret it aright, there arose a widespread skepticism

---

1.   John T. McNeill, "Natural Law in the Teaching of the Reformers," *Journal of Religion* 26 (1946): 168.

2.   Evangelical Lutheran Church in America, *A Social Statement on Human Sexuality: Gift and Trust*. This statement, as amended, was adopted by a two-thirds majority at the ELCA's eleventh biennial Churchwide Assembly, August 19, 2009. Available online at http://www.elca.org/What-We-Believe/Social-Issues/Social-State ments/JTF-Human-Sexuality.aspx (accessed November 2, 2010).

3.   Utilitarianism is the theory of morality that asserts that what determines right from wrong conduct is the degree of its usefulness in providing pleasure and happiness.

4.   Positivism is a theory of knowledge that holds that all real knowledge must be based on sense perceptions subject to empirical verification.

about the ability of reason to discern a universal moral order in human society. That prepared the way for the administration of law to become subject to those who hold the instruments of power. The slogan "might makes right" expressed the prevailing sentiment within the totalitarian states ruled by Fascist and Communist ideologies. The totalitarian states under Hitler and Stalin manipulated laws to promote the self-interests of dictators who held a monopoly of power and disregarded the welfare of citizens. For the most part, the churches were powerless to mount any effective resistance; a measure of their impotence can be traced to their own lack of support for the validity of a universal natural moral order as the highest court of appeal.

A RECONSIDERATION OF NATURAL LAW

After World War II, churches and theologians began to have second thoughts about the relevance of natural law to Christian ethics. Churches realized that they share responsibility for the process and quality of law in society and the nation. But if there is no natural law to appeal to as common ground with those who do not acknowledge the authority of Scripture, what other foundation might there be to establish consensus and collaboration in a pluralistic secular society? The World Council of Churches and the Lutheran World Federation sponsored international conferences to explore the possibility of a rebirth of natural law as an antidote to legal positivism.[5] Might it be that Christian ethics and natural law are not in fact antithetical to each other?

I was a young professor of dogmatics at the Lutheran School of Theology at Chicago in the early 1960s when I was asked to lecture at various sites in Europe and Britain under the auspices of the Lutheran World Federation on the Lutheran doctrine of the law. That was the beginning of my long-standing effort to overcome the chief Protestant theological objections to natural law. Some of the usual objections include the following: Natural law does not take seriously the power of sin. Natural law seems to suggest that the original creation has not been totally corrupted by Adam's fall from grace. It assumes that human reason

---

5.   Legal positivism is a school of thought that maintains that laws are human constructs posited by social conventions and have no necessary connection with objective moral standards.

is not blinded by sin, rendering it incapable of perceiving the will of God through the way things are made. The Formula of Concord reiterates the teaching of the Apology of the Augsburg Confession that the image of God in humankind (*imago Dei*) is not so totally destroyed by sin and the fall as to leave human beings totally incapable of discerning the difference between what is right and wrong, good and evil, true and false.[6] The natural law is essential to the human quest for justice and in defense of human rights. The Church needs to respect the common search for justice and law in an imperfect world and to promote cooperation between Christians and non-Christians in all spheres of public life.

Natural Law and the Orders of Creation

Catholic moral theology has shown no such hesitation to support natural law as has generally been the case in Protestant ethics. This helps to explain why the Roman Catholic Church has produced a comprehensive body of social teachings on most issues of common human concern. Even when we do not agree with the Roman Catholic application of natural law in every case of moral dispute, there is much to admire about a church that knows where it stands on the critical issues of the day and offers cogent arguments to explain its teachings. The sources of Catholic moral theology include the Bible, the ancient creeds and councils of the Church, and the fathers and doctors of classical Christianity. In addition, it has incorporated the tradition of natural law that began with the Greek philosophers into its arsenal of theological argumentation.

The concern of some Protestant theologians (particularly those in the school of Karl Barth; 1886–1968) that natural law stems from pagan metaphysics rather than biblical revelation is overcome in Catholic moral theology by integrating it into the dogmatic theology of revelation and Christology. Natural law does not function in an autonomous realm independent of the eternal law in the mind of God. The God who

---

6.   After the fall, human beings lost their freedom to relate positively to God, that is, in spiritual and divine matters. This was asserted against Pelagianism. Yet, humans retain something of their reason and free will to know and discern the difference between good and evil with respect to earthly temporal matters. This was asserted against Manichaeanism.

designed the structures of the world to correspond to human reason is the living God of the Bible, so that we are not confronted by two sets of morality, one for Christians and a different one from non-Christians.

Lutheran theology similarly has integrated natural law into a biblical theology of creation. The Lutheran doctrine of the "orders of creation" maintains that Christians, along with all other human beings, exist in a framework of universal structures that are there prior to and apart from biblical revelation and the Church. God placed all human beings in particular structures of existence, such as ethnicity, race, sexuality, family, work, and governance. The law of God and His commandments are revealed through these common forms of human existence and function apart from the Gospel and faith in Christ. Luther claimed that God does not need to have Christians as magistrates; the ruler does not need to be a Christian in order to rule; it is sufficient that he be in command of his reason. Certainly, after the fall, the orders of creation are subject to the conditions of sin. Still, God preserves them as media through which He addresses the conscience of all human beings. Spanning the entire spectrum of creation, whether in terms of politics, religion, or sexuality, God is present and active through the law written on human hearts.

The doctrine of the orders of creation goes hand in glove with the doctrine of the two kingdoms as well as the important distinction between Law and Gospel. Christian theology practiced by Lutherans is treated as a fine art of drawing the proper distinction between two quite different ways that God is active in the world to achieve His ends. Based on a twofold revelation of God, universal (general) and particular (special), the whole of theology is composed of a series of necessary distinctions, such as God hidden (*absconditus*) and revealed (*revelatus*), creation and redemption, the left hand and the right hand of God (the two kingdoms), the old creation and the new, being righteous and yet sinful (*simul iustus et peccator*), Law and Gospel, *opus alienum* and *opus proprium* (the strange and proper work of God's love). There is one God, but He relates to the world and humanity in two different modes of activity. The God of the Gospel is the same God who is at work through the Law in the secular realm where believers in Christ share common ground with others of different belief systems.

There is no such thing as a secular world from which God is absent. Christians are not commissioned by God to introduce Him to the world for the first time. God is always present in the world beforehand through the law engraved in the nature of the things He creates. God is universally present as the authority that drives people to do what they must do to sustain life, to administer justice, to play by the rules, and to care for their families and communities. Luther spoke of the orders of creation— family, state, or work—as the masks of God (*larvae Dei*), masks of the hidden living God. This is God incognito, whose power we humans experience in the demands He makes upon us in daily life.

KARL BARTH'S REJECTION OF NATURAL LAW

Karl Barth held that Christian ethics had no use for the natural law; he also led the assault on the Lutheran doctrine of the orders of creation. What did Barth offer in its place? He wrote that Christian ethics "is always an individual command for the conduct of this man, at this moment and in this situation; a prescription for this case of his; a prescription for the choice of a definite possibility of human intention, decision and action."[7] This kind of thinking is the theological launching pad of the infamous "situation ethics" popularized by Joseph Fletcher.

Barth had his followers. One was a French professor of law, Jacques Ellul, who wrote *The Theological Foundations of Law*.[8] Following Barth, he argued for a Christological basis of all law and justice. This represents a massive confusion of Law and Gospel and of the two kingdoms of God. The problem with a mono-Christological basis of natural law is that only Christians are privy to it; hence, no common ground exists, no point of contact between Church and world. This results either in a triumphalist theology of glory according to which Christians must seek to dominate the public square or in a sectarian withdrawal into Christian communes in which members pledge to live by the Sermon on the Mount.

If the secular world were void of God's presence apart from the revealed Word of God in Christ and the Bible, then a coalition of true believers would be needed to invade the public square and fill it with their Christian convictions of what is right and wrong, good and bad. This assumes that Christians are the only ones in the position to know

---

7.   Karl Barth, *Church Dogmatics: The Doctrine of Creation* 3/4 (Edinburgh: T. & T. Clark, 1961), 3:11–12.

8.   Jacques Ellul, *The Theological Foundations of Law*, trans. by C. Hanks (Grand Rapids: Eerdmans, 1985).

what God intends to accomplish in the world of politics, economics, and cultural life. Knowing the Bible and holding church membership would become the Christians' litmus test on what political party to support or what candidate to vote for. Luther had a different opinion; he said he would rather be governed by a wise Turk (a Muslim) than a stupid Christian.

The Barthian view was championed by one of my teachers at Harvard Divinity School, Paul Lehmann. He renounced natural law in favor of what he called "koinonia ethics."[9] Following Barth, Lehmann rejected the idea "that there is a common link between the believer and the non-believer grounded in the nature of human reason which enables both believer and nonbeliever to make certain ethical judgments and to address themselves in concert to commonly acknowledged ethical situations."[10] This is a complicated way of saying that only Christians know what is best to do in a particular situation that calls for a moral decision.

A similar view is promoted by Stanley Hauerwas, who writes: "Christian ethics does not have a stake in 'natural law' understood as an independent and sufficient morality."[11] I would agree that an appeal to natural law by itself does not provide a "sufficient morality," for that would mean to separate it completely from theology, treating it as an autonomous resource for ethical discourse. Our claim is that while not in itself sufficient, natural law has a necessary role to play in Christian ethics, political philosophy, and legal theory.

The common criticism of natural law theory is that it is a medieval relic, based on a rigid non-historical view of the world, determined by absolute laws and immutable orders that preexist in a timeless realm removed from the flux of historical change and societal developments. Contemporary advocates of the natural law—Catholic and Protestant— cannot be so easily dismissed by such a caricature. The writings of scholars such as John Courtney Murray, Robert P. George, Russell Hittinger, Stephen J. Grabill, J. Daryl Charles, and David VanDrunen exhibit the

---

9.   Paul Lehmann, *Ethics in a Christian Context* (New York: Harper & Row, 1963).

10.   Lehmann, *Ethics in a Christian Context*, 148.

11.   Stanley Hauerwas, "Natural Law, Tragedy and Theological Ethics," in *Truthfulness and Tragedy: Further Investigations in Christian Ethics* (South Bend, IN: University of Notre Dame Press, 1983), 58.

power of natural law arguments to deal with the critical life-and-death issues within the wider culture.[12]

WHY THE NATURAL LAW IS NECESSARY

No contemporary thinker is interested in a wooden repristination of the natural law that is tied necessarily to the particular metaphysical foundations in the Thomistic–Aristotelian synthesis. The history of natural law shows a wide variety of interpretations and applications. But they all have some elements in common. They all oppose cultural relativism, the notion that laws are mere moral conventions that vary among societies, with no transcendent ontological claim to being universally valid and binding. To the contrary, those who hold to the natural law believe that for a law to be just, it must conform to the structure of reality itself and not depend on the shifting opinions and preferences of human beings. The law must be the same for all human beings and at all times, so that if murder is morally wrong in America, it is equally so in Asia and Africa. If torture is to be condemned as evil in Jerusalem, it must be equally so in London and Tehran. The United Nations' Declaration of Human Rights formulates rules with respect to freedom and equality that are binding on all nations and peoples, not because of any majority vote, but because of an inherent correspondence between reason and nature. That is what is meant by saying that the law is "written on the hearts" (Romans 2:25) of all human beings.

This brief essay cannot flesh out the full extent of what it means to incorporate natural law into the body of Christian ethics. Such a project entails a number of moves. The first calls for clearing of the ground: there is nothing in the Lutheran confessional documents that speaks against the natural law. They clearly acknowledge what the Scriptures teach,

---

12. John Courtney Murray, *We Hold These Truths: Catholic Reflections on the American Proposition* (New York: Sheed and Ward, 1960). Robert P. George, *In Defense of Natural Law* (Oxford: Clarendon, 1999). Russell Hittinger, *The First Grace: Rediscovering the Natural Law in a Post-Christian World* (Wilmington, DE: ISI Books, 2003). Stephen J. Grabill, *Rediscovering the Natural Law in Reformed Theological Ethics* (Grand Rapids: Eerdmans, 2006). J. Daryl Charles, *Retrieving the Natural Law: A Return to Moral First Things* (Grand Rapids: Eerdmans, 2008). David VanDrunen, *Natural Law and the Two Kingdoms* (Grand Rapids: Eerdmans, 2010).

namely, that the Gentiles are able to know the law of God through the works of creation by means of reason and conscience.

Second, a high evaluation of the natural moral Law of God does not detract from the integrity and uniqueness of the Gospel of God. The Gospel is totally other and exclusively given to the Church of Christ to make known to the nations for the salvation of the world. The Gospel is unlike the Law; it is not "written on human hearts" from the outset. Rather, it comes from the outside, always by means of the external Word (*verbum externum*).

Third, a Christian theological affirmation of natural law will be different from a purely philosophical assessment, because the idea that the original creation and human reason have been deeply affected by sin is based on biblical revelation, to which philosophy can make no appeal.

Fourth, Christian ethics based on the Bible will necessarily include the perspective of eschatology, based on the idea of the kingdom of God in the message of Jesus. Natural law or the law of creation (*lex creationis*) refers to the way God orders the world between the times, between the fall and the parousia. In the eschatological kingdom of God, the earthly orders of creation will be transfigured into a new creation of celestial glory as it is portrayed in the Book of Revelation by symbols that seem opaque to ordinary reason. Natural law cannot go there. Its use is limited to the conditions of historical existence on the way to the final judgment and consummation. Its validity is penultimate, but nonetheless to be taken with utmost seriousness.

CONCRETE APPLICATIONS

We might ask, what is the value of natural law in reaching a moral judgment with respect to some of the most controversial issues in today's Church and society? If space permitted, we would wish to demonstrate the applicability of natural law arguments regarding a host of hot-button issues, such as capital punishment, "just war" theory, weapons of mass destruction, abortion, euthanasia, eugenics, cloning, stem cell research, universal health care, and gays in the military. When the Church and its officials make moral pronouncements on any of these topics, it makes no sense if all they do is preach Christ or quote the Bible. Their position statements will be persuasive to non-Christians solely on the condition that they are backed by reasonable arguments intelligible to those who do not happen to believe in Christ and the Bible. The age of Christian society is past, when declarations of the Church could be announced to the world with unquestioned authority.

For many churches today, homosexuality has become a critical moral issue. In the light of natural law and a plain sense reading of the Bible, homosexual behavior can easily be seen as a disordering of God's creation. That homosexual behavior is contrary to nature is knowable by reason, and that it is morally wrong is grasped by conscience. It is amazing that the mainline Protestant churches seem to give greater weight to modern cultural trends than to two thousand years of Christian consensus on the ethics of human sexuality.

When post-Enlightenment movements in philosophy and theology rejected the natural moral law and postmodern hermeneutics applied its critical methods to the Bible, the way was paved for moral relativism and Antinomianism. The dike was breached. Previously condemned patterns of behavior were now considered licit in some situations, all depending on the quality of the relationships. The twin authorities of natural law and revealed truth collapsed, creating great uncertainty among Christians about whether they share a consensus regarding the difference between right and wrong, good and evil.

It is well known that millions of non-Christians and people in non-Western cultures who do not read the Bible or believe in Christ oppose same gender sexual relations. By the light of reason, human beings the world over, since the dawn of human civilization and across all cultures, have known that the male and female sexual organs are made for different functions. Humans know what they are; they are free to act in accordance with them or in opposition to them. Humans' reason and conscience are illuminated by the law of nature written on their hearts by God the Creator. No books on anatomy, psychology, or sociology are needed to teach people what they already know by nature.

When God created the world and human beings, He designed all things to obey certain laws. There is the law of gravity; God invented it. There is the second law of thermodynamics. Scientists discovered it, but it is part of God's original design. There is the law called *suum cuique* (to each his own, to each what rightfully belongs to him) on which the principle of justice is based. The Golden Rule is universal, "Do unto others as you would have them do to you." People do not need to learn from the Bible that cheating is wrong, whether it is cheating on one's spouse or in a game. Nor do people first learn from the Bible what sexual organs are made for. Male and female sexual organs are complementary. The human race depends for its very existence on males and females doing what comes naturally. Same gender sex is procreative of nothing.

Biblical scholars say that there are seven explicit passages in the Bible that condemn homosexual acts as contrary to the will of God. This used to be sufficient to settle the matter for churches that claim that their teachings are derived from Scripture. But for many Christians today, this no longer settles the matter. Why not? The answer is that that they no longer hold to what the natural law, transparent to reason, tells us about human sexuality. The biblical strictures against homosexual behavior are true because they perfectly set forth God's creative design for human beings and their bodies. The law of creation written into the nature of things is the antecedent bedrock of the natural moral law, knowable by human reason and conscience.

2

What Is the Natural Law?

Medieval Foundations and Luther's Appropriation

Gifford A. Grobien

Introduction

Natural law refers to a commanding principle in a substance, which regulates all substances of the same kind. Questions about the source, scope, and force of this principle, however, have suggested various refinements to this definition in different cultures and eras. The task of this essay is to define the natural law, more specifically, according to Martin Luther and the Scholastic tradition he received. Because of the foundational divergence of modern natural law doctrine from its medieval and Reformation-era precursors, it is necessary to step back intellectually through the modern era in order better to appreciate the position of Luther and the medievalists.

After a brief explanation of this modern divergence, the first main part of this essay describes a general account of the Western medieval Scholastic theological tradition of the natural law, the tradition Luther inherited and out of which he operated.[1] The second main part of this essay describes Luther's understanding of the natural law, highlighting differences from the medieval understanding. Throughout I argue that, while reason and the given structures of nature are foundational to the natural law, a substantive, useful construction of the natural law cannot be developed by rational appeal or scientific observation. Instead, such a construction is informed and elaborated by the authorities, values, and concepts of one's culture and tradition. Consequently, while the natural law provides a means for engaging non-Lutheran or non-Christian traditions in moral or theological matters, much of this engagement, at least initially, must uncover differences in the traditions' assumptions about reason, authority, and values, and then work to build commonality in these areas as a foundation for apologetics, ethics, or policy discussion.

The Natural Law in the Modern Era

Since the seventeenth century, Western natural law thinkers have generally understood the natural law to be a moral order built, in some way, into human nature, not conditioned by culture or religion, from which a set of universal norms can be rationally derived. This order might have been established by a creator, but the necessity of a creator is

---

1.   I rely heavily on Jean Porter's work, *Natural and Divine Law* (Grand Rapids: Ee-rdmans, 1999) and *Nature as Reason: A Thomistic Theory of the Natural Law* (Grand Rapids: Eerdmans, 2005), for the account of the medieval Scholastic natural law tradition included in this essay. I do so because she is especially concerned with interpreting the Scholastics in their historical and intellectual context, and I find credible her criticism that many contemporary natural law theorists misunderstand the Scholastics because they overlook the historical and intellectual context of twelfth- and thirteenth-century Western Europe. For the most important alternative view of Thomas Aquinas's teaching on the natural law, see John Finnis, *Aquinas: Moral, Political, and Legal Theory* (Oxford: Oxford University Press, 1998). By medieval Scholastics, Porter means, primarily, theologians and canon lawyers, not secular lawyers, who understood the natural law in a fundamentally different way. See *Natural and Divine Law*, 47.

denied.[2] This conceptual elimination of the necessity of God is a modern development that began with Hugo Grotius (1583–1645) and continued with Thomas Hobbes (1588–1679), John Locke (1632–1704), and other Enlightenment thinkers. Grotius said that the intrinsic principle of the natural law does not depend on a theological account of divine reason or will.[3]

This line of argument was taken up by most Enlightenment thinkers after Grotius. They sought a foundation for law that would appeal to all people, despite the growing diversity of religious opinions in the Reformation and post-Reformation era. As public and private religious authority was breaking down, political philosophers introduced a concept of natural law that was intrinsic to nature, not relying on God or any particular idea of Him. Furthermore, in an age of increasing exploration and encounter with non-Christian and non-European societies, such a foundation for the natural law also promised a method for interacting with other cultures, for understanding, negotiating, and judging each other's laws and norms.[4] By positing nature as an autonomous source of law, modern thinkers argued that a naturally based body of norms could be accessed through reason, offering a systematic account of morality and law that was scientific, secure, and undoubted.[5] The authority and clarity of the natural law depended on the human capacity to comprehend it and implement it through human law.

This modern natural law theory generally operates out of the assumptions that the natural law is autonomous (even if one personally believes it to be an expression of divine law), that it is universally accessible by reason, and that several or more precepts can be systematically derived and received as binding on all people in all eras and conditions. Disagreement in moral conclusions is due to a failure to perceive the law or a refusal to recognize it, not to any deficiency in the scope or pervasiveness of

---

2.   Patrick D. Hopkins, "Natural Law," in *Encyclopedia of Philosophy*, 2nd ed., ed. Donald M. Borchert (Detroit: Macmillan Reference USA, 2006), 6:510.

3.   Hugo Grotius, *Prolegomena to the Law of War and Peace*, trans. Francis W. Kelsey (Indianapolis: Bobbs-Merrill, 1957), 8–11.

4.   Porter, *Natural and Divine Law*, 27–29, 31–32; Hopkins, "Natural Law," 510.

5.   For example, Hobbes argued that reason is a science dealing with proper terminology, syllogistic connection between facts, and the consequences of these connections. Through the science of moral philosophy, Hobbes derived nineteen laws of nature that are immutable and acceptable to all, because they are logical conclusions from the first, fundamental law of nature. See Thomas Hobbes, *Leviathan*, ed. C. B. Macpherson (London: Penguin, 1968), 115, 189–90, 215–17.

the natural law.[6] Significantly, in this paradigm, natural law and divine law have been separated. The natural law has become autonomous and, through basic reflection on it, provides a standard from which to develop human law. Divine law, if it exists, is supplementary, accessible only to some via revelation, and unnecessary. Divine law becomes merely positive law, God's expression of or supplement to the primordial natural law, and is similar to human positive law.

THE MEDIEVAL SCHOLASTIC NATURAL LAW TRADITION

Looking back to the Scholastics, a completely different connection is made: the divine law is affiliated foundationally more with natural law than with human law. The modern mind-set may consider it contradictory to equate the divine law with the natural law, if it understands natural to mean that which is given or perceived apart from revelation. Yet, for the Scholastics, the natural law is not an established order that, once built into creation, operates autonomously from divine direction. Rather, the natural law is the continued participation of creation—each kind according to its nature—in the divine law. It is inconceivable for the Scholastics to consider a natural law operating somehow apart from the

---

6.   I do not mean to suggest that there has been no refinement, variation, or development of natural law theory since the seventeenth century, but that the autonomous conception of the natural law has been a foundational characteristic in prevailing theories since that time. Depending on the theory, this moral order can be grasped either (1) through reason or (2) through the intrinsic structure of natural design. (1) If the moral order is understood through reason, the good is self-evident or derived through rational reflection, and one should act in a way to bring about this good. By reason, a property unique to the human person among all other earthly creatures, a person discerns those basic precepts that should govern human life. (2) If the theory holds that moral order is grasped through the design of nature, this design has moral significance and suggests right action. Morality is not perceived by reason, but through the design and inclinations of the prerational human nature. In this conception, reason works instrumentally: it is used to consider which action or course of actions will result in obtaining the natural good. In some variations of this conception, action in accordance with the natural law is prerational. That is to say, the natural law operates in a realm prior to and apart from reason, while reason presumably involves itself with speculative and pragmatic matters. Whether the theory is of the rational kind or the natural design kind, the modern conception of the natural law typically can be described by a comprehensive set of precepts or commands. See Porter, *Nature as Reason*, 28–40.

divine reason and purpose. The divine and the natural are closely related, even identical, while positive law can vary by culture and convention, yet still be an acceptable derivation from the natural law. Divine and natural law are both "preconventional."[7] Human beings properly rely on the precepts of divine and natural law to serve as the foundation and the boundary for human law, which may vary widely without violating the natural law. Various conventions may be equally valid expressions of the natural law.

Because they understand the divine and natural laws to be closely connected, the Scholastics readily assume the equivalence between the natural law and the moral law taught in Scripture. As the authoritative revelation of God, Scripture proclaims the will of God—including the divine law. While modern thinkers may be inclined to consider scriptural law to be positive law because of its explicit promulgation, the Scholastics distinguish scriptural law from positive law because Scripture is not of human origin or custom. Divine moral law is the explicit content and expression of the natural law and proceeds from the same source.[8]

The Scholastics also differ from modern thinkers in the method by which they treat the natural law. While a modern thinker might consider it important methodologically to consider the natural law by pure reason or the plain observation of the natural, the Scholastics treat the natural law as they do all fields of study—that is, by reading, reflecting on, and responding to authoritative texts on law and doctrine handed down from antiquity. The natural law is not deduced from pure reason operating in a reflective vacuum, but learned from prior respected articulations that also teach the natural law. This may be the most difficult point for the modern thinker to understand, but the Scholastics saw no contradiction in considering the natural law in the context of the deep tradition of Christian theology and classical jurisprudence. They received all expressions of truth, regardless of the sources or methods of expression. They were not concerned with culling the layers of tradition and commentary that had accumulated through the centuries. On the contrary, the Scholastics received those contributions and sought to harmonize them into a cohesive, systematic body of thought.[9]

---

7. Porter, *Natural and Divine Law*, 77–79.
8. Porter, *Natural and Divine Law*, 134.
9. Porter, *Natural and Divine Law*, 41–48. The Scholastic method typically involved some kind of statement of a topic or problem, excerpts from authorities express-

Therefore, even in considering the properties of preconventional nature and what it commands, the Scholastics relied on a body of thought—we may even say conventional thought—to inform them. Nature itself could only be defined in certain basic, foundational ways; however, the sources for this definition were not restricted to the natural. In other words, in treating the natural law, although the Scholastics were attempting to understand and define only the natural, they did not limit themselves only to natural sources in understanding this truth.

The Scholastics relied on standard compilations of these textual authorities. In the field of law, the standard was Gratian's *Decretum*, a digest of texts assembled in the early twelfth century. The *Decretum* harmonized various ancient sources on law and became the standard basis for commentary on law from the mid-twelfth century.[10] Besides the textual authorities, Scripture also stood as the supreme authority. Scholastics included Scripture in their arguments, integrating it into their method of dialectic, while recognizing its authoritative place. In this way, Scripture conversed with other authorities, yet also stood above them.

The Scholastic doctrine of the natural law may be outlined according to the following three characteristics: (1) the distinction of preconventional norms—both natural and divine—from human custom and law; (2) the recognition of several kinds of natural law, due to the different definitions of "natural" in the source texts;[11] (3) the dialectical method of reflection on the natural law, consisting of the interaction between nature, reason, and Scripture,[12] which suggests that the purpose of the natural law is to judge proposed or existing rules and conventions with respect to their natural origin, and to defend (or refute) their rationality and morality on that basis.[13]

---

ing various opinions, and a resolution or harmonization offered by the scholar, perhaps with particular responses to the more challenging or divergent authorities.

10. J. Rambaud-Buhot, "Decretum of Gratian (Concordia Discordantium Cano-num)," *New Catholic Encyclopedia*. 2nd ed. (Detroit: Gale, 2003), 6:420–21. The excellence of the *Decretum* is due not only to the vast number of texts included but also to the unifying way in which the texts are presented.

11. Porter, *Nature as Reason*, 11–12.

12. Porter, *Natural and Divine Law*, 51.

13. Porter, *Natural and Divine Law*, 36.

Preconventional Norms: Divine and Natural

The Scholastic understanding of preconventional norms was the category linking the natural and the divine, as distinct from conventional human norms and customs. This integrity between the divine and the natural suggested one definition of the natural law for the Scholastics: it was the participation of the natural (through some property generic to each species) in divine reason.[14] The distinction between the preconventional and the conventional does not mean there is no interconnection between them. Human conventions are particular determinations and expressions of the preconventional. Conventions are informed by the natural and are an expression of the natural. A good convention is one expression of the natural, but not necessarily the *only* one. A convention is not a spontaneous, necessary manifestation of the natural law, but the natural law applied in a particular place and time and under certain conditions.[15]

Furthermore, as a scriptural doctrine, the natural law was defined as the law of God written on the hearts of all people (Romans 2:14–15), as the Golden Rule (Matthew 7:12 and Luke 6:31), and, less frequently, as the law of love (Romans 13:8–10; Luke 10:27).[16] Because of the disruptive effects of sin, the natural law is illumined by revelation in the Ten Commandments. Scripture and the natural law are not equivalent, because revelation includes other truths differing from the moral law, such as the ceremonial laws and the Gospel, but scriptural moral principles are the basic expression of the natural law. Therefore, the moral principles of the Ten Commandments were widely understood by the Scholastics to be fundamental precepts stemming from the natural law. Because of the continuity of the natural law with the divine law, the Scholastics were not limited to deducing the precepts of the natural law by rational reflection alone, but they gleaned the precepts from the Scriptures.[17]

---

14. Thomas Aquinas, *Summa Theologica*, I–II.91.2
15. Aquinas, *Summa Theologica*, I–II.91.3.
16. Porter, *Natural and Divine Law*, 142; Aquinas, *Summa Theologica*, I–II.103.1 ad 1.
17. Porter, *Natural and Divine Law*, 129–36. See also Aquinas for comparison to the Golden Rule, *Summa Theologica* I–II.94.3 ad 1; for comparison to the Ten Commandments, I–II.100.3; for the use of the Ten Commandments to make up for defects in reason after the fall, 99.2 ad 2.

VARIETY OF THE NATURAL

How, then, do the natural aspects of the human person have moral significance? Or, to put it another way, to what extent does human nature actually inform moral action? The natural structures, inclinations, and limits of human nature suggest both what is foundational to human action and what its limitations are.[18] Thomas Aquinas (1225–1274) says, "All those things to which man has a natural inclination, are naturally apprehended by reason as being good, and consequently as objects of pursuit."[19] That is, to whatever a person tends by nature, whether a basic bodily need, the desire of the senses, or the fulfillment of the intellect, are natural goods. Of themselves, those tendencies and desires have no *moral* force. So, for example, eating fulfills a physical good—the nourishment of the body. Enjoying music or relishing the taste of chocolate are goods of the physical senses. Enjoying companionship is a good of the soul. None of these desires in itself is a moral good, and depending on the circumstances, may be either morally good or evil. Reason, the unique natural gift to the human "animal," provides actual moral force to these activities. Reason commands the natural activities of the human person in a moral way. The conditions, intention, and end of the act—qualities associated with reason and the will—qualify an action with moral goodness. In this sense, natural inclinations suggest possible good actions, thereby offering the possibilities and boundary for action. Reason directs the will to choose what is morally good from among the possibilities of action, discerning from intention, conditions, and end. Thus, by offering these natural possibilities and boundaries to action, nature informs action.[20]

---

18. There are also limits on the Scholastic understanding of what is natural. Naturalness does not include mere essence or fact apart from some kind of arrangement or purpose. Creation, as an expression of God's mind and will, is orderly, with various species working in harmony with one another; each species is created with its unique structure and inclinations aiming toward its purpose and serving as principles of action. Nature, then, for the Scholastics, assumes some kind of intelligibility. Nature is essence directed toward the purpose of the species. See Porter, *Natural and Divine Law*, 77–78.

19. Aquinas, *Summa Theologica* I–II.94.2. English translations are taken from the edition translated by the Fathers of the English Dominican Province (New York: Benzinger Bros., 1947–1948), found online at http://www.ccel.org/ccel/aquinas/summa.html.

20. For a more extensive explanation of the Scholastic understanding of the link between the prerational nature and human action, see Porter, *Nature as Reason*,

More directly, for human beings, reason itself is not sharply distinguished from the natural. While animals act according to the order of nature through instinct, the human person acts by reflecting on his possible options, informed by inclination and senses, and chooses the option that seems to accomplish a good purpose. This process of reasoning is natural. Reason differs from other aspects of nature, such as physical or bodily structure or instinct. Yet reason is considered part of nature because it is a property enjoyed by all human beings according to their species.[21]

Thus, if that natural law is the participation of the natural in divine law, reason, then, as the unique, natural gift to human beings, is the way human beings participate in the divine law. Right reason comprehends the law of God and commands actions pertaining to the law. In this way, the Scholastics also developed an understanding that reason itself is the natural law, for it is a property of human nature that comprehends law and directs action.[22] The natural law as reason can be further understood as the capacity to make judgments, and conscience is the natural capacity of the human person in understanding both the natural and revealed law.[23]

Thomas Aquinas took it as self-evident that the first principle of practical reason—and, thus, of the natural law—is that good is to be done and evil avoided.[24] This may seem extremely general, to the point of being unusable, but the generality is in accordance with the universal and preconventional aspects of the natural law. That good should be done and evil avoided is the most general moral precept, and it requires more specific precepts to command moral action in context. To put it another way, reason participates in the divine law most foundationally in recognizing that there is a good, and that it should be pursued. In this narrow sense, only human beings are under the natural law, for only

---

68–82.

21. Porter, *Natural and Divine Law*, 86.

22. Porter, *Natural and Divine Law*, 86–89.

23. Porter, *Nature as Reason*, 11–12.

24. "'Good' is the first thing that falls under the apprehension of the practical reason, which is directed to action: since every agent acts for an end under the aspect of good. Consequently the first principle of practical reason is one founded on the notion of good, viz. that 'good is that which all things seek after.' Hence this is the first precept of law, that 'good is to be done and pursued, and evil is to be avoided'" (Aquinas, *Summa Theologica* I–II.94.2).

through reason can they follow it properly. Animals follow the created order according to instinctual principles, which are analogous to the natural law in that they conform to the natural order, but animals differ from humans in that following their instinctual animal nature does not require rational reflection and the exercise of the will.[25]

Does the natural law command anything other than humans to do what is good and to avoid evil? As noted earlier, the moral precepts of the Decalogue were understood by the Scholastics as the basic expression of the natural law. Thomas, like other Scholastics, also spoke of other precepts of the natural law, which he said pertain to three categories of general inclinations: the preservation of being (an inclination shared with all substances), the procreation and education of the species (an inclination shared with all animals), and the desire to live in society, including friendship with God (rational inclinations, unique to human beings).

Yet Thomas never actually lists what these precepts could be. Instead, he says that these precepts are apprehended by a person for his good, and that inclinations should be directed according to reason.[26] Precepts derived from the natural law are determined by reason according to the contingencies surrounding action.[27] Thus, it is more appropriate to refer to specific precepts as *derivative* or *pertaining* to the natural law, rather than saying they are further precepts of the natural law itself, which

25. Porter, *Natural and Divine Law*, 126.
26. Aquinas, *Summa Theologica* I–II.94.2.
27. "As to the proper conclusions of the practical reason, neither is the truth or recti-tude the same for all, nor, where it is the same, is it equally known by all. Thus it is right and true for all to act according to reason: and from this principle it follows as a proper conclusion, that goods entrusted to another should be restored to their owner. Now this is true for the majority of cases: but it may happen in a particu-lar case that it would be injurious, and therefore unreasonable, to restore goods held in trust; for instance, if they are claimed for the purpose of fighting against one's country. And this principle will be found to fail the more, according as we descend further into detail, e.g. if one were to say that goods held in trust should be restored with such and such a guarantee, or in such and such a way; because the greater the number of conditions added, the greater the number of ways in which the principle may fail, so that it be not right to restore or not to restore.

"Consequently we must say that the natural law, as to general principles, is the same for all, both as to rectitude and as to knowledge. But as to certain mat-ters of detail, which are conclusions, as it were, of those general principles, it is the same for all in the majority of cases, both as to rectitude and as to knowledge; and yet in some few cases it may fail, both as to rectitude, by reason of certain ob-stacles (just as natures subject to generation and corruption fail in some few cases on account of some obstacle), and as to knowledge" (Aquinas, *Summa Theologica* I–II.94.4).

would apply in every circumstance and in all places. It is at this point that the natural meets the conventional, and that conventional norms can be said to be an expression of the natural law. But the conventional, properly speaking, should not be understood as actual precepts of the natural law.

Method and Purpose with the Natural Law

It may seem that, in the Scholastic conception, the natural law tradition has little constructive purpose. On its own, natural law commands a person to do good, but it says very little of what that good is. For the content of the natural or divine law, the Scholastics usually looked to the Scriptures. It is here that another notable difference from the modern thinker arises. Although the modern thinker may hope that the natural law offers common content to be embraced by all people, the Scholastics use the natural law not to supply content to the law, but as a rational method for judging law. Reason and the Scriptures contribute mutually in a dialectical way. While the Scriptures provide foundational content and precepts of the natural law to overcome the clouding effects of original sin, reason serves moral thinking through the interpretation of Scripture.

The Scholastics used their understanding of the natural law to interpret divine commands appropriately. Those commands or aspects of commands that call for moral action are unchanging principles of the natural law. Those commands that have to do with ceremonial action or offer some other kind of symbolic meaning are not interpreted as moral commands, but as typological, spiritual, or prophetic. Natural law theory offers a method for distinguishing between moral and ceremonial commands, and allows Christians to understand what is still morally applicable for conduct.[28] By interpreting scriptural precepts through the lens of what is natural and reasonable, the Scholastics determine which of these precepts are of the natural law, and therefore principles for moral action.

The Scholastics further used the natural law to apply the precepts of the divine law. When they recognize reason as nature, they recognize the ongoing, practical work of reason in determining right action. The natural law is not statically developed in a comprehensive structure of precepts. It reminds and challenges the human person through reason to

---

28. Porter, *Natural and Divine Law*, 137–38.

reflect upon options and to take one's moral responsibilities seriously. It challenges a person to consider the various purposes and ends available through choice, and to make those choices that really will promote and result in what is good.

Finally, the correspondence between Scripture and the natural law is significant for the Scholastics because it indicates that God's revelation affirms and is in harmony with human reason and the created order. God's redemptive and gracious work does not contradict or nullify creation, but it restores and perfects it. The harmony of the human person as both physical and spiritual is brought out in the harmony of the divine, spiritual law with the natural law.[29]

THE *VIA MODERNA* AND NATURAL LAW

One of the scholarly problems in determining Luther's reception of the medieval natural law tradition is determining his attitude toward Scholasticism in general. Further complicating the issue is that Luther's own Scholastic training followed the *via moderna*, rather than the *via antiqua*, in which much of the Scholastic tradition of the natural law was developed. The *via moderna*, inspired by William of Ockham (1285–1349), operated out of the premise of God's absolute freedom and power. The basis for God's action was not an eternal or divine law, but God's divine will. Although God bound Himself to agreements and covenants for the sake of human beings, He could, in His freedom, act unbound by any established law. This way of thinking suggests doubt about the consistency of a natural law.

Ockham's school of thought, also called *nominalism*, further challenged the speculative power of human reason, claiming that reason alone could not reflect on purely abstract categories. Reason could only reflect on an individual thing presented to it.[30] This also suggests doubt regarding the metaphysical foundations for a natural law. God, in His radical difference, could not be grasped by reason, and therefore could be

29. Jean Porter, "Natural Law as a Scriptural Concept: Theological Reflections on a Medieval Theme," *Theology Today* 59:2 (July 2002): 235–36.

30. Martin Brecht, *Martin Luther: His Road to Reformation*, trans. James L. Schaaf (Philadelphia: Fortress, 1985), 1:36–37; Bernhard Lohse, *Martin Luther: An Introduction to His Life and Work* (Philadelphia: Fortress, 1986), 13–14.

known only by revelation. This led to a third difference from the older Scholastics, in that Ockham challenged the earlier integration of philosophy and theology, such as we see from Thomas Aquinas. Theology depended on revelation and had to be believed, while philosophy was distinguished as those things related to the world understood apart from revelation.[31]

Despite Ockham's metaphysical commitments, it does not appear that Ockham departed significantly from the natural law tradition he inherited from the earlier Scholastics. His conception of the natural law did not develop out of theoretical reflection on the nature of God and the universe, but it relied on the textual tradition that preceded him. Like the Scholastics before him, he commented on and clarified the understanding of natural law presented in Gratian's *Decretum* and passed preserved in other texts and commentaries. The *Decretum* and other commentators, not some novel metaphysical system, were the context for Ockham's reflection and opinions when it came to the natural law.[32]

Ockham defines the natural law in three general ways, none of which radically departs from the earlier Scholastics.[33] First, natural law follows established and unchanging natural reason and is expressed in the Ten Commandments. This is in contrast to the common view that Ockham understood law to be arbitrary or even unpredictable, depending on the current will of God. Rather, Ockham taught that the rational creature makes use of reason to comprehend the intent, scope, and application of laws. God reveals the natural law in the Decalogue, not as a limited or narrow expression of the divine will, but for clarity, so that reason can make use of these precepts to govern the subject further.[34] Second, natural law is the judgment of justice in accordance with reason, more foundational than human custom. This corresponds to the Scholastic understanding of the natural law as the capacity for judgment.[35] Third,

---

31. Brecht, *Martin Luther: His Road to Reformation*, 35.

32. Brian Tierney, *The Idea of Natural Rights: Studies on Natural Rights, Natural Law and Church Law 1150–1625* (Atlanta: Scholars Press, 1997), 8, 175–77.

33. See also H. S. Offler, "The Three Modes of Natural Law in Ockham: A Revision of the Text," *Franciscan Studies* 37 (1977): 207–18.

34. Tierney, *The Idea of Natural Rights*, 177.

35. Tierney, *The Idea of Natural Rights*, 177–78. Ockham seems to indicate that, after the fall, this judgment of reason allows for customs different from those which would be allowed prior to the fall, especially in matters of private property and slavery. But the result of this opinion is not fundamentally different from earlier Scholastics, who saw private property and slavery to be the reasonable application

natural law are the laws and judgments made in accordance with prevailing conditions. These are precepts that are reasonable to institute, assuming certain conditions, situations, and contingencies. Ockham called it the *suppositional* natural law. These precepts can be likened to those conventions that "pertain" to the natural law, discussed above.[36]

While, in theory, a radical Ockhamist could deny the natural law, Ockham himself generally continued the tradition of the natural law passed on to him through the Scholastic method and understood in the Scriptures.[37] The notion of the natural law in its specifically scriptural character was retained by Ockham.

LUTHER'S SCHOLASTIC HERITAGE

It is important to recognize that Luther's worldview and scholarly perspective cannot be attributed to any one philosophical or theological school. Educated during the rising influence of the Renaissance, like other scholars of his day, Luther studied a variety of sources while improvising, modifying, and restructuring them to operate within his own convictions. His training was in a moderate form of nominalism, refined by Gabriel Biel (d. 1495); he was familiar with the *via antiqua*, including having firsthand knowledge of some of Thomas's work.[38] Luther drew influence also from Augustinianism, humanism, mysticism, monasticism, and his contemporaries.[39] Often he developed his theological stance as a reaction to these ways of thinking, not as an appropriation of them.

---

of the natural law or accommodations permitted by the natural law. Compare Aquinas, *Summa Theologica* I–II.94.5 ad 3, II–II.57.3 ad 2 (on slavery), and II–II.66.1, 2 ad 1 (on property).

36. Tierney, *The Idea of Natural Rights*, 178–79.

37. I am not suggesting that Ockham agreed with the earlier Scholastics regarding every detail of natural law theory, nor even that all the earlier Scholastics agreed with one another. Rather, I have shown that the general contours of the medieval Scholastic natural law tradition include a close connection between the divine and natural law in distinction from positive law, several kinds of natural law with the natural law as reason or judgment being the proper sense for the human person, and the mutual reliance of reason and Scripture in developing and applying the natural law.

38. Denis R. Janz, *Luther on Thomas Aquinas: The Angelic Doctor in the Thought of the Reformer* (Stuttgart: Franz Steiner Verlag Wiesbaden GmbH, 1989), 100–113.

39. Robert Kolb, *Martin Luther: Confessor of the Faith* (Oxford: Oxford University Press, 2009), 26–41.

Luther received from the *via moderna* an emphasis on the absolute power and otherness of God, and the necessity of revelation for coming to know God—not just in understanding, but in faith. This seems to be a lasting appropriation that remains central to Luther's theological perspective, and belongs to his identity as a biblical theologian. Luther continually wrestled with the biblical text and grew to recognize that it is divine revelation, not only in revealing information about God that could not be known through reason, but as the means by which God approaches a person and works repentance and salvation in him. By the Scriptures, God addresses the hearer or reader personally, condemning sin, announcing grace, and bestowing the life of Jesus Christ on the recipient.[40]

Luther's theology of revelation becomes more apparent in his opposition to the method of Scholastic theology. His work as a biblical theologian inspired a break from the Scholastic tradition. The Bible itself impressed upon Luther the profound difference between the biblical and Scholastic methods of theological study.[41] Although the Scholastics had recognized the supreme authority of the Bible, Luther recognized that the power of the Scriptures and its quality as God's Word established it as a fundamentally different kind of authority from the other texts in the Scholastic tradition. The authority of Scripture was not merely in its truth, content, and information, but in the manner in which it is used and its spiritual force. For Luther, the Bible was to be announced and wielded rhetorically, as a sword is wielded in battle. The Scholastics limited and categorized the Bible as one kind of authority, taming it under the rationally precise Scholastic method, even if only unwittingly. On the contrary, for Luther, the Scriptures were to be proclaimed with a view toward the full force of the saving work of Christ, which work is powerfully accomplished in the proclamation. Reading and preaching the Scriptures did not just provide more information; it acted on the reader or hearer in a salvific way.[42]

---

40. Kolb, *Martin Luther: Confessor of the Faith*, 42–50.
41. Leif Grane, "Luther and Scholasticism," in *Luther and Learning*, ed. Marilyn J. Harran (Selinsgrove, PA: Susquehanna University Press, 1985), 55–56.
42. Grane, "Luther and Scholasticism," 57–61.

Luther on the Natural Law

Because Luther's attack on Scholasticism was methodological, he did not reject the content of Scholastic teaching outright. His hermeneutic had been transformed, but that did not mean that every theological conclusion would differ from the Scholastics. It appears that Luther received the basic tradition of the natural law from the Medieval Church while emphasizing two aspects: the natural law as the law of love and the corruption of human reason through sin.

Luther's teaching about the natural law follows three basic points: (1) In its narrow sense, the natural law is the law of reason, written on the heart of humanity, in contrast to a principle of instinct or physicalism. This law is expressed most foundationally by the Golden Rule, yet the corruption of human reason through sin severely distorts one's capacity to know and act on the natural law. (2) The precepts of the natural law are further expressed in the Ten Commandments, yet the Old Testament commandments are to be judged according to the natural law and the New Testament revelation, to distinguish the universal theological and moral meaning from the ceremonial and civil aspects. (3) The natural law is also defined as the principle of loving one another. This is a departure from many Scholastics, though it follows some. However, the innovative way in which Luther understands the natural law as the law of love departs even from those Scholastics who held this identification.

The Natural Law as Reason and the Golden Rule

The divine law is written on the hearts of all men (Romans 2:14–15); this law is according to the unique property of man, that is, reason. The natural law is not instinct that drives a person to action without reflection. Law is unique to human beings, and commands what *ought* to be done, not simply what is. No law—no precept—directs instinct, so instinct is not properly called law, natural or otherwise.[43] Natural law, on the other hand, says not how things are, but commands the way things ought to be. Consequently, to understand and obey, intellect and will are required of those who would obey this command. A person must both know and understand the command, and desire and be able to carry

---

43.   Martin Luther, "How Christians Should Regard Moses," AE 35:164–68; Martin Luther, *Table Talk*, AE 54:103–4.

it out for him to be able to fulfill it. Using terms very close to Thomas Aquinas, Luther called the natural law the first principle of morality: it commands good and forbids evil.[44]

For Luther, this left the natural law in an unusual place theologically. On the one hand, he affirmed the natural law as a scriptural doctrine according to Romans 2:14–15. Yet the tradition taught that the natural law is a participation of reason in the divine law. Because of Luther's view of sin and the need for God's Word to act on a person in order to forgive and regenerate, the participation had to be highly qualified.

In the state of innocence, the natural law indeed was a rational participation in the divine law. However, after the fall and the corruption of the human person, including reason, the human person is no longer able naturally to understand or participate in the mind of God except in an extremely dim way. Sin has blinded the person's ability to receive and understand the law in its full, spiritual, and loving meaning. Although the natural law has not changed, the human person's understanding of it has changed, so that he no longer understands God's will. The dim vestige of divine knowledge that remains tells us nothing about divinity, other than that it is greater than we are, and is therefore to be obeyed and worshiped.[45] In other words, the natural law implies a legislator, which, as the source of nature can be called "god" in some sense, but the full expression of His will with respect to His stance toward us and our proper response to this stance is incomprehensible to corrupt reason.[46]

The human person, therefore, imagines his own content for the natural law, according to the standard of the corrupt sinful nature. This imagination is a dim mimicking of the true law, just as the unregenerate person's concept of God is a dim likeness of the true God. The unbelieving sinner recreates the natural law, as he does God, in the image of himself. The Golden Rule: "Whatever you wish that others would do to you, do also to them" (Matthew 7:12), apart from spiritual insight, has an egoistic perspective.[47]

---

44. Luther, *Table Talk*, AE 54:293.
45. Martin Luther, *Lectures on Genesis*, in AE 1:62–67, 113–14; "Against the Heavenly Prophets," AE 40:96–97.
46. Johannes Heckel, *Lex Charitatis: A Juristic Disquisition on Law in the Theology of Martin Luther*, trans. and ed., Gottfried G. Krodel (Grand Rapids: Eerdmans, 2010), 54–55.
47. Heckel, *Lex Charitatis,* 55–57.

Thus, although a person self-evidently knows the Golden Rule according to his nature, even corrupted by sin,[48] Luther does not rely on the innate knowledge of people or their ability or willingness to reflect on the Golden Rule to ensure true understanding of the natural law. In this way, he is similar to the Scholastics: Luther supports his understanding of the natural law as the Golden Rule by appealing to Scripture (Matthew 7:12; Luke 6:31). The Golden Rule is taught to all hearts, but because of sin, the proclamation of Scripture is added to it in order to illumine its true meaning, not only to teach the precepts of the natural law, but also to convict people of sin.

The promulgation of law clarifies the content of the law for the mind of man, which is corrupt and unable to discern the true content of the law on its own. However, this preached and taught law has internal force and conviction because of the natural law written on the heart. This internal recognition of the law is the knowledge that there is good and evil, the content of which biblical revelation teaches. Outward commands are felt in the conscience because of the natural law.[49]

Scripture and Reason

Luther understands the relationship between the Ten Commandments and the natural law in a dialectic manner, similar to his Scholastic predecessors. In their historical context, the Ten Commandments are limited in jurisdiction to the Hebrews under the old covenant. The Ten Commandments were not given to all people, and therefore, in a strict sense, do not apply to non-Hebrews. The ceremonial nature of the First and Third Commandments buttressed Luther's argument: the use of images or statues and the literal observation of Sabbath rest were nullified by the New Testament, so that they cannot be part of the natural law.[50] On the other hand, the Golden Rule and the command to love

48. Luther assumes the equation of the natural law with the Golden Rule, and that the Golden Rule is self-evident, e.g., in "How Christians Should Regard Moses," AE 35:171; "Against the Heavenly Prophets," AE 40:96–97; "Temporal Authority: To What Extent It Should Be Obeyed," AE 45:118–19; "Trade and Usury," AE 45:287, 292–94, 303; "Whether Soldiers, Too, Can Be Saved," AE 46:114.

49. Luther, "Against the Heavenly Prophets in the Matter of Images and Sacraments," AE 40:97.

50. Luther, "How Christians Should Regard Moses," AE 35:167–70; "Against the Heavenly Prophets," AE 40:95.

one another have been preached to all nations. Their universality proves their identity with the natural law, so that, strictly speaking, the natural law—not the Ten Commandments—rules the Church and the nations.[51]

Luther, however, goes on to argue for the right use of the Ten Commandments: to the extent that they agree with the natural law, they should be taught in order to expound the natural law and reveal where people fall short.[52] The natural laws were never so orderly and well written as by Moses; therefore, the Ten Commandments serve not only the ancient Israelites but also the faithful in all generations by expressing the basic precepts of the natural law. The natural law is fundamentally and clearly expressed in the Ten Commandments when the ceremonial and civil aspects are eliminated.

Note the similarity between Luther and the Scholastics in their dialectical treatment of the Commandments and the natural law. Luther judges the Commandments by the natural law, but he also understands the content of the natural law to be best expressed in the Commandments. Like the Scholastics, Luther links natural and divine law as to their direct divine source—their preconventional character—in distinction from human custom and positive law, which originate in society as particular expressions of natural law.

THE LAW OF LOVE

Finally, the natural law is equivalent to the law of love, "Love your neighbor as yourself" (Romans 13:9).[53] Yet Luther acknowledges that this is not the natural law as it is usually understood. Only the Christian can know and express true love. Only the Christian can recognize the natural law as the law of love. Only after one is regenerated by the Holy Spirit and alive in Christ do one's faculties begin to be restored and to grasp the true original meaning of the divine natural law. This is a perception that is granted by grace and is grasped only to the extent that one is a Christian, walking by faith (2 Corinthians 5:7).[54] The self-evident

---

51. Luther, "How Christians Should Regard Moses," AE 35:171.
52. Luther, "How Christians Should Regard Moses," AE 35:166, 171.
53. Luther, "Against the Heavenly Prophets," AE 40:97. See also "Temporal Authority," AE 45:128.
54. Heckel, *Lex Charitatis,* 46–48, 88–93. For Luther's extended and eloquent comments on this, see his "Sermon for the Fourth Sunday after Epiphany—Rm 13:8–

nature of the command to love is clouded by sin, but revealed by the Word through faith.[55]

The non-Christian can do works of love, when understood as the outward expression or action of a loving work. It is in this limited way that a non-Christian might even understand the law of love. "Love your neighbor as yourself" can be accomplished to some extent in the secular realm, but not like a heart motivated by true charity. Charity is the true love of God poured out into the believer in Christ, motivating both the good intention and action. Apart from the true charity of the Holy Spirit, the love command can only be acted on in reference to one's self-love, rather than as enlivened by the Spirit of God.

The natural law is restored to its fullness only when the person is restored to righteousness. In sin, apart from faith, there can be no participation in divine reason, but only a distortion of the divine reason, so that one's self becomes the measure of good and evil. The natural law actually serves as a tool of condemnation, testifying that the sinner must seek after the divine and do what is good, but also that he fails to do the good. This testimony, however, is silenced by the overwhelming corruption of reason, which supplants the divine natural law with a personal standard of self-love. Only in his regenerate state can a person begin to grasp the scope and meaning of the natural law. This natural law is the law of love, a love not only of neighbor for neighbor, but a love that finds its source in God, and a human love that is inspired and grows out of this divine love.

SUMMARY REFLECTIONS

Both Luther and the medieval Scholastics hold a notably different view of the natural law from that generally espoused by modern thinkers. Rather than developing their views through the autonomous work of reason or a scientific account of natural being, they rely on a tradition informed by classical and Christian opinions, normed by Scripture. The natural law is the principle of practical reason, commanding good and

---

10" in *The Complete Sermons of Martin Luther*, vol. 4, ed. John Nicholas Lenker (Grand Rapids: Baker, 2000).

55.   Notably, Thomas also acknowledges that the self-evident nature of the law of love might be perceived only through faith. See Aquinas, *Summa Theologica* I–II.100.3 ad 1.

forbidding evil. Scripture fills in the content of the natural law, beginning with its definition as the Golden Rule and by including the basic precepts of the natural law in the Ten Commandments. Rational reflection guides practical action and interprets the Ten Commandments for application in the conditions and circumstances of daily life. Luther's methodological departure from Scholasticism drives him to emphasize the corruption of human reason after the fall, so that any rational participation in the divine law is but a dim vestige. On the other hand, for the Christian, the presence of God by grace through His Word bestows and pours forth the true life of charity, the rich and full expression of the natural law.

This essay suggests that a Christian doctrine of the natural law is part of a tradition informed by sources other than reason and natural observation. A robust and comprehensive doctrine of the natural law is not self-generating or self-sustaining. It relies on a worldview to give structure and content to the concept of rationality and the good. The bare natural law merely teaches that there is a good to be done; but apart from other sources it does not teach what it is that should be done. It is, simply, a capacity for judgment—a capacity that needs other precepts—as well as a context for reflection to consider what particular action shall actually fulfill the good.

In engaging non-Christians with the natural law, one may not assume a set body of precepts that will become universally acceptable upon clear presentation. The doctrine of the natural law teaches us that non-Christians recognize some kind of good and evil, but that they will understand the good differently from the Christian. In fact, the non-Christian will be influenced by his own traditions, values, and concepts, just as the Christian is influenced by his.

Even if we cannot assume that appeals to the natural law will result in a common body of moral precepts, natural law theory still provides great potential. For one, it provides within the Christian tradition, as it did in the medieval and Reformation periods, a principle for practical action informed by Scripture. Further, it serves in conversation with other traditions on a foundational level as a basis for examining presuppositions, for reflecting on long-term and ultimate goods, and for comparing and contrasting worldviews. We cannot assume that the appeal to the natural law will result in a common body of moral precepts, but it calls all of us to think rationally, to recognize how our traditions value different goods, and to consider carefully how our practical action pursues the good. Most significantly, the natural law testifies to God, but it is finally only God's own witness in Jesus Christ that shows true love to be the ultimate fulfillment of this law.

3

Luther's Pragmatic Appropriation of the Natural Law Tradition

Thomas D. Pearson

Introduction

T
he question of just how to situate Martin Luther within the natural
law tradition that he inherited—or whether he should be situated
within that tradition at all—is a deeply congested matter. The difficulty
inherent in clarifying Luther's relation to, and use of, the natural law tradition, however, is a reflection of the struggle to disentangle the jumble
of themes that gradually coalesced around the notion of natural law over
two millennia in the Western intellectual community. From its early

expression in Sophocles[1] and Socrates,[2] through Cicero,[3] the Stoics,[4] and the Fathers of the Christian Church,[5] then reaching a depth of complexity in the medieval constructions of Hugh of St. Victor,[6] Aquinas,[7] Bonaventure,[8] and Ockham,[9] the natural law tradition initially embraced principles of ethics and civil (positive) law, grew to encompass normative formulations in social theory and political philosophy, and finally in the later Middle Ages became the locus for metaphysical and epistemological assertions within a framework of Christian theology.

How did Luther respond to this saturated tradition, so firmly in place in his own day? Did he rest comfortably within the broad scope of natural law conventions in Western thought? Or did he reject them outright? Did he perhaps selectively modify elements of the natural law argument in order to harmonize those claims with his own theological assertions? There is little agreement among Luther's commentators on this question. In the nineteenth century, Ernest Troeltsch portrayed Luther as one who held strongly to a primitive notion of natural law that "is at every point a crude, raw and aphoristic theory," but who nonetheless advanced the idea of natural law into the modern period.[10] Subsequently, Karl Holl offered the corrective that "Luther, in fact, totally rejected the natural

1. See Sophocles, *Antigone* (New York: Dover, 1993).
2. Although the *Republic* and *The Laws* contain significant discussions of the relation of law and morality, the most extended examination of the natural law basis for civil legislation is contained in the *Minos*, Loeb Classical Library, vol. 12 (Cambridge: Harvard University Press, 1927).
3. Cicero, *De Republica* (New York: Oxford University Press, 2006).
4. Epictetus, *Discourses*, Loeb Classical Library, vol. 1 (Cambridge: Harvard University Press, 1925).
5. See, for instance, Augustine, *Commentary on the Sermon on the Mount* (Washington, DC: Catholic University of America Press, 2001); Ambrosiaster, *Commentary on Romans* (Downers Grove, IL: InterVarsity Academic, 2009); Lactantius, *Divine Institutions*, Ante-Nicene Fathers, vol. 7 (Peabody, MA: Hendrickson, 1994).
6. Hugh of St. Victor, *Hugh of St. Victor on the Sacraments of the Christian Faith (de Sacramentis)* (Eugene, OR: Wipf & Stock, 2007).
7. Thomas Aquinas, *Summa Theologica,* I–II, Q. 91, aa. 1–6 (Indianapolis: Hackett, 2000).
8. Bonaventure, *Collations on the Ten Commandments*, vol. 6 (St. Bonaventure, NY: Franciscan Institute, 1995).
9. William of Ockham, *A Dialogue on Imperial and Pontifical Power*, in "A Letter to Friars Minor," and Other Writings (Cambridge, UK: Cambridge University Press, 1995).
10. Ernest Troeltsch, *Die Religion in Geschichte and Gegenwart*, 3rd ed. (Tubingen, Germany: 1957–1965), 4:697ff.

law concept" and that the Reformer "contributes nothing to its historical development"[11] The Calvinist scholar John T. McNeill, on the other
hand, acknowledged that "[natural law] remains something of an alien in
the republic of his [Luther's] theology," but nonetheless that "natural law
is determinative for Luther's political thinking."[12] Finally, if we turn to
the recent work of William Lazareth, we find the judgment that "Luther's
liberating conclusion is that Christians are bound only by God's universal
natural law, some of which, however, is also embodied in the Mosaic
moral law. . . . For Christians [according to Luther], natural law can still
regulatively demonstrate what love alone normatively motivates."[13] Is the
collapsing of natural law into the principle of Christian love, as recommended by Lazareth, an accurate description of Luther's position on the
subject?

What this mélange of different verdicts on Luther's appropriation of
the natural law tradition may reflect is that Luther himself had difficulty articulating a consistent account of natural law, a difficulty accented
by his avoidance of natural law when he addresses strictly theological
matters, and his loose deployment of natural law when dealing with
matters of practical and political significance. Indeed, as will be seen in
what follows, Luther routinely moves between endorsing and ignoring
natural law at various times and in differing contexts, with no apparent
uniform pattern emerging from his scattered comments. Nevertheless,
Luther's very inconsistency on this point reveals an underlying methodological commitment throughout his writings: in spite of the fact that
the natural law tradition he received fails to portray accurately the human
condition *coram Deo*, natural law can therefore play only a limited role
in proper biblical exegesis and theological reflection per se. The diverse
postures of that tradition may at the same time serve as a reference point
for pragmatically adjudicating conflicts in the public and political realm.
Put differently, Luther's description of natural law divides along the
fault lines of the "two kingdoms" doctrine. Natural law does scant work
throughout Luther's biblical and theological endeavors, but it does substantial, albeit often conflicted, work when his focus is on the domain of

11. Karl Holl, *The Cultural Significance of the Reformation* (Cleveland: World, 1959), 50.
12. John T. McNeill, "Natural Law in Luther's Thought," *Church History* 10, no. 3
    (September, 1941): 224, 227.
13. William Lazareth, *Christians in Society: Luther, the Bible, and Social Ethics* (Minneapo-
    lis: Fortress Press, 2001), 157, 225.

civil righteousness. It is important to keep all this in mind when reading Luther; he produces a bewildering miscellany of views on a single subject. Luther did not, in fact, regard natural law as a single subject with a secure center, but rather as an inchoate set of common prejudices shared by people everywhere.

This claim suggests Luther understood "natural" to mean the historic sinful condition of humanity; "human nature" to designate the created collection of innate yet incontinent human powers rendered inert by sin; and "natural law" to refer to the basic instincts of human beings expressed within the context of a sinful existence. None of this is congruent with the classical natural law tradition in the West; Luther subsumes his treatment of natural law under the more comprehensive rubric of Christian liberty. I argue for this multifarious conclusion, in a very preliminary and narrow manner, in this essay.

Natural law functions for Luther as an ingredient in maintaining the integrity of the left-hand kingdom of civil order, but not as a fit subject on which to ground theological discourse within the kingdom of the right. I will examine Luther's early writings on Romans and from the *Disputation on Scholastic Theology* to establish his initial manner of distancing himself from the prevailing natural law theory of his time. In connection with this, I will look at a key passage from two decades later—Luther's 1535 *Commentary on Galatians*—which, although it comes from Luther's maturity, maintains the effort to set aside the fundamental theological and philosophical premises on which the natural law tradition rests. I will then turn to several assorted works from the 1520s that demonstrate Luther's freewheeling approach to questions that would typically have been resolved by an appeal to natural law, but which Luther treats in an entirely different manner while still invoking the authority of natural law. The cumulative verdict from inspecting these texts of Luther's is that he freely revises the entire concept of "natural law" in an effort to secure liberty of action for those who must make difficult decisions in congested circumstances in public life. Indeed, it would seem that Luther puts nature and grace in opposition to one another, such that the divine law is an imposition on nature rather than an essential feature of it. As we shall see, Luther spurns the classical natural law teaching that grace works through nature and perfects nature, arguing instead that grace belongs to the theological category of justification, while divine law has been bestowed on humankind in order to interdict the waywardness of human nature.

This essay explores these questions in three sections, with each section focused on a single question. First, what is the natural law tradition as Luther would have received it from his teachers? Second, what does Luther reject in that tradition, and what does he affirm? Third, how does Luther handle matters of moral, legal, and political importance that would normally be referred for judgment to the precepts of the natural law as traditionally understood?

What Is the Natural Law Tradition?

Classical natural law theory makes four closely interrelated claims. First, there is a natural moral order to the universe that is teleological in character; that is, all things in the cosmos, including human beings, seek to fulfill their basic and created purposes and functions, and doing so represents what is the "good" for each thing, including human beings. Second, this teleological order is discernible in fundamental behavioral inclinations or tendencies in things. For human beings, this means our common human inclinations are indications of what is the "good" for us, and what it is that enhances human flourishing. Third, these inclinations, and the way they promote the genuine "good" for things, are rational and can be discovered by human reason. Indeed, the principles (or "precepts") of the natural law are embedded in our human reason—they are "written on the heart"—so that we "can't not know" them.[14] Fourth, because the moral precepts of the natural law are also the moral precepts of human reason, expressed not only within individuals but also collectively, the civil laws and legal procedures of a "good" society will be derived from the precepts of the natural law.

Central to these four theses of natural law theory is the presumption that "nature" refers to a self-contained and self-sustaining order within creation. All persons embody this natural order within themselves. Within the Christian account of natural law, however, human beings are fallen creatures, and thus are unable to fully actualize that fulfillment toward which we naturally strive. The freely given gift of grace from God

---

14. See J. Budziszewski, *What We Can't Not Know: A Guide* (Dallas: Spence Publishing, 2003).

is the remedy for this human inadequacy, working to repair our fallen natures and restore to us the possibility of perfecting our being.

It was the Roman jurists—in particular, Cicero, Ulpian, and the legal specialists working under Justinian—who first ratified this understanding of natural law into a moral and legal tradition. Cicero had insisted that "there was one immutable, eternal and unchangeable law" that properly governed human affairs,[15] while Ulpian distinguished between the "law of the nations" (*ius gentium*) from "natural law" (*ius naturale*) by specifying that natural law was what "nature teaches all animals," such as procreation and marriage, with the law of the nations being that aspect of the natural law particularly applicable to human governance.[16] Although *ius gentium* and *ius naturale* are often collapsed into a generic natural law theory in the subsequent tradition, it is important to note this difference inasmuch as it turns out to be a distinction Luther will later take advantage of. Finally, Justinian's scholars, borrowing heavily on Ulpian, add to the definition of natural law the stipulation that the natural law is rational and originates with the source of all reason, the Christian God.[17]

The development of natural law throughout the medieval period is an exceedingly complex story. By the time we reach the thirteenth century, we can see that a theoretical description of natural law can be constructed out of an assortment of philosophical rudiments: nature, reason, animal instinct, human inclination, Scripture, and the Golden Rule, among others. But with Thomas Aquinas, we encounter a thoroughgoing approach to ordering dialectically these diverse treatments, offering a polished presentation of natural law that has dominated analyses of the subject, both from secular and theological sources, ever since.

For Aquinas, God is essentially reason; God's will is informed and directed by His reason. Natural law, according to Aquinas, is the presentation of God's rational nature as that nature is revealed in creation; God has ordained that His creatures know Him by means of His eternal law made accessible through natural law. Thus God, in His ordained power, is intelligible to human reason, and we must be reconciled to God rationally, through submission to His eternal and natural law.

---

15. Cicero, *De Republica*, 3:22.
16. Ulpian, *Digest,* I,1,1, 3 (Charleston, SC: BiblioBazaar, 2010).
17. Justinian, *Institutes*, I, 2, 11 (New York: Thomas Nelson and Sons [Nabu Press], 2010).

This is a weighty and comprehensive scheme of moral and positive law, and Aquinas argues that God's grace is necessary for humans to accomplish the goals of the system. Christ provides access to the resources of grace by which we can be reconciled to God through maturing into persons who are exemplars of fully realized human beings in the image of God. Because we are rational creatures, we possess the faculties necessary to engage the rational structure of the natural law and to understand its precepts. The most critical faculty we are gifted with is *synderesis*, which is a power of conscience that is able to intuit the precepts of the natural law. If the natural law is written on the heart, then it is *synderesis* that reads the heart.[18]

There is in Aquinas no sense of a malignant force (i.e., sin) that might disturb the metaphysical tranquility of this schema. Because of the fall, human beings may fail to acknowledge the natural law and, therefore, make mistakes or otherwise succumb to human weakness, which is the real source of sin. But the system itself is uncontaminated by sin.

The rendition of natural law provided by Aquinas is a complete natural ontology of law. There is no sense here that law is an artifact of human communities, manufactured for pragmatic political goals; there is no social contract in Aquinas. Nor is there the possibility that law is a provisional arrangement, always subject to change, owing to the variety of sinful proclivities continually expressed by human beings. Instead, the structures of law have ontological status as rooted in nature; sin is the name for those transgressions that occur when this ontological reality is neglected. We will soon see that Luther's understanding of natural law turns this model upside down.

WHAT DOES LUTHER REJECT AND AFFIRM IN THE NATURAL LAW TRADITION?

Luther employs locutions such as "natural law," "laws of nature," and "command of God" 583 times as translated in the American Edition of his works.[19] These references cover Luther's writings from early to late, composed in a variety of contexts. As indicated earlier, although Luther

---

18. Aquinas, *Summa Theologica*, I, Q. 79, a. 12.
19. David M. Whitford, "Cura Religionis or Two Kingdoms: The Late Luther on Religion and the State in the Lectures on Genesis 1," *Church History* 73:1 (2004).

does indeed directly mention natural law in a number of his writings, he does not employ any vestige of the traditional apparatus of classical natural law theory.

Luther appears to distance himself from the natural law tradition early in his career. In his university lectures on Paul's Epistle to the Romans, delivered at Wittenberg in 1515–1516, Luther offers striking interpretations of his analysis of Romans 2:14–15, interpretations that are at variance with the usual natural law conclusions. The familiar Romans passage reads as follows:

> For when Gentiles, who do not have the law, by nature do what the law requires, they are a law to themselves, even though they do not have the law. They show that the work of the law is written on their hearts, while their conscience also bears witness, and their conflicting thoughts accuse or even excuse them.

Luther first tries to determine to whom the appellation "Gentiles" refers in this passage. He concludes that it must be "people who are in the middle between the ungodly Gentiles and the believing Gentiles." Ungodly Gentiles cannot be the group Paul describes here, because they would not "do instinctively (by nature) what the law requires." But why could not "believing Gentiles" be the subjects of this law that is done "by nature"? Luther writes:

> But neither does he [Paul] speak of the first group, that is, the believers in Christ, for this interpretation of "by nature" is forced, and I cannot see why the apostle wanted to use this particular expression, unless he wanted to hide from his reader what he really intended to say, especially since elsewhere he does not speak in this way.[20]

What is it that makes φύσει, "by nature," seem to Luther forced in this context? It is because these Gentile Christians have been "by the Spirit of the grace of Christ restored from a nature that had been corrupted by sin."[21] That little word *from* in this sentence is critical: those who are rooted in Christ are being restored to a right relationship with God *from* a previous natural condition of estrangement from God brought about by sin. Here we see that Luther understands φύσις, "nature," as posited in

20. AE 25:185–86.
21. AE 25:185.

opposition to grace. Grace does not perfect our sinful nature, but operates independently to separate us from our sinful nature; grace stands to justification as nature stands to unbelief. Thus, for Luther, Christians (including, in this case, Gentile believers) are positioned in a different relationship to the law than are non-Christians: the former do not receive the law, nor do they perform the works of the law, naturally. The early Luther does not endorse the possibility that the Christian could rightly apprehend the precepts of divine law through the natural exercise of right reason, nor effectively implement those precepts, because right reason has been permanently impaired by sin. This is a position contrary to the traditional stance of natural law.

This dissonance with natural law is further emphasized in Luther's consideration of Romans 2:15. He first notes that the text says, "the works of the Law are written on their hearts," and declares that this is decidedly different from a statement that "The Law is written on their hearts."[22] The works of the law are known naturally to everyone precisely as *works*; and as works, they are performed under the auspices of sin, and so are able only to convict us of our unrighteousness. Luther says:

> Therefore I believe that the sentence "The law is written on their hearts" is the same as "God's love has been poured into our hearts through the Holy Spirit" (Rom. 5:5). This is, in the real sense, the law of Christ and the fulfillment of the law of Moses. Indeed, it is a law without a law, without measure, without end, without limit, a law reaching far beyond everything that a written law commands or can command. But the words "The work of the law is written" mean that the knowledge of the work is written, that is, the law that is written in letters concerning the works that have to be done but not the grace to fulfill this law. Therefore until the present day they have of necessity remained tied to the letter that kills, for they have had nothing else but the works of the Law written on their hearts.[23]

If the natural law is congruent with knowledge of the works of the law written on the heart, then natural law is associated with "the letter that kills," and not with the Spirit that gives life. If it were simply God's law itself written on the heart, such a law would be indistinguishable

---

22. AE 25:187.
23. AE 25:187.

from God's love bestowed on Christians, the love that fills and renews and restores us. But Luther insists that Paul is not here (Romans 2:14–15) talking about the law written on the heart (the law of love), but the deadly works fixed by the written law known to the natural light of reason that are inscribed within all human hearts.

Arguments similar to these found in the *Lectures on Romans* are reprised in the 1517 *Disputation Against Scholastic Theology*. Luther prepared these propositions to be defended at the University of Wittenberg at a time when he was working through Aristotle's *Physics* and struggling to make sense of the congealed arguments of his Scholastic contemporaries. Here are selections of theses from the *Disputation*; note the parallels to Luther's concern over questions about "nature" and "human nature" that he had expressed just a few years earlier:

17. Man is by nature unable to want God to be God. Indeed, he himself wants to be God, and does not want God to be God.

18. To love God above all things by nature is a fictitious term, a chimera, as it were.

20. An act of friendship is done, not according to nature, but according to prevenient grace.

21. No act is done according to nature that is not an act of concupiscence against God.

30. On the part of man, however, nothing precedes grace except ill will and even rebellion against grace.

34. In brief, man by nature has neither correct precept nor good will.

36. For ignorance of God and oneself and good works is by nature always invincible.

39. We are never lords of our actions, but servants.

69. As a matter of fact, it is more accurate to say that the law is destroyed by nature without the grace of God.

70. A good law will of necessity be bad for the natural will.

71. Law and will are two implacable foes without the grace of God.

83. But even the Decalogue itself and all that can be taught and prescribed inwardly and outwardly is not good law either.

> 88. And from this it is clear that everyone's natural will is iniquitous and bad.[24]

These are becoming familiar themes for Luther: the "natural" is no medium for discovering the divine order of creation; human nature with its handmaid of right reason is no suitable venue for moral performance. It is obvious that there is little here a traditional natural law theorist could affirm. By 1517, Luther has put considerable distance between the theoretical foundations of Scholastic natural law and his emerging sense of the boundaries defining evangelical theology.

Turning now to his 1535 *Commentary on St. Paul's Epistle to the Galatians*, Luther offers up the following set of judgments that resonate well with his earlier contentions from twenty years before:

> For albeit that all men have a certain natural knowledge implanted in their minds (Rom. ii. 14), whereby they naturally perceive that they ought to do unto others as they would have others do unto them (and this and other such opinions, which we call the natural law, are the foundation of human right and of all good works); yet notwithstanding man's reason is so corrupt and blind through the malice of the devil, that it understands not this knowledge wherewith it is born; or else, being admonished by the Word of God, it understands it, and yet (such is the power of Satan) knowingly neglects and condemns it.[25]

As with so much of Luther's writing on biblical texts, this passage is a rich porridge of assertions, qualifications, and scoldings. Despite the density of Luther's comments here, one thing stands clear: Luther does believe in the existence of something called natural law. But it comes with a typically fatal qualification, namely, that this natural law is effectively disabled by sin's thorough contamination of our reason. Advocating for natural law as a theological insight into the divine order of things placed within us by God is, for Luther, equivalent to comforting a man whose kidneys have permanently shut down with the fact that God endowed him with those kidneys. Luther's position here is fully consistent with his comments from 1515–1517. Given this sort of textual evidence, it

---

24. Martin Luther, *Disputation Against Scholastic Theology*, in *Selected Writings of Martin Luther*, ed. Theodore G. Tappert (Philadelphia: Fortress, 1967), 1:35–42, *seriatim*.

25. Martin Luther, *A Commentary on St. Paul's Epistle to the Galatians*, text prepared by Philip Watson (Cambridge, UK: James Clarke, 1953, 1978), 66.

would be difficult to sustain an argument that Luther changed his mind on natural law and adopted a more congenial attitude toward the natural law tradition as his theological acuity matured. Luther, both early and late, was always skeptical (at best) of reason's ability to grasp divine truth, and equally convinced of human moral incompetence.

So just what is the natural law good for? What, if anything, does Luther affirm in the natural law tradition he inherited? An array of Luther's writings from the 1520s furnishes a preliminary indication of an answer to this question.

How Does Luther Handle Matters of Moral, Legal, and Political Importance in the 1520s?

Exactly how Luther employs natural law can be seen in those texts that most frequently appeal to this idea, the majority of which come from the period around 1525, when Luther was dealing with violence and public disorder connected with the uprising of the peasants, and with the efforts of radical reformers such as Karlstadt and Muntzer.

Consider first Luther's words in the *Admonition to Peace* from 1525, subtitled *A Reply to the Twelve Articles of the Peasants in Swabia*, where he reproaches the peasants for their bloody revolt against the political authorities.

> Now you cannot deny that your rebellion actually involves you in such a way that you make yourselves your own judges and avenge yourselves. You are quite unwilling to suffer any wrong. That is contrary not only to Christian law and the Gospel, but also to natural law and all equity. . . .
>
> Now in all this I have been speaking of the common, divine, and natural law which even heathen, Turks, and Jews have to keep if there is to be any peace or order in the world. Even though you were to keep this whole law, you would do no better and no more than the heathen and the Turks do. For no one is a Christian merely because he does not undertake to function as his own judge and avenger but leaves this to the authorities and

the rulers. You would eventually have to do this whether you wanted to or not. But because you are acting against this law, you see plainly that you are worse than heathen or Turks, to say nothing of the fact that you are not Christians. . . . you are so far from being Christian, and your actions and lives are so horribly contrary to his law, that you are not worthy to be called even heathen or Turks. You are much worse than these, because you rage and struggle against the divine and natural law, which all the heathen keep.[26]

Luther here reproves the Swabian peasants for seeking to avenge themselves against their oppressors, accusing them of doing what is contrary to natural law and equity. *Equity* is a term originally employed by Aristotle that became an adjunct to discussions of natural law in the Western tradition. An approximate meaning is "justice," understood as giving to each one what is due to her or him. "Prudential justice" is perhaps the closest English cognate.

In this passage, Luther is indicting the peasants for attempting to usurp the place of the local ruler in the community, passing judgment on the ruler's culpability when the peasants are in no position to do so. To act as judges in the case of their own grievances is an affront to equity. In doing so, the peasants also violate the "Christian law," which for Luther is generally the law of love. But Luther does not rest his judgment of the Swabian peasants on this Christian law. He admonishes them on the basis of the natural law, which even the "heathen, Turks and the Jews" have to keep "if there is to be any peace or order in the world." There are two critical points here. First, doing the right thing—even the morally right thing—does not identify a person as a Christian. Following the precepts of the natural law is not authentically distinctive of Christian morality and should not be pursued because it promises to achieve some particular Christian good. There is clearly a different spirit at work here in Luther from that of Aquinas or his predecessors.

Second, this passage underscores Luther's conviction that the value of the natural law is fundamentally pragmatic and instrumental. Natural law ought to be observed "if there is to be any peace or order in the world." It is not the case, Luther implies, that we should follow the precepts of

---

26. Martin Luther, *Admonition to Peace: A Reply to the Twelve Articles of the Peasants in Swabia*, in ed. Theodore G. Tappert, *Selected Writings of Martin Luther* (Philadelphia: Fortress, 1967), 3:325, 327.

the natural law because it is the way that each individual member of the human species can, in proper teleological fashion, realize the good for herself or himself. Instead, it is the case that we should adhere to the natural law because it produces a salutary outcome for society. I can find nowhere in Luther's writings an endorsement of the traditional notion that the value of natural law lies in the prospect that individual members of the human species can use reason to order their lives in accordance with the moral precepts of the natural law. On the contrary, Luther's counsel to Christian individuals is to hear what God's law demands of them, to repent of their sin, and to cling through faith to the promises of God in Christ.

Finally, Luther offers an argument in the midst of discussing the third of the twelve complaints of the Swabian peasants that demonstrates how far he has moved away from the traditional outlook of natural law theory. From the beginning, classical natural law theory held that all persons were equal on the basis of the "higher law," and that natural justice required that civil law recognize the fundamental equality of each human being, regardless of the political consequences. Luther disagrees.

> You assert that no one is to be the serf of anyone else, because Christ has made us all free. That is making Christian freedom a completely physical matter. Did not Abraham [Gen. 17:23] and other patriarchs and prophets have slaves? Read what St. Paul teaches about servants, who, at that time, were all slaves. This article, therefore, absolutely contradicts the gospel. It proposes robbery, for it suggests that every man should take his body away from his lord, even though his body is the lord's property. A slave can be a Christian, and have Christian freedom, in the same way that a prisoner or a sick man is a Christian, and yet not free. This article would make all men equal, and turn the spiritual kingdom of Christ into a worldly, external kingdom; and that is impossible. A worldly kingdom cannot exist without an inequality of persons, some being free, some imprisoned, some lords, some subjects, etc.; and St. Paul says in Galatians 5 that in Christ the lord and the servant are equal.[27]

The problem is that "a worldly kingdom cannot stand" if there is not a publicly maintained inequality of persons. Once again, we see that

---

27. Luther, *Admonition to Peace*, 3:339.

Luther's worry is for the pragmatic effects of the natural law, and not with enshrining natural law as a necessary point of departure for establishing moral and civil rectitude. If invoking natural law proves to have deleterious social consequences in a given situation, so much the worse for natural law.

But note the reference in this passage to "Christian freedom" and Luther's distress at the prospect that this might become a "physical matter." The problem is that the Swabian peasants are translating Christian liberty into political freedom, when for Luther there is no connection between the two. Christian liberty for Luther is an attitude, a disposition of love toward God and regard for the neighbor unfettered by social convention, legal precedent, ecclesiastical rule, or personal status. Christian liberty is a passport to compassionate creativity in seeking solutions to practical problems where human need is paramount and human well-being is at stake. Luther holds that one can enjoy Christian liberty while politically enslaved; to believe otherwise is to turn Christian liberty into an exercise in carnality. When Luther invokes natural law in contexts such as these, he intends to align natural law with Christian liberty, such that the former becomes an expression of the latter. In this sense, what is "natural" for Luther is the specific human capacity for responding effectively (as far as possible under the onerous bondage to sin) to situations in which our neighbors are in need, for figuring out what best accomplishes the end of neighbor-love. Natural law is thus the practice of Christian liberty.

Because Luther nowhere offers a systematic account of natural law, we are forced to cobble together this description of his attitude toward it from the fragmentary comments he makes in texts such as the *Admonition*. Within a larger purview, Luther's stance as presented in this source is closely related to a contemporary populist version of the *ius gentium*, in which natural law is portrayed as the consensus position of human beings in all nations as they address the practical needs of their communities. Everyone cherishes peace and order, Luther believes, and thus natural law indicates that the ruler must do whatever is necessary to ensure peace and order. There is no indication in Luther that he shared the conviction of Aquinas that the natural law descends from divine law via eternal law. Divine law has an entirely different function in Luther. For the reformer, divine law expresses itself in two ways: first, as a set of strong commands that we cannot satisfy and through which we are confronted with our sin, and second, as the "Christian law," the law of love. Natural law becomes then an independent source of practical deliberation, rooted not in some metaphysical human nature, but in the common interest of all people for peace, order, and equity.

Another example of this attitude of Luther's is his reply to a question about bigamy—"Whether [a] person may have more than one wife"—which Luther takes up in a letter written to Joseph Levin Metzsch in December 1526. Luther's response here is a precursor of his action in the infamous case of Philip of Hesse some thirteen years later. Luther writes:

> Moreover, although the patriarchs had many wives, Christians may not follow their example, because there is no necessity for doing this, no improvement is obtained thereby, and, especially, there is no word of God to justify this practice, while great offense and trouble may arise from it. Accordingly, I do not believe that Christians any longer have this liberty.[28]

Note the texture of Luther's argument here. He does not argue that bigamy is a violation of the natural law, that the practice would disturb a natural order in creation (i.e., marriage), or even that this arrangement is opposed to the common judgment of humankind. Instead, he argues against it largely on instrumental and practical grounds—there is no necessity for bigamy, it produces "no improvement" and provokes "great offense and trouble." In short, it generates negative effects, and those effects far outweigh any prospective benefits. To be sure, Luther adds that he can find no Word of God to justify the practice. But he does not rest the argument on that point. However, even if he had built his contention on the lack of any Word of God on this subject, that is not a natural law position.

Another source just prior to this time period that demonstrates Luther's free rearrangement of the natural law tradition is the treatise *On Temporal Authority* (1523). In this text, Luther combines natural law, the law of love, and the Golden Rule into a single principle that rides rough-shod over the careful and elaborate construction of natural law theory he inherited.

> For nature teaches—as does love—that I should do as I would be done by [Luke 6:31]. Therefore, I cannot strip another of his

---

28. The text of this letter is printed in W. H. T. Dau, *Luther Examined and Reexamined: A Review of Catholic Criticism and a Plea for Reevaluation* (St. Louis: Concordia, 1917), 227.

possessions, no matter how clear a right I have, so long as I am unwilling myself to be stripped of my goods. Rather, just as I would that another, in such circumstances, should relinquish his right in my favor, even so should I relinquish my rights.

Thus should one deal with all property unlawfully held, whether in public or in private, that love and natural law may always prevail. For when you judge according to love you will easily decide and adjust matters without any lawbooks. But when you ignore love and natural law you will never hit upon the solution that pleases God, though you may have devoured all the lawbooks and jurists. Instead, the more you depend on them, the further they will lead you astray.[29]

Both natural law and the law of love teach the same thing, namely, the Golden Rule. The Golden Rule, in turn, is a representation of reason, which manifests itself as "free good sense." The exercise of reason is nothing more than the activity of love and natural law, and this activity produces "good judgment," which is the application of the Golden Rule. So Luther's argument here is indelibly circular, but no matter; the point is that the Golden Rule is the fundamental moral principle at work in human interactions, and both nature and the requirements of neighbor-love teach this principle. Natural law, understood in its classical sense, is a divinely established system of moral goodness, of which the Golden Rule may serve as a summary expression. This summary principle in no way replaces natural law as the mechanism by which all persons may reliably understand what is necessary for human flourishing. But for Luther, natural law plays exactly this kind of secondary role as pointing out the primary function of the Golden Rule in guiding the "good judgment" of persons acting in the public domain. Once again, natural law in Luther's hands describes, not a hallowed and rational moral order rightly governing human conduct, but a set of innate instincts that operate merely as a useful instrument for directing our attention toward appropriate actions that serve the neighbor. Thus, there is nothing in Luther that resembles the complete natural ontology of law we found in Aquinas.

---

29. Martin Luther, *On Temporal Authority: To What Extent It Should Be Obeyed*, in ed. Theodore G. Tappert, *Selected Writings of Martin Luther* (Philadelphia: Fortress, 1967), 2:318.

So what does a "good judgment," informed by the Golden Rule and endorsed by natural law and the law of love, look like? Luther will illustrate.

> This story is told of Duke Charles of Burgundy. A certain nobleman took an enemy prisoner. The prisoner's wife came to ransom her husband. The nobleman promised to give back the husband on condition that she would lie with him. The woman was virtuous, yet wished to set her husband free; so she goes and asks her husband whether she should do this thing in order to set him free. The husband wished to be set free and to save his life, so he gives his wife permission. After the nobleman had lain with the wife, he had the husband beheaded the next day and gave him to her as a corpse. She laid the whole case before Duke Charles. He summoned the nobleman and commanded him to marry the woman. When the wedding day was over he had the nobleman beheaded, gave the woman possession of his property, and restored her to honor. Thus he punished the crime in a princely way.

> Observe: No pope, no jurist, no lawbook could have given him such a decision. It sprang from untrammeled reason, above the law in all the books, and is so excellent that everyone must approve of it and find the justice of it written in his own heart. St. Augustine relates a similar story in *The Lord's Sermon on the Mount*. Therefore, we should keep written laws subject to reason, form which they originally welled forth as from the spring of justice.[30]

What can Luther possibly mean here? Luther is presumably relying on some notion of equity as the basis for his approval of this episode, an equity that satisfies the primitive desire for retributive justice. This is the work of "unfettered reason," the reason that is not to be held captive to letters, nor even captive to the Word of God, but is instead captive to the popular and universal opinion of the public. Luther seems to have collapsed natural law completely into *ius gentium* and regards *ius gentium* as equivalent to the acceptable instincts of the people. But is it really the case that such a judgment as the one enacted by Duke Charles, which

---

30. Luther, *On Temporal Authority*, 2:318–19.

earns approbation from Luther, is the result of natural law and the law of love? The traditional teaching of natural law would only commend this type of action under the most extreme of circumstances. But Luther endorses it enthusiastically and without hesitation. If natural law fosters an outcome that the general public will applaud for its crude equity, then appeals to natural law are appropriate.

Luther's sermons during this period of social upheaval also contain references to the subject of natural law. But these sermons continue the themes Luther has already been sounding: natural law is a synopsis of the type of dispositions we happen to find in all persons; it is expressed in what moves and affects people and is not the product of reason; and it functions instrumentally to propose those decisions and actions that will generate the pragmatic goods of peace, order, and justice. In a sermon preached in January 1525, Luther reiterates his understanding that natural law rests on a single foundational principle that is logically prior to any of the precepts of the classical natural law, namely, the familiar principle of the Golden Rule. Luther says:

> Where are to be found any who comprehend the meaning of the little phrase "thy neighbor," notwithstanding there is, beside this commandment, the natural law of service written in the hearts of all men? Not an individual is there who does not realize, and who is not forced to confess, the justice and truth of the natural law outlined in the command (Matt. 7:12), "All things therefore whatsoever ye would that men should do unto you, even so do ye also unto them." The light of this law shines in the inborn reason of all men. Did they but regard it, what need have they of books, teachers or laws? They carry with them in the depths of their hearts a living book, fitted to teach them fully what to do and what to omit, what to accept and what to reject, and what decision to make.[31]

It sounds at this point as if Luther is suggesting that all a person needs to do, in order to know explicitly what is morally required for service to "thy neighbor," is to inspect the inner workings of this law "written in the hearts of all men." However, as Luther continues, he will insist once again that this light of inborn reason has dimmed considerably, and that

---

31. Martin Luther, "Sermon for the Fourth Sunday After the Epiphany, January 29, 1525," Weimar Ausgabe 17.1.2:88–104.

it is futile to attempt to construct an ethic out of the natural law thus instilled in human beings. Luther concludes his discussion of natural law with a motif that will resound in his writings on this topic from this point forward: the effects of the fall on the human psyche:

> But evil lust and sinful love obscure the light of natural law, and blind man, until he fails to perceive the guide-book in his heart and to follow the clear command of reason. Hence he must be restrained and repelled by external laws and material books, with the sword and by force. He must be reminded of his natural light and have his own heart revealed to him. Yet admonition does not avail; he does not see the light. Evil lust and sinful love blind him. With the sword and with political laws he must still be outwardly restrained from perpetrating actual crimes.[32]

This entire sermon is a polemic against the effort to establish a law-like model for human moral conduct. Luther argues that all people in their natural condition, including Christians, are unable because of sin—"evil lust and sinful love"—to utilize the resources of the natural law written on their hearts. Luther lectures his congregation in this sermon on the folly of legislating our response to the neighbor. As he describes it, the law is purely negative in its function: it cannot tell us (because of our sin) what is the good that we should do, but can only work to prevent us from doing evil. Of course, one would need to read the entire sermon to see this recurring emphasis.

This sermon is typical of Luther's scattered comments on natural law (and typical of such comments by the other sixteenth-century Lutheran reformers). There is a natural law, but the practical reality is that, because the created order has been made so dysfunctional by sin, this natural law is useless to human beings as they seek to understand how to live rightly and serve the neighbor.

It is sometimes argued that Luther's catechetical exposition of the Ten Commandments makes them into exemplars of natural law. But Luther was ambivalent about the precise relationship of the Decalogue and the natural law, particularly during the 1520s, when his thoughts were concentrated on questions of how Christians can know what is right and good when the structures of authority were crumbling all around them.

---

32. Luther, "Sermon for the Fourth Sunday After the Epiphany, January 29, 1525," 17.1.2:88–104.

In a typically blunt sermon preached in August 1525, when Karlstadt had tentatively softened his extreme iconoclasm and doctrine of the Eucharist, and Luther was trying to separate the younger man from more radical elements, he took issue with those who insisted that observance of the Ten Commandments was a requirement of the faithful Christian life.

> To be sure, the Gentiles have certain laws in common with the Jews, such as these: there is one God, no one is to do wrong to another, no one is to commit adultery or murder or steal, and others like them. This is written by nature into their hearts; they did not hear it straight from heaven as the Jews did.

> We will regard Moses as a teacher, but we will not regard him as our lawgiver—unless he agrees with both the New Testament and the natural law.[33]

At least on this occasion, Luther suggests that it is not the case that natural law is derived from the Ten Commandments, but that the Ten Commandments are derived from the natural law. As a result, natural law, which Luther has exhibited a strong tendency to treat as an expression of the "natural" interests of the people, is also a template by which the Decalogue is to be measured. Jews and Gentiles have many of the same laws; these common statutes comprise the most important legal precepts. How did the Gentiles receive them? By an alternate route: engraved on the hearts rather than written in stone. Because this alternate route is prior to and more basic than revelation, Luther seems inclined to regard these generic laws as something like a set of authentic instincts in people that represent their most fundamental desires for the quality of their public life. Luther does not deal with these "natural instincts" (e.g., for peace and order) as rational or even as cognitively apprehended. What Aquinas would have seen as explicitly and essentially rational, Luther regards as precognitive and essentially affective. Luther continues:

> Therefore it is natural to honor God, not steal, not commit adultery, not bear false witness, not murder; and what Moses commands is nothing new. For what God has given the Jews from heaven, he has also written in the hearts of all men. Thus I keep the commandments which Moses has given, not because Moses

---

33. AE 35:164, 165.

gave the commandment," but because they have been implanted in me by nature, and Moses agrees exactly with nature, etc.[34]

Luther concludes this sermon with a threefold distinction: human desires expressed through the natural law, the law of Moses, and the teachings of Christ.

> I have stated that all Christians, and especially those who handle the word of God and attempt to teach others, should take heed and learn Moses aright. Thus where he gives commandment, we are not to follow him except so far as he agrees with the natural law. Moses is a teacher and doctor of the Jews. We have our own master, Christ, and he has set before us what we are to know, observe, do, and leave undone.[35]

One additional issue pertinent to this discussion of Luther's treatment of the Ten Commandments should not be overlooked. It has been occasionally suggested by his commentators that Luther understands the Decalogue to be a reduced rendition of the natural law. Thus, Paul Althaus argues that, for Luther, the Mosaic law functions to "renew the primal natural law," and that it "reminds us of the one natural law and expresses it in a way that has never been equaled."[36] William Lazareth echoes this assertion when he speaks of the Decalogue as "God's natural law summary."[37] But if we turn to Luther's most extensive treatment of the Ten Commandments, found in the Large Catechism of 1529, we see that he discusses there the meaning and application of the Decalogue in ways that no Scholastic natural law theorist would recognize.

In his lengthy examination of the Fourth Commandment, for instance, Luther ignores any precept of the natural law that might inform a child of his responsibility to honor his parents. With regard to such children, Luther says, God "keeps after them with the reminders and proddings of the commandments, so that everyone might think what his parents did for him."[38] A classical natural law theorist would insist that this moral consciousness arises naturally, from an inspection of right

---

34. AE 35:168.

35. AE 35:173–74.

36. Paul Althaus, *The Ethics of Martin Luther* (Philadelphia: Fortress, 1972), 27–28.

37. Lazareth, *Christians in Society*, 225.

38. F. Samuel Janzow, *Getting Into Luther's Large Catechism* (St. Louis: Concordia, 1978), 49.

reason in relation to family obligations. But such a position is nowhere to be found in Luther's Large Catechism presentation of this, or any other, commandment.

Luther further claims, in his discussion of the Fifth Commandment, that "desire for revenge clings to our nature," and so God "wants us to develop the habit of keeping this commandment before our eyes at all times, of seeing ourselves mirrored in it, and of respecting God's will, so that we may confidently and prayerfully commit to Him any wrongs we have suffered."[39] Luther unmistakably contrasts "nature" with "habit" here. "Habit" is not a natural human inclination, but a product of God's gracious encouragement to follow his positive commands. It is also apparent in reading Luther on the Fifth Commandment that he takes the liberty of inflating "thou shalt not kill" to a rubric of "do no harm to anyone," and then expanding the negative injunction against harm to a positive appeal "to take the opportunity to do good to the neighbor."[40] Neither the methods nor the specific content of the natural law is evident in Luther's free construal of the Decalogue in the Large Catechism.

Finally, we see again Luther's distrust of human nature inspected by right reason as a reliable source for discerning divine truth about good and evil in his consideration of the Sixth Commandment. As he has earlier, in the *Lectures on Romans* and the *Disputation Against Scholastic Theology*, Luther assesses human nature, including its rational faculties, as functionally disabled by sin. The enduring and pervasive fact of sin in this life means that human inclinations will invariably slide off in the direction of moral dissolution. In this section of the Large Catechism, Luther writes:

> Where nature as implanted by God has its way, it is not possible to remain chaste except within marriage. For flesh and blood remain flesh and blood, and the natural tendencies and attractions proceed without restraint or hindrance, as everyone can see or sense.[41]

"Nature as implanted by God" is hopelessly corrupt when it comes to figuring out, or living up to, the stipulated divine requirements. This stance eviscerates the vital organs from the body of natural law theory

---

39. Janzow, *Getting into Luther's Large Catechism*, 58.
40. Janzow, *Getting into Luther's Large Catechism*, 58.
41. Janzow, *Getting into Luther's Large Catechism*, 62.

as that theory had developed over a millennium and a half by Luther's time. In its place, Luther offers a model of Christian liberty in moral deliberation, in which God's positive commands pragmatically ground our actions in the public sphere. These positive divine commands do what nature and right reason cannot do: they point us toward the norms of good and evil as established by God. Instead of right reason as the universal arbiter of human flourishing, Luther suggests a "pragmatic reason" that is directed not at a speculative system of ordered ethical precepts, but at the neighbor, and at evaluating in approximate ways what the neighbor's genuine needs might be in a given circumstance. Luther gives every evidence of being concerned with ethical decision-making in real time instead of crafting a timeless structure of moral norms stretching from heaven to earth.

So Luther treats natural law as a manifestation of human affective states implanted in us by creation, to which Mosaic law must conform if the latter is to be authoritative in the Christian life. The Mosaic law has no religious sanction of its own for Christians. But both natural law and Mosaic law are subordinated to the teachings of Christ, which are the normative standards for the Christian. Again we see that Luther avoids offering any kind of divine ontology for moral law, contrasting the earthbound claims of natural law with the spiritual mandates proclaimed by our Master, Christ.

This will turn out to be the consistent trajectory in Luther's account of the natural law. We have seen that this account consists of four related assertions. First, Luther's understanding of the "natural" element in natural law is reduced to something like "natural instinct," or the affective dimension of human life. There are things in life that we "naturally" seek out, and these include peace, prosperity, good order, family, friendship, and other similar goods (this is Luther's version of the *ius gentium*). But these are not rational precepts. For Luther, nature and reason have come apart, and thus natural law seems more aligned with animal instinct than with rational apprehension. So Luther agrees this far with Aquinas: human dispositions are signs of the natural law. But for Aquinas these dispositions are rationally construed to indicate a divine moral order; with Luther, these dispositions are natural only in the sense that all people agree on the common objects of their desires.

Second, insofar as these natural instincts can be translated into moral maxims, they represent for Luther practical considerations rather than divine commands. The precepts of the natural law are ends to be pragmatically achieved within human communities, and not laws to be obeyed regardless of consequences. In our fallen condition, no law of divine origin can be adequately obeyed anyway. All persons desire peace, and so Luther believes it incumbent upon the prince to figure out suitable strategies for securing peace. This is the proper use of reason, as far as Luther is concerned: to reckon the best means for accomplishing the ends toward which we are naturally disposed.

Third, the result of all this is that Luther refuses either to create or to approve an ontology of moral deliberation and action. He will not ratify the Thomist version of natural law, nor the nominalist rendition, and he will not construct his own system. It does not go too far to suggest that Luther thinks of ethics as fundamentally local and circumstantial. In ethics the "natural instincts" of human persons are universal. But the rendering of those instincts into a series of practical judgments applied to specific situations in order to realize the goods embedded in those instincts is something for Luther that can only take place on the ground, in the midst of the immediate context where the opportunities for right action actually present themselves.

Finally, Luther understands natural law not as a Christian teaching, but as an observation of human nature in general. It is apparent that, since the fall, human reason is disordered and cannot be relied on for identifying those goods that lead to human flourishing. The Jew, the Turk, and the heathen employ the same tactics of ethical deliberation, the same resources of the natural law, that Christians do. In this sense, there appears to be no such thing as "Christian ethics" for Luther. There are just ethics, human activities fueled by natural desires, satisfied by practical arrangements, enforced by political structures, producing at their best the conditions under which each one may serve his neighbor and live in peace.

Ultimately, Luther creates a new account of natural law morality: instinctive, not rational; provisional, not ontologically secured; pragmatic, not divinely commanded; chastened by sin, not robust with natural human possibilities. When Luther invokes natural law, it is with a different insight than that supplied to him by the classical natural law tradition.

4

Natural Law in the Lutheran Confessions

Roland Ziegler

The Lutheran Confessions, contained in the Book of Concord, address the doctrinal controversies of their time. The Confessions also summarize the Christian faith; here the three Ecumenical Creeds, the Augsburg Confession, the Small Catechism, and the Large Catechism serve as examples. However, because natural law was not the object of doctrinal controversy in the sixteenth century and because it had not been a central focus of the Christian faith, it does not occupy a prominent place in the Confessions. Nevertheless, when the Confessions treat the law, which according to their soteriological focus is an important topic, they do mention natural law. Yet the Confessions are primarily concerned about the proper distinction of Law and Gospel. This distinction is indispensable for the proper teaching of justification, the chief article of the Christian faith.[1] Thus, the primary focus of any discussion of the law in the Confessions, including natural law, consists of its function as revealing the sinfulness of man and the wrath of God, the so-called *usus elenchticus*.

The Confessions rarely refer to the natural law as a law internal to creatures governing their behavior. Further, the Enlightenment concept that man is endowed with certain inalienable rights as part of "natural law," which played such an important role in the development of the United States of America, is not present in the Confessions. In most monographs on the Confessions, the topic of natural law does not take up much space. There are two exceptions: Edmund Schlink's *Theologie der lutherischen Bekenntnisschriften* and Holsten Fagerberg's *Die Theologie der lutherischen Bekenntnisschriften von 1529 bis 1537.*[2] In the 1930s, a heated debate about the natural knowledge of God was carried on in Germany. Followers of Karl Barth denied any knowledge of God outside of Christ, and thus also any form of the knowledge of natural law as God's law. This found its most famous expression in the Barmen Declaration, which denied that there is any revelation outside of Christ and any authority that should be obeyed besides Christ.[3] The Declaration was primarily a response to Adolf Hitler's ascendency to power in 1933, and the subsequent nazification of the Evangelical Church in Germany. The Barmen Declaration rejected the interpretation of the "orders of creation" doctrine promoted by the German Christians of that era. This interpretation, which had crept into the Lutheran and Reformed Churches in the seventeenth century, suggested that those orders included one's own people (in this situation, those of pure Aryan blood). Since the orders of creation were God's law, they could make a claim on the Christian's life. Because of

---

1. See Ap IV 5f. The standard, critical edition of the Book of Concord is *Die Bekenntnisschriften der evangelisch-lutherischen Kirche* (Göttingen: Vandenhoeck & Ruprecht, 1930) and later editions. The edition quoted in this essay is *Die symbolischen Bücher der evangelisch-lutherischen Kirche, deutsch und lateinisch. Besorgt von J. T. Müller. Mit einer neuen historischen Einleitung von Th. Kolde. 10. Auflage* (Gütersloh: Druck und Verlag von C. Bertelsmann, 1907). All English translations are mine.

2. Edmund Schlink: *Theologie der lutherischen Bekenntnisschriften.* 2. Aufl. (München: Chr. Kaiser Verlag, 1946) [Einführung in die evangelischen Theologie; Band VIII]; Holsten Fagerberg, *Die Theologie der lutherischen Bekenntnisschriften von 1529 bis 1537* (Göttingen: Vandenhoeck & Ruprecht, 1965).

3. *Die erste Bekenntnissynode der Deutschen Evangelischen Kirche zu Barmen. II. Text— Dokumente—Berichte.* Ed. by Gerhard Niemöller, Göttingen: Vandenhoeck & Ruprecht, 1959, 198ff. [Arbeiten zur Geschichte des Kirchenkampfes; Band 6].

this, under Barth's influence the Barmen Declaration rejected any notion of the natural knowledge of God, including the notion of natural law. Some Lutherans objected to the Barmen Declaration precisely because of this. They maintained that the natural knowledge of God and natural law were part of the Lutheran confessional heritage.[4] Other Lutherans, however, were of a different mind. For example, Edmund Schlink, a Lutheran close to Barth on this question, sought in his book to show that a close reading of the Confessions gave no support to the concept of natural law as a guide independent of revelation. Situated in the Swedish discussion, Holsten Fagerberg suggested that the natural law was simply the commandment to love one's neighbor. On this basis, nothing more about the natural law could be said; each Christian has to decide with his or her reason in the concrete situation what this means.[5]

THE TEACHING ON NATURAL LAW IN THE CONFESSIONS

THE FACT OF THE NATURAL LAW

In the background of the Confessions' teaching on natural law is Romans 2:14–15: "For when Gentiles, who do not have the law, by nature do what the law requires, they are a law to themselves, even though they do not have the law. They show that the work of the law is written on their hearts, while their conscience also bears witness, and their conflicting thoughts accuse or even excuse them." Even though the Confessions never explicitly quote this passage, they do use the metaphor of the law being written in man.[6] The writing of the law into man's existence is something that has its origin in creation itself.

God wrote the law into the heart of our first parents, Adam and Eve.[7] But God's writing of the law did not stop there; the law is also rewrit-

---

4.   See Paul Althaus, *Die Christliche Wahrheit* (Gütersloh: C. Bertelsmann Verlag, 1947), 1:272.
5.   Fagerberg, *Die Theologie der lutherischen Bekenntnisschriften von 1529 bis 1537*, 66–77.
6.   LC II 67 uses it; Ap IV 7 speaks of the law written "in the mind."
7.   FC Ep VI 2.

ten on the Christian's heart, so that he or she is like our first parents in this respect. A restoration of creation occurs in the order of salvation.[8] Natural law talks about the nature and extent of the law inscribed into man's existence. Like everything else after the fall, this inscription of the law has also been corrupted, so that it has to be renewed.

The Formula of Concord's Solid Declaration expresses the corruption of the knowledge of the law in fallen man in this way: a "dark spark of the knowledge that there is a God, Romans 1, and also of the teaching of the law" (FC SD II 9), remains in man after the fall. This knowledge is situated in man's reason.[9] Also, in the Apology Melanchthon talks about human reason having an understanding of the law by nature. Having established that the Confessions refer to the natural law, the next step is to investigate what the content of that law is and what influence sin has had on it.

The Content of the Natural Law

Melanchthon defines "law" in Apology IV 7 immediately before presenting the natural knowledge of the law. For Melanchthon, the law is the Ten Commandments or the Decalogue, not the Mosaic ceremonial and civil laws. The German translation of Apology IV 7 clearly identifies the natural law with the Decalogue: "For since the natural law, which agrees with the law of Moses or Ten Commandments, is innate in all men's hearts and written in it."[10] In his one remark on natural law contained in the Confessions, Luther also identifies natural law with the Ten Commandments: "The Ten Commandments are also written in men's

---

8.   FC SD VI 5.

9.   See Ap XVIII 4 [70]: "Human will has freedom in choosing works and things which reason understands by itself. It can somewhat effect civil righteousness or the righteousness of works, it can talk about God, show to God a certain worship with an external work, obey magistrates, parents, in choosing an external work it can restrain the hand from killing, from adultery, from theft. Since there is a relic of reason in man's nature and a judgment on the things subject to the senses, also left is the choice of these things and the freedom and ability to effect civil righteousness. For this the Scripture calls the righteousness of the flesh, which the fleshly nature, that is, reason by itself, effects without the Holy Spirit."

10.   Luther continues: "Therefore I keep the commandments which Moses has given, not because they are commanded by Moses, but since they are implanted in me by nature and Moses here agrees with nature." WA 24:10.3–5 (*How Christians Should Regard Moses*, 1525).

heart, but faith cannot be understood by any human ingenuity and has to be taught solely by the Holy Spirit."[11]

The Confessions claim that the Ten Commandments are the content of natural law, a law that is innate to human beings. Further, the Confessions do not restrict the second table of the law (i.e., the Fourth through Tenth Commandments) to natural law. Rather, they indicate that the first table (i.e., the First through the Third Commandments) is part of the law given to every man. Natural law not only regulates the relations between human beings (Commandments Four through Ten), but also the relations between God and human beings (Commandments One through Three). Hence, the First Commandment is part of natural law.[12] For Luther, this is made clear by the fact that worship is a universal human phenomenon. All societies form some form of cultus; all idolatry is rooted in the sin-perverted knowledge of the commandments of the first table.[13]

On the other hand, not everything in the Ten Commandments is natural law. The Sabbath is not part of natural law, because the particular day to worship was abolished in the New Testament (AC XXVIII 58–60). Thus, the New Testament and its reception of the Old Testament must be taken into account in the discussion about the content of natural law.

The ongoing discussion—whether natural law can be reduced to the command to love or to decisions made by reason, which takes into account the need of the neighbor who meets the Christian—played quite a role in twentieth-century theological discussions in Scandinavia. These

---

11. LC II 67: "Additionally, the Ten Commandments are written in men's heart, but no human wisdom can understand the Creed, and it has to be taught solely by the Holy Spirit."

12. See WA 16:371.5–372.3: "Nevertheless these laws are given to all peoples, as that there is one God, not to do injustice" (*Sermons on Exodus*, 27 August 1525, Rörer's notes).

13. See LC I 16–21. For Luther, knowing about God and worshiping Him go together. This means that, if there is a distorted knowledge of God and of the First Commandment, there is also a distorted worship of a false God. Luther also includes the Third Commandment in this discussion, because its content as part of natural law is not to have a day of rest, but to listen to the Word of God. Luther did not believe that a day off per week is part of the natural law but rather an opportunity to sanctify the day, that is, to invoke God and cherish His revelation. See LC I 82, where the "crude", i.e., literal understanding of the commandment is classified together with other parts of the Mosaic law that are not binding for Christians; but see also WA 18:81.4ff., where Luther admits that nature teaches that there must be some rest from time to time.

discussions originated out of Luther's sometimes rather critical statements about the Mosaic law as the "Jewish civil code," and the corresponding claim by Luther that a Christian can make new Decalogues.[14] For Luther, this does not mean a Decalogue commanding different things, but rather that the Christian, led by the Holy Spirit, knows the law of God through the Holy Spirit. As the later Antinomian controversies showed, by suggesting that the written law has no positive significance for the Christian, some early Lutherans misunderstood the law. However, the Confessions indicate that the Decalogue is part of man's moral fiber. This is proven by the biblical metaphor of God writing the law in Adam's heart and rewriting it in the Christian's heart. Natural law conceived as materially different from or contrary to the Decalogue is inconceivable for the Confessions.[15]

But is natural law limited to the Ten Commandments? That would make natural law rather restricted. What about the task of government? Does natural law have any impact on statutory law besides what is explicit in the Ten Commandments? Here, in view of contemporary discussions, we should remember that while homosexual unions are not explicitly mentioned in the Ten Commandments, the Six Commandment forbids all sexual unchastity, not just adultery, which is explicitly mentioned.

---

14. See WA 24:1–16 (*How Christians Should Regard Moses*).

15. Werner Elert was skeptical about Luther identifying natural law with the Ten Commandments, although Elert conceded this for Melanchthon. According to Elert, Luther identified the "orders of creation," including the difference of individual peoples, with natural law. See Werner Elert, "Morphologie des Luthertums," vol. 2 of *Soziallehren und Sozialwirkunges des Luthertums* (München: C. H. Beck'sche Verlagsbuchhandlung, 1932), 338. Thus, for Elert, all law is natural law insofar it is law of the state as order of creation. Cf. also the quote from Luther, Elert, ibid., 339 (WA 51:212.14ff.) where natural law is devalued in favor of governmental rule. The quote reads as follows: "If natural law and reason would stick in all heads, men's head are equal, then fools, children and women could rule as well and lead wars as David, Augustus, Hannibal, and Phormios must be as good as Hannibal. Yea, all men should be equal and no one would rule the other. What a rebellion and lawless thing should come out of that? But God has created it thus, that men are unequal and one should govern the other, one should obey the other. Two can sing together (that is all equally praise God), but not talk together (that is rule). One has to talk, the other to listen. Therefore one finds that among those who claim or boast of natural reason or law are many splendid and great natural fools. For the precious jewel which is called natural law and reason, is a rare thing among the children of men." Because the discussion of Luther is outside of the scope of this essay, the reader is referred to the pertinent essay in this volume. Even if Elert's interpretation is correct, it is not found in the Book of Concord.

Although countries such as Iran or Saudi Arabia make homosexual acts a capital offense, most Western societies have decriminalized these acts. Thus, discussions about natural law and the state in some countries may meet resistance.[16]

The Confessions do not discuss the relationship between natural law and positive law. Rather, the Confessions declare that the Gospel does not introduce new laws and that Christians are conscience-bound to submit to the government and obey its laws. Governments are compared to seasons; as Christians are subject to the seasons, they are also subject to the government (Ap XVI 6 [58]). Although Christians are subject to legitimate governments and can execute imperial and other law (Ap XVI 1 [53]), the Confessions do not explicitly define legitimate government. The Confessions also do not indicate if there are any limitations to imperial, national, and local laws, whereby a Christian would be relieved from his or her obligation to obey them, except when they violate God's law. (For this, AC XVI 7 quotes Acts 5:29.) From a historical perspective, at the time of the Augsburg Confession, legitimate governments in the Holy Roman Empire were the emperor, elected by the princes that were electors; the princes, either secular (legitimated through descent from the former prince) or spiritual (bishops and abbots, elected according to the laws of the diocese or monastery by a certain group, confirmed by the pope); and city councils, elected by whatever group was enfranchised. Thus, government can be legitimized in different ways—from the hereditary principle to elections by a group.[17] The laws to which the Christian is to subject himself can also be pagan laws; there is no restriction to laws from a Christian perspective (Ap XVI 3 [55]). Melanchthon rejects as insanity Andreas Bodenstein of Karlstadt's idea to reinstate the Mosaic law as civil law (Ap XVI 3 [55]).

Fundamentally, government is an institution from God and can therefore be seen as part of natural law (AC XVI 1ff.). In fact, government

16. Some moral infractions, such as adultery, still violate state statutory law in some states in the U.S. See Jonathan Turly, "Of Lust and Law," *Washington Post,* September 5, 2004, B01, available online at http://www.washingtonpost.com/wp-dyn/articles/A62581-2004Sep4.html.

17. In order to understand what a legitimate government is for the reformers, modern readers have to divest themselves of their democratic prejudices and concepts such as popular sovereignty. Though not incompatible with their teachings, the idea that political power resides in the people and is delegated by them to the government—*the consent of the people* making a government legitimate—was not even entertained by the reformers.

might even be called a sacrament (Ap XIII 15). Government is an extension of the paternal authority (LC I 141, 150). If we look at the purpose of government, it is the same as for parents and neighbors: to be God's hands, channels, and means through which God extends His goodness. The government gives goods (LC I 26). Through the government, God offers daily bread and provides the comforts of this life (LC III 74). Thus, even though the Ten Commandments do not explicitly state this, parents, masters, government, and others in authority should not act like criminals or tyrants. Rather, they should care for those under their authority with provisions for this life and raise them to God's praise and honor (LC I 167f). The government should defend marriage and invite people to marry, since upholding public discipline is part of the government's mission (Ap XXIII 55). The government is instituted to uphold civil righteousness. Luther wished that the government would also interfere in the economic sphere and curtail the demands of artisans and day laborers who charge highly for their labor. A well-ordered government, as in Roman times, would prevent this (LC I 239).[18] But it would also interfere against a behavior that charges the poor for goods irrespective of their situation (LC I 246–248). Even though Luther sees that he can only preach against the lack of care for the neighbor, he does assign the government a role in enforcing civil righteousness that includes care for the neighbor.

The government also has a duty to govern marriage. The Roman Catholic Church had made marriage into a sacrament, taking marriage out of the realm of civil law and placing it into canonical law. In addition, the Roman Church forbade marriage between those who were "spiritually related," that is, between baptismal or confirmation sponsors. Remarriage of an innocent party following a divorce was also prohibited. The Confessions condemn the Roman Church's acceptance of secret engagements as unjust and condemn the requirement of clerical celibacy. Since the ecclesiastical courts for whom the bishops were responsible continued to enforce unjust laws, the civil authorities were to take over jurisdiction by *divine right* (Tr 77f). The government thereby reinstitutes the true law of God for marriage, because the legal ordering of marriage is not by divine right a matter of the Church. Any legal jurisdiction bishops

---

18. For Luther's economic thought, especially his advocacy of price and wage controls, cf. Hans-Jürgen Prien, *Luthers Wirtschaftsethik* (Göttingen: Vandenhoeck & Ruprecht), 1992.

and the church had at the time of the Reformation they had by human right (AC XXVIII 29), because marriage, even though instituted by God, is a secular estate.[19]

This gives us some insight at least into what the Confessions see as natural law in the realm of marriage. Because of natural law, a "spiritual relationship," which is not mentioned in Scripture, does not impede marriage. Following a divorce, the innocent party, whether Christian or non-Christian, may remarry. Secret engagements are null and void, most likely because they are made without parental consent and thereby violate parental authority over their children. All of this goes far beyond the mere wording of the Sixth Commandment. The rejection of a spiritual relationship can be seen as a simple reduction of human regulations, but it is more: it assumes that the Church has no authority to limit marriage by its own laws beyond the laws of nature. The same is true with celibacy. It is against divine and natural law (Ap XXIII 6). The reformers not only reject a false ecclesiastical authority, but they also reestablish the natural law that resides in creation. Man is created with an inclination toward woman, woman with an inclination toward man. But Melanchthon does not argue here with biological facts, or, more generally speaking, by analyzing the human condition. He simply quotes Genesis 1:28 (Ap XXIII 7). Nevertheless, Melanchthon expressly agrees with the legal scholars that marriage is as a divine institution also by natural law.[20] In this way, Melanchthon acknowledges natural law in the area of marital law, but he

---

19. See Luther's Marriage Booklet (*Die symbolischen Bücher* etc., cf. Footnote 1, 764): "So many lands, so many customs, goes the common saying. Therefore, since marriage and the estate of marriage are a worldly business, it behooves us ministers or servants of the church to order or govern nothing in it, but to allow every city and country its custom and habit, as they come." Although marriage is a secular matter, this does not mean that it lies outside of the scope of God's law as an autonomous institution. In fact, traditional civil law used natural law to rule out certain degrees of consanguinity, or kinship, between potential husbands and wifes. Melanchthon's remark above allowed for remarriage *by the innocent party* after a divorce. The shift in civil marriage law away from what the reformers perceived as part of God's universal law did not begin with same-sex marriage. In fact, the universal acceptance of no-fault divorce would have been abhorrent to the reformers.

20. (Ap XXIII 9) "And because this creation or divine order in man is natural law, therefore the jurists have wisely and rightly said that the union of male and female belongs to natural law."

does not give us a method to evaluate what it is materially besides what is said in Scripture.[21]

Beyond that, Melanchthon addresses Emperor Charles: "You owe this duty most of all to God, to preserve the true doctrine and propagate it to posterity, and to defend those who teach right things. For this God demands when he honors kings with his name and calls them gods, saying: 'I have said: Ye are gods.' (Psalms 82:6 [KJV]), so that they care about preserving and propagating divine things, that is the gospel of Christ, and, so to say as vicar of God, defend the life and well-being of the innocent" (Ap XXI 44). Charles as emperor therefore has also a duty in regard to the true worship of God and in regard to the eternal welfare of his subjects. This might seem alien to us, we who cherish religious freedom, but for the reformers it is not religious freedom, but freedom for the Gospel and the true worship of God and its defense and care for by the government that is part of natural law.

The statements on the duties of government show that especially Luther uses the commandment to love one's neighbor to flesh out the meaning of natural law. Thus, the Decalogue is not seen as limiting natural law, but rather as its summary. The command to love one's neighbor is the summary of natural law and has to govern also civil authorities.[22]

This leads us to the fundamental problem of natural law: How does one define what natural law is besides quoting Scripture? Can one analyze the human condition and from its factual state derive natural law, so that the *ought* follows from the *is*? Or should one compare cultures and find natural law in the common denominator of their ethical prescripts? What one finds depends, of course, on whom one includes, and what are the criteria for that? Neither way seems workable theologically, because since the fall, human nature is sinful and corrupt. Because of this, a clear criterion that distinguishes between corruption and incorruption must first be found. Thus, for this task law must be presupposed in the analysis of

---

21. In AC XXIII, the argument from natural law against clerical celibacy is thus summarized: "Since God's Word and command cannot be changed through a human vow or law, therefore and for other reasons the priests and other ministers have married" (AC XXIII 9). God's Word and command are taken from 1 Corinthians 7:2, 9; Matthew 19:11; Genesis 1:27. Experience is only adduced as a confirmation that voluntary chosen celibacy outside of this order is not a lifestyle that can be maintained without sin.

22. The commandment to love does not rule out the use of force, when it is in exercised to preserve public order, which in itself is an order of love.

the human condition in order to find law. The way from *is* to *ought* is therefore theologically impossible. Accordingly, this way is never used in the Confessions. The closest to it is the statement that no law can nullify nature; consequently, laws concerning celibacy and monastic vows are null and void (Ap XXIII 15–16). Even here Melanchthon does not simply start with the fact of sexual desire and the necessity for its relief in sexual intercourse, but he quotes 1 Corinthians 7:9. We know that sexual desire and its *telos*, its intended fulfillment, is in marriage (not in fornication or adultery) and that it is neither inherently evil nor controllable by mere willpower through God's Word, not through an analysis of the phenomenon and its "natural solution."[23]

But is the natural law, written in man's heart, clear enough that an analysis of innate ideas themselves, or at least how these innate ideas have manifested themselves in cultures, lead to a knowledge of natural law? The statements of the Confessions about the knowledge of the law in sinful man as a "dark spark" does not give much hope that this is a feasible way to go.

The Confessions do not answer the question of how natural law can be known without the Word of God. They simply describe the phenomenon: People do act in such ways that in their actions there is somewhat of the understanding of the law of God. Of course, people also act also in ways that are totally contrary to God's Word. Laws and customs do not always reflect natural law; they can be completely corrupted. One may only think of the treatment of unwanted infants in Sparta. Spartans had no moral qualms about committing infanticide; indeed, the human law *demanded* the exposure of weak children.[24] All human laws are imperfect due to sin.

---

23. We have to remember that for some people their deviant behavior feels natural to them. Man can effectively silence God's voice in natural law, working through his conscience, when it comes to certain actions. See the position of the Epicureans as described by David Hume, *David Hume: The Philosophical Works* (London: Longmans, Green and Co., 1882), 3:198: "When by my will alone I can stop the blood, as it runs with impetuosity along its canals, then may I hope to change the course of my sentiments and passions. In vain should I strain my faculties, and endeavor to receive pleasure from an object, which is not fitted by nature to affect my organs with delight."

24. See Plutarch's *Life of Lycurgus* that documents also the different view of marriage in Sparta where progeny was more important for marriage than sexual faithfulness. Hence, an older man married to a younger wife without offspring could invite a younger man to be his substitute.

For though human morality has its root in God's law, it is corrupted in such a way that it never clearly shows the will of God. The natural law enables the sinner to understand somewhat the revealed law of God as it is preached. However, sinful human reason impedes a true understanding of the law, because the sinful human being believes that the law can be fulfilled and that through it righteousness before God can be obtained. Reason does see that certain works are required, but the Decalogue truly requires things that are beyond reason: truly to fear God, truly to love Him, and truly to call upon Him. Sinful human reason believes that sinners can be justified by the law. This shows that sinful reason is deluded about its abilities and that it is deluded about the content of the law. The natural knowledge of the law leads to a false understanding of righteousness before God: "For all human reason and wisdom cannot judge otherwise than that one has to become pious before God through the law, and who keeps the law externally is holy and pious."[25]

Thus, non-Christian religions are a manifestation of natural law: They acknowledge that there is a God and that man has a duty to worship Him. They are also a manifestation of sin: non-Christians do not worship the true God, but idols, and they worship in a manner that is not divinely ordained (LC I 18).[26]

Therefore, natural law has the same ambiguity as natural revelation. God did not leave man without witness to Himself; man does know something about Him. However, such knowledge is a mixture of truth and error. The natural knowledge of God does not simply serve as a stepping-stone to the true knowledge of God, it also serves as a witness in man's conscience that atheism and materialism are self-defeating ideologies. Even if individuals do not realize this, natural law still serves as a

25. "For all human reason and wisdom cannot judge in any other way than that one has to become pious through law, and that he who keeps the law externally is holy and pious." (Ap IV 159, only in the German of Justus Jonas's paraphrase of the Latin. Even though it is therefore not part of the confessional document itself, it accurately reflects Melanchthon's thinking, as a comparison with Ap IV 288 shows: "And this mode of justification [namely through works], can be understood and somewhat accomplished, because it is according to reason and completely turned towards outward works.")

26. See also FC SD V 22: "As Doctor Luther has practiced this distinction with special assiduity in almost all his writings, and has shown explicitly, that it is a vastly different knowledge of God that comes from the gospel than that which is taught and learned by the law, since also the pagans have somewhat of a knowledge of God from natural law, even though they have neither properly known him nor honored him, Romans 1."

means to maintain some form of civil order and as a basic knowledge about the difference between good and evil. The preaching of the revealed law will deconstruct and reconstruct that basic knowledge. Thus, natural law does leave men "without excuse" (Romans 1:20).

CONCLUSION

Natural law is a topic in the current debate about the moral foundations of a society. Modern Western societies do not have the cohesion of a common religion, because they have consciously secularized themselves through the abolition of state churches and the consequent privatization of religion. Nevertheless, societies need some basic moral convictions that are shared by the population. This service formerly was provided by shared theological and philosophical principles. The problem is not that a diminishing of such shared convictions might result in a civil war (though this lack of shared values was once a problem that led to the Civil War in the United States), but that there is a shift in convictions and thus in laws, as especially the sexual revolution has brought about. The use of "natural law" in the discussion about abortion and same-sex marriage is an effort to establish a nonsectarian basis in political lobbying.

Of course, nothing prevents the Church from proclaiming that both abortion and same-sex marriage are sinful and condemned by God. Nevertheless, in a religiously pluralistic society, this is a particularistic point of view. One trying to push for legislation in these matters naturally encounters the accusation of fostering his or her religious values. This in itself is considered to be a breach of the basic conviction and law of the land that religious freedom is to be protected. A more promising strategy may be to argue from a natural law perspective—a universal, nonsectarian perspective—because many important historical documents appeal to natural law. Even though contemporary discourse has shifted from natural law as natural obligations to natural rights, and natural law at least in legal contexts has also been secularized, some headway may be made. Although not without some difficulties, the Confessions lend themselves to the modern discussion because of their insistence that religion is part of natural law.

Moreover, the modern idea of human rights as some form of natural law is not only a shift in terminology, but also a shift in content. If one compares the second table of the Ten Commandments with lists such as those enumerated in the Declaration of Independence of the United States of America (1776), the Declaration of Rights of Man and of the Citizen of the National Assembly of France (1789), or the Universal Declaration of Human Rights by the General Assembly of the United Nations (1948), one sees similarities and differences. Property and life are protected, too; but adultery is not treated, nor coveting one's neighbor's wife, servants, or property.[27]

For the reformers, political rights are not part of natural law.[28] Political rights include individual freedoms, such as freedom of religion, freedom of speech, and freedom of assembly. In the contemporary understanding, these "negative" rights are to be protected from governmental interference. The shift in the way we treat natural law today is due to the fact that modern natural law discourse is derived from several sources, including classical Greece and Rome and the work of Enlightenment philosophers such as John Locke, not just the Christian tradition. Therefore, the term *natural law* itself becomes somewhat equivocal. Lutheran Christians and those who define their understanding of natural law in the tradition of modern Western political thought do not agree on the content of natural law. Additionally, the most enticing feature of the thought of natural law, namely, that it is universal and consequently evident to everybody, must take into account that sin has effaced and distorted it.

The task of the Church is to preach the law, also the *usus politicus legis,* in season and out of season to everyone, so that through the Gospel the Law is again inscribed into the hearts of men by God (FC SD VI 5). Although, due to sin, sinful human beings perceive natural law imperfectly, it is not totally alien to them. As such, an ally exists in everybody's heart for the preaching of God's law.

---

27. As revolting as it is to our modern sensibilities, for the reformers the right to individual freedom grounded in the fact of self-possession (as opposed to forms of slavery of serfdom) was not part of natural law. Thus, Luther's critique of the demands of the peasants in the Peasants' Revolt in 1525, see WA 18:326.14–327.10.

28. The closest one gets to something like civil liberties are the statements concerning the freedom to marry and the freedom for the Gospel (not religious freedom!).

5

NATURAL LAW AND THE ORDERS OF CREATION

Armin Wenz

The need to find clarity again concerning the relevance, contents, and implications of the natural law among Lutherans is obvious when we perceive the contradicting notions of that theological topic, as they can be discovered in current ethical discourses. One example is the conflict concerning abortion. Some Protestant theologians in Germany argue that, whereas the Roman Catholic Church has perceivable material norms based on an objective revelation (natural or supranatural), "Protestant Ethics" in all its variants finds its prime paradigm in Luther's protest of a pious individual against an almighty powerful clerical institution and in the notion of "the freedom of a Christian."[1] The impression

---

1. Friedrich W. Graf and Stephan Schleissing, "Es gibt eine Zeit zum Streit," in *Frankfurter Allgemeine Zeitung,* July 7, 1999, 45.

one gets here is this: natural law is a specifically Roman Catholic doctrine, which has no relevance among Lutherans or Protestants in general because they base their judgments on their conscience alone, not on external, objective norms.

In this very discourse concerning abortion, we not only find such blatant negations of natural law, but also attempts to claim Luther as authority for a dynamic transformation of the traditional notion of natural law that would help the Church to cease "making inappropriate appeals over against state parliaments concerning the lawful prohibition of divorces or abortions in a constitutional state," in order to open the road for a "true" humanization of society.[2] In a public discussion with Igor Kišš in "Das Neue in Luthers Verständnis vom natürlichen Gesetz," from *Luther*, the theological quarterly of the German "Luthergesellschaft," Wichmann von Meding rightfully refutes this distortion of Luther's theology when he writes, "When Luther talks about natural law, he does not refer to a 'law that is adapted to mankind's sinful situation,' but to the Decalogue which confronts sin and only by doing so, enables man to receive knowledge of sin." The difference between the dynamic notion of natural law (as represented by Igor Kišš) and Luther's notion, according to von Meding, is "the question whether abortions can be perceived as human and just acts taking into account man's sinful condition, or whether they clearly contradict the Fifth Commandment."[3]

In a recent publication, German theologian Gunther Wenz identifies natural law with the Decalogue,[4] thus following the line of thought in the Lutheran Confessions. At the end of his explanation of the Creed in the Large Catechism, Luther notes that whereas "no human wisdom can comprehend" the Creed that "must be taught by the Holy Spirit alone," "the Ten Commandments are written in the hearts of all men" (LC II 67). The Formula of Concord claims: "Therefore both for the penitent and impenitent, for regenerated and unregenerate people the

2. Igor Kišš, "Das Neue in Luthers Verständnis vom natürlichen Gesetz," *Luther: Zeitschrift der Luther-Gesellschaft* 70 (1999): 32; 38.
3. Wichmann von Meding, "Luthers Rede vom Naturgesetz: Eine kleine Antwort an Igor Kišš," *Luther: Zeitschrift der Luther-Gesellschaft* 71 (2000): 40. My translation.
4. Wenz, who is not related to the author of this essay, also combines the notion of "natural law" with the notion of "order of creation," cf. Gunther Wenz, "Die geschöpfliche Bestimmung des Menschen nach Luthers Dekalogauslegung," *Denkraum Katechismus. Festgabe für Oswald Bayer zum 70. Geburtstag,* ed. Johannes von Lüpke and Edgar Thaidigsmann (Tübingen: Mohr Siebeck, 2009), 279.

law is and remains one and the same law, namely, the unchangeable will of God" (FC Ep VI 7). Nevertheless, the notion of "natural law" is mentioned in the Lutheran Confessions only occasionally because it was not a church-divisive factor in the sixteenth century. In any case, the theology of creation, which is the basis also for the notion of "natural law," plays an important role in the Confessions. And in this context of a theology of creation the Lutheran Confessions find and use another notion much more frequently than the notion of "natural law." This notion, though related to natural law, is the notion of divine orders (*ordinationes Dei*) or institutions (*institutiones Dei*), which are of universal relevance because they shape the lives of all human beings according to God's will as it is revealed in the Bible.

These creational orders or institutions in the Confessions[5] are perceived as having the same structure as God's orders and institutions for the Church: they are founded on words of institution that combine a divine mandate (*mandatum*) and divine promise (*promissio*). In the orders of salvation, these words, of course, are Christ's solemn institutions, surrounding His death and resurrection, of the preaching office, of the keys, of Baptism and Holy Communion. In the orders of creation, though, these words are located in Genesis concerning the creation of mankind.[6] God's words are perceived as most effectively bringing about what they say. In both realms, God's words do not aim at blind obedience, but at man's trust and sure confidence that he, in, with, and under the reality of these orders and institutions and their representatives, has to do with God Himself in His blissful and life-giving and life-preserving mercy. This line of thought is prevalent in Luther's explanation of the Fourth Commandment in the Large Catechism, although it is already summarized in his explanation of the First Commandment:

> Although much that is good comes to us from men, we receive it all from God through his command and ordinance. Our parents and all authorities—in short, all people placed in the position of neighbors—have received the command to do us all kinds

---

5. Concerning political rule: AC XVI 5–7; Ap XVI 1 (53): "that legitimate civil ordinances are good creatures of God and divine ordinances, which a Christian can use with safety." Concerning marriage and family: AC XXIII 15–23; Ap XXIII 14. Luther in the Smalcald Articles (SA II 3) talks about "offices and callings ordained by God" ("von Gott gestifte Ämpter und Orden").

6. Cf. AC XXIII 5–9; XXVII 19–21; Ap XXIII.

of good. So we receive our blessings not from them, but from God through them. Creatures are only the hands, channels, and means through which God bestows all blessings. For example, he gives to the mother breasts and milk for her infant, and he gives grain and all kinds of fruits from the earth for man's nourishment—things which no creature could produce by himself. No one, therefore, should presume to take or give anything except as God has commanded it. We must acknowledge everything as God's gifts and thank him for them, as this commandment requires. Therefore, this way of receiving good through God's creatures is not to be disdained, nor are we arrogantly to seek other ways and means than God has commanded, for that would be not receiving our blessings from God but seeking them from ourselves. (LC I 26–27)

Just as the Christian draws certainty concerning his salvation in Christ on the basis of the divine institutions for the Church, so on the basis of the divine institutions for the world as God's creation he draws certainty that his love and sanctification lived out in the framework of these institutions has the approval and blessing of his heavenly Father. Albrecht Peters writes fittingly: "This threesome—God's blessing as Creator, God's foundations and callings, and God's Commandments—bestows on the Christian ethos a sacramental dimension, as it were. As the all-sovereign Redeemer reveals Himself for our salvation only under Word and Sacrament, so the omnipotent Creator wants to be found in His institutions and Commandments."[7]

Thus, in the Lutheran Confessions, this approach of a theological ethic as trustful reception of the biblical commandments and orders of God the Creator is an implication of a specifically structured biblical hermeneutics, which perceives the solemn Words of Institution marked by divine self-commitment through commandment and promise, as key texts whose total relevance for the history of salvation is expounded in broad and manifold ways in the great narrative parts of Scripture, as well as in its liturgical (Psalms) and poetical parts. These solemn words of universal validity are to be considered among the very clear stars in the

---

7.   Albrecht Peters, *Commentary on Luther's Catechisms: Ten Commandments* (St. Louis: Concordia, 2009), 126.

Scriptures that throw their light upon all parts of the biblical revelation and from which and toward which the Scriptures are to be interpreted.

The Church obediently applies this canonical structure by shaping the contents of her proclamation and catechesis and her worship life in its narrow, liturgical, and its broad, diaconical dimension according to God's biblical institutions and commands. The Church's worship life in its narrow sense is determined by the institution of the means of grace as it is expounded by Luther in the Catechisms and in his instruction concerning Confession and Absolution. The Christian worship in everyday life is determined by the rediscovery of the Creator's institutions and orders as they are expounded on broad biblical bases in the Table of Duties as well as in Luther's "Marriage Booklet."[8] The Decalogue impresses both, in its First Table obedience over against the divinely instituted means of grace, as well as in its Second Table reverence over against the holiness of human life in its different aspects and relations as they are ordained by the Creator and are protected and guarded by His very commandments. Marriage and family, food and goods, good reputation and vocation are perceived as divine gifts protected by God Himself through His commands.

The Christian is free to make use of God's life-preserving gifts in the relations he lives in, within the family, the economy, and the state. The divine institutions and orders these relations are based upon thereby constitute space and time for the human being. And the divine commandment through which God protects and preserves these relations demarks the framework—indeed, the borderlines—for this time and space in which God presents His gifts as Creator. Thus, these realms and relations the Christian lives in are not constituted from scratch through faith or a sanctified life. Instead, the justified and sanctified Christian acknowledges or rediscovers these realms as gifts and commands, which his heavenly Father, in whose fellowship he has entered through Christ, always had in mind for the creation and preservation of his life in which he now lives in faith and holiness in Christ. Sanctification, therefore, does not constitute a special Christian ethic (*Sonderethik*), but leads into a rediscovery and theological and practical reaffirmation of those gifts and activities that the Creator universally bestows on us humans in the realm of the political use of the law (*usus politicus legis*).

---

8.   Both are parts of Luther's Small Catechism, printed in the Book of Concord.

Even Jesus' commandment to love one's foes is justified by the practice of the heavenly Father Himself who (in the realm of His creation)
lets the sun shine and rain for all His humans (Matthew 5:43–45). The
principle *sola gratia* is not only valid for salvation but also in creation and
preservation. Luther makes this quite clear in his explanation of the First
Article when he concludes his list of divine gifts that serve the Creator to
preserve our lives: "All this he does out of his pure, fatherly, and divine
goodness and mercy, without any merit or worthiness on my part. For
all of this I am bound to thank, praise, serve, and obey him" (SC II 2).
Theological ethics, first of all, has to do with enjoying the gifts of God's
creation and serving Him and one's neighbors in these orders, which on
a secondary level due to man's sin necessarily find their protective power
in the Commandments of the Decalogue.

To the extent that the Decalogue obviously presupposes these divine
gifts in the realm of creation and draws a protective borderline around
them, one can say, following Sasse[9] and Elert,[10] that the notion of the
orders of creation is the Lutheran equivalent to the classical notion of

---

9. Cf. Hermann Sasse, "Vom Sinn des Staates," *In statu confessionis,* ed. Friedrich Wilhelm Hopf (Berlin/Schleswig Holstein: Furche-Verlag, 1976), 2:331–66. Sasse first
refutes the notions of natural law in Roman Catholic and Enlightenment theology, before concluding (355): "Dennoch gibt es nach evangelischer Lehre etwas,
was dem Gedanken des Naturrechts entspricht: Es ist der Gedanke der *Schöpfungs-
sordnungen,* d. h. Ordnungen, durch die Gott seine Schöpfung erhält." ("Yet, there
is, according to evangelical doctrine, something that corresponds to the notion of
natural law: it is the notion of orders of creation, that is, orders, through which
God preserves His creation.") My translation.

10. Also, according to Elert, a whole "system" of "natural law"-thinking as in Roman-
Catholic theology is not possible due to the reality of sin and evil in our fallen
world, but the task is to find those orders of being which can be viewed as "prescribed according to nature" (*naturgesetzlich*) since they find their foundation in
God's creational and governing activity and are therefore presupposed in God's
written law. The law presupposes these orders by introducing and sending us into
them. "Es kommt vielmehr . . . darauf an, die . . . im kreatorischen und guberna-
torischen Tun Gottes begründeten und *darum* auch naturgesetzlichen Seinsord-
nungen aufzufinden, die vom geschriebenen Gesetz Gottes vorausgesetzt werden.
Sie werden von ihm vorausgesetzt, indem wir in sie eingewiesen werden." Werner
Elert, *Das christliche Ethos* (Tübingen: Furche-Verlag, 1949), 108. Cf. *The Christian Ethos,* trans. Carl J. Schindler (Philadelphia: Muhlenberg Press, 1957), 74. This
translation seems to be slightly deficient here, translating "*naturgesetzlich*" merely
as "natural." This would be a fitting paraphrase of Elert: "We are not attempting to
develop a system of natural law but to discover those orders of existence which are
grounded in the creative and governing activity of God and are therefore natural
orders of existence which the law presupposes. Their existence is taken for granted
insofar as we are assigned to them."

"natural law." When we talk about "orders of creation," we are aware that this terminology has not been used in the Church before the nineteenth century. Sasse, in another essay, suggests using the term *divine order* instead.[11] And it is quite obvious that the Confessions and traditional Lutheran theologians use a variety of synonymous terms.[12] Nevertheless, for the sake of being able to mark the differences among those institutions and orders that serve our salvation and shape the life of the church, the term *order of creation* seems to be a helpful choice because it points to the structural parallels between the orders in both realms (divine command, divine promise, divine blessing), as it is repeatedly expounded by Albrecht Peters in his commentary on Luther's Catechisms. At the same time this term marks the clear difference: We are not talking about orders that bring about eternal salvation in God's judgment, but we are talking about orders through which the very same triune God continues to create new life and to preserve His whole creation to the earthly benefit of the very same people He wants to save in Christ and through the work of the Spirit. Parallel to the "means of grace," through which God the Spirit bestows on us our salvation in Christ, one could talk about "means of earthly bliss" through which God continues to create and preserve the very world into which His church and His Christians are sent to serve Him, their Creator and Savior.

Whereas the term *law* reminds us that even unbelievers or non-Christians will be judged by the very same law that is—as natural law—written into their hearts despite the darkness of sin, thus making the sinner without excuse, the term *order* on the other side points to the fundamental character of God's activity in creation and to the very framework in which He shapes and preserves His creation. The biblical term in the

---

11. Cf. Hermann Sasse, "The Lutheran Confessions and the Volk" (1933), in *The Lonely Way. Selected Essays and Letters. Vol. I (1927–1939)* (St. Louis: Concordia, 2002), 136: "Thus the confusing term 'order of creation' (*Schöpfungsordnung*) should be avoided where possible. The order of the state, for instance, does not have anything *directly* to do with creation. The expression 'order of preservation' is problematic, because it is not specific enough (preservation of the world in general, or preservation of the fallen world). Theology would do well to return to the old term 'divine order' (*göttliche Ordnung*), or 'God's order' (*Gottesordnung*)."

12. Carl E. Braaten observes that the "orders of creation" are discussed in Luther's theology under a manifold terminology such as: "*ordo, ordo divina, ordo naturalis, ordinatio, ordinatio divina, creatura Dei, weltlich Regiment, potestas ordinata.*" Braaten, "God the Creator Orders Public Life," *No Other Gospel! Christianity among World Religions* (Minneapolis: Fortress Press, 1992), 119.

Greek for order is *taxis* and its components. Throughout the Bible, *taxis* denotes pairs or relations between things or persons that are at the same time distinct from each other and, nevertheless, joined together by the Creator for a common purpose that can be fulfilled only together.

According to 1 Corinthians 14:33, "God is not a God of confusion, but of peace." Confusion, chaos, is the opposite of order. Luther renders this verse: "*Gott ist nicht ein Gott der Unordnung, sondern des Friedens*" (God is not a God of disorder, but of peace). This motif runs throughout the Scriptures starting with creation in Genesis 1. God creates the world for the sake of us human beings by giving the life-threatening primeval chaos (in the Hebrew: *tohu wabohu*) an ordered form in which life can thrive. The Creator separates light from darkness and thus creates the polarity of day and night. The firmament separates the waters; the lights separate night and day. Man and animals are created male and female. Each creative work in Genesis 1 constitutes pairs joined together by God. Only together all these pairs serve the preservation and reproduction of life on earth. God creates by commanding and by putting the created things in their determined order when He gives them names and joins them together with their respective opposites. Man has the ability to distinguish the animals by giving them names (Genesis 2:19ff). God the Creator relates to His creatures by giving different things different names. In the same way, man, as God's earthly representative, relates to his fellow creatures as their lord who exercises his authority by putting everything in the very same order God the Creator has established before. The scientific ability of mankind to distinguish and give names to the creatures around him, and thus to perceive the world in an orderly manner, mirrors God's way of creating by putting things into their order.

Creation's being ordered implies that each work of creation has its specific shape and glory (1 Corinthians 15:40–41), function and *boundary!* Psalm 74:16–17 says: "Yours is the day, Yours also the night; You have established the heavenly lights and the sun. You have fixed all the *boundaries* of the earth; You have made summer and winter." And Psalm 104:5–9: "He set the earth on its foundations, so that it should never be moved. You covered it with the deep as with a garment: the waters stood above the mountains. At Your rebuke they fled; at the sound of Your thunder they took to flight. The mountains rose, the valleys sank down to the place that You appointed for them. You set a *boundary that they may not pass*, so that they might not again cover the earth."[13] It is this well-ordered creation which God judges as being "very good" (Genesis 1:31). Thus, the order of creation in its original state reflects God's very perfection.

This is the reason why in the Old Testament the well-ordered works of creation do proclaim the glory of their Creator together with and in accordance with the law through which God orders the life of His people (Psalms 19; 36:6–7; 119:89–94; 148). The same qualities that are ascribed to the law are ascribed to creation: Beyond and despite all the dangers experienced in life, the order of creation is permanent, firm, and reliable. Psalm 148:6 says concerning God's creatures that fill the heavens: "And He established them forever and ever; He gave a decree, and it shall not pass away." The Hebrew word חֹק,[14] which some render as "bounds," in the Luther Bible is translated as "order"/"Ordnung." This word in the Old Testament most of the time is used as a term for regulations of the law. The same is true for Jeremiah 31:35–36: "Thus says the LORD, who gives the sun for light by day and the fixed order of the moon and the stars for light by night, who stirs up the sea so that its waves roar—the LORD of hosts is His name: 'If this fixed order departs from before Me, declares the LORD, then shall the offspring of Israel cease from being a nation before Me forever.'" Psalm 119:90–91 uses another term taken from the context of the theology of the law and justice for grounding the stability of the earth in God's creative activity: "Your faithfulness *endures* to all generations; You have established the earth, and it stands fast. By Your appointment they stand this day,[15] for all things are Your servants." All these texts bring to mind God's promise after the primeval flood in Genesis 8:22: "While the earth remains, seedtime and harvest, cold and heat, summer and winter, day and night, shall not cease." God's "very good" as judgment concerning His creation thus can be reflected even under the conditions of the fallen world in the liturgical praise of the people of God, when Psalm 104:24 says: "O LORD, how manifold are Your works! In wisdom have You made them all; the earth is full of Your creatures."

---

13. Also see Job 26:10, 38:10; Psalm 148:6; Proverbs 8:29; Jeremiah 5:22.

14. The Septuagint (LXX) renders: πρόσταγμα (Psalm 148:6). Cf. Jeremiah 31:36, where the plural of חֹק, חֻקִּים, is translated as οἱ νόμοι.

15. The Hebrew here has לְמִשְׁפָּטֶיךָ; the LXX renders: τῇ διατάξει σου διαμένει (German: *deine Ordnung bleibt*).

This wisely ordered creation is the place where man lives his life in an environment in which, on the one hand, God takes care of him and preserves him by means of the creatures and gifts around him, and in which, on the other hand, man has the task to cultivate his world and multiply himself. Man lives as a child God himself takes care of; and at the same time, man is assigned to live as a king, carefully ruling the world entrusted to him.[16] Scripture clearly reveals that the whole creation is a divine gift and displays a divine task for us humans. This revelation can be seen in the total story of the Bible and especially in the Psalms. But it is made even clearer in the very divine words of institutions in which commandment and promise are joined together. God's creation thus is revealed as a total gift (*elementare Gabe*), which man is free to work with and enjoy. These concrete commandments and promises of God denote man's specific place and task in the creation: Human beings are first of all designated to live from the fruits of creation through which God sustains their life, and at the same time they are to respect the one boundary that God puts up around the tree of the knowledge of good and evil (Genesis 2:16ff).[17] Second, man receives dominion over the surrounding creation; he is neither supposed to demonize it nor to adore or deify the creatures, but to rule them as free lord and king whose sole ruler is the Creator Himself (Genesis 1:28; 2:15–19).[18] Third, mankind receives both God's life-sustaining care and gifts and the task of ruling and cultivating the world in the relationship of man and woman, husband and wife, joined together as one flesh by the Creator Himself, thus being enabled to pass on life from one generation to another (Genesis 1:27ff; 2:18).

Because the Creator of the world in the biblical canon is the same God who calls Israel out from the Gentiles in order to prepare the way for the Savior of mankind, God's primeval institutions and orders are of great relevance for the history of Israel and mankind. The orderly working together of the pair-wise works of creation, both human and nonhuman, is the fundamental presupposition for the continuous thriving of life on earth and for man's self-perception as a historical being in the succession

---

16. Cf. Armin Wenz, "Der Mensch als Kind und König (Bibelarbeit über Genesis 1:26–2:3)," *Lutherische Beiträge* 9 (2004): 139–61.

17. Oswald Bayer, following Luther, sees Genesis 2:16 as foundation of the church as "order of creation," which was disturbed as consequence of the fall. Cf. Bayer, *Freiheit als Antwort: Zur theologischen Ethik* (Tübingen: J.C.B. Mohr, 1995), 85, 118–20.

18. Cf. Genesis 1:28 (LXX): καὶ κατακυριεύσατε αὐτῆς.

of generations. The very fact that the Creator gives man a fruitful place to live and a perspective of life in time comprising generations past and future, is established in the primeval history of mankind and later on realized and specified in God's promises to the fathers of His chosen people, Abraham, Isaac, and Jacob. One of the prime motifs in the history of the patriarchs (Genesis 12–50) is the promise of future offspring and the often highly difficult preparation, constitution, and preservation of the indispensable marriages and births, the repeated redemption of the chosen family from a variety of dangers and temptations.

We also have to mention here the genealogies that are quite often interwoven with the narrative parts of the canon to the annoyance of uninformed Bible readers.[19] These lists make transparent that the primeval blessing of the Creator (Genesis 1:28) is very effective, both in the history of mankind as well as in the history of the people of God. In the New Testament, it is the Gospels of Matthew and Luke that follow this Old Testament tradition.[20] Thus, at the beginning of the New Testament the reader realizes it is God's creational order and institution of marriage and family that serves not only for the preservation of mankind in general, but also for the preservation of God's people. Ultimately, this order, in, with, and under the preservation of mankind, above all is instrumental for the sake of the incarnation of the eternal Son of God through the Virgin Mary.

Parallel observations can be made concerning mankind's kingship over creation as it is reflected in the institution of political rule and power. Even those governments that act as enemies of God and His chosen people, in a hidden way have to serve God's plans for the sake of judging and saving Israel and His Church. This is true, to cite but a few examples, if we look at the Egyptian pharaoh, the Babylonian Nebuchadnezzar, the Persian Cyrus all the way down to the Romans Augustus and Pontius Pilate who all play prominent roles in the Bible.[21] It was the roads and sea-routes of the Roman Empire that served the Gospel and allowed the young Church to be spread out among the Gentiles. The "peaceful and quiet life, godly and dignified in every way" (1 Timothy 2:2), which is guaranteed by stable governments and is hardly possible in a state of

---

19. Cf. e.g., Genesis 5; 10; 11:10–32; 25:12–18; 36; 1 Chronicles 1–9.
20. Matthew 1; Luke 3:23–38.
21. Concerning Pontius Pilate and the hidden role he plays in God's hands and plans, see John 19:11; for an Old Testament parallel, see Daniel 5:18.

anarchy, dare not be confused with passive "quietism," but serves as a presupposition for the immense (e.g., traveling) activities of the apostles and the first parishes. Petitions and prayers brought forth for the sake of the earthly governments and obedience toward their authority, unless this collides with the First Commandment (Acts 5:29), therefore are an integral part of Christian worship life.[22]

Thus, it comes as no surprise that God in the Decalogue not only reminds His people of its salvation from bondage in Egypt at the beginning of His history as chosen and saved people of God (Exodus 20:2), but also of His creative work at the beginning of the world (Exodus 20:11). This double reference to God's creating and saving actions is reflected in the double structure of the commandment of love and of the Decalogue as a whole. The Decalogue first presents rules for the relation between God and His people. In the second table, though, human life in all of its aspects and relations is put under the protection of God's jealous holiness and judgment.[23] The prophets, in their proclamation of God's judgment on Israel, resume this connection over and over again, when they claim that the conditions for a good and blessed life of God's people are endangered and destroyed where God's commandments and orders are despised. In the Scriptures, the abolition and destruction of the Creator's good order for life is a symptom of man's enmity against God and for his lawlessness (Antinomianism). And at the same time, in its catastrophic cosmic effects, this suspension of God's order is a result of the divine wrath and judgment, which according to Jesus and His apostles, will dramatically increase toward the end times.[24]

---

22. 1 Timothy 2:1–4; Matthew 22:21; Titus 3:1; Romans 13:1–7; 1 Peter 2:13–17.

23. Cf. Luther's question at the end of his explanation of the Decalogue (SC I 21): "What does God declare concerning all these commandments? Answer: He says, 'I the Lord your God am a jealous God, visiting the iniquity of the fathers on the children to the third and the fourth generation of those who hate Me, but showing steadfast love to thousands of those who love Me and keep My commandments.' " (Deuteronomy 5:9–10).

24. Matthew 24:6–7; 12:29; Mark 13; Romans 1:18–32; 2 Peter 3:10; Revelation 8:5–13; 9:1–18. According to Christ's words testified in the first Gospel, the loss of love, as it is rooted in utter lawlessness (Matthew 24:12), belongs to the eschatological plagues, under which Christ's flock will have to suffer, for the prophets who preach this lawlessness in God's name go forth right from its midst.
    Schniewind, in his commentary on the Gospel of Matthew writes that the message of the Antichrist is described in a very similar way, e.g., in 1 John 2:18; 2 Thessalonians 2:9–12; Revelation 13:3–8; 13–17. The Antichrist is called the man of lawlessness (2 Thessalonians 2:3). Schniewind also points to 1 John 3:4;

When discussing the question concerning a God-pleasing life with the Pharisees, Jesus Himself goes back behind the manifold man-made regulations, even back behind the Mosaic legal regulations for Israel, all the way to the basic realities of the primeval history in Genesis 1–3. In this way, Jesus specifically fights against the contempt of marriage and family. It is important to note that Jesus deals critically with the Mosaic law. However, it is most important to perceive *how* He applies such criticism. In Mark 10:4–6, Jesus, in the conflict with the Pharisees concerning the Mosaic allowance to write "a certificate of divorce" (Deuteronomy 24:1), remarks: "Because of your hardness of heart he wrote you this commandment. But from the beginning of creation, 'God made them male and female'." Jesus thus falls back upon the words of institution for marriage from Genesis 1:27 (Mark 10:6), and He immediately adds the divine commentary on occasion of the creation of Eve from Genesis 2:24: "Therefore a man shall leave his father and mother and hold fast to his wife, and the two shall become one flesh. So they are no longer two but one flesh" (Mark 10:7–8). In another conflict with His opponents, Jesus goes back behind pious Jewish traditions upon the Decalogue: "You have a fine way of rejecting the commandment of God in order to keep your tradition! For Moses said, 'Honor your father and your mother'; and, 'Whoever reviles father or mother must surely die.' But you say, 'If a man tells his father or his mother, Whatever you would have gained from me is Corban' (that is, given to God)—then you no longer permit him to do anything for his father or mother, thus making void the word of God by your tradition that you have handed down. And many such things you do" (Mark 7:9–13).

Christ's apostles take up this approach of their Lord. Neither the cultic, social, nor economic regulations of the Mosaic laws are mandatory for Christianity. Rather, Christian behavior is bound to the Decalogue and its summary in the twofold commandment of love.[25] The New

Matthew 7:23, and 13:41 and claims that Jesus' struggle with the teachers of the law, the Pharisees, was a struggle against their lawlessness (Matthew 23:28). Schniewind concludes that the greatest threat for Christianity is to misinterpret the salvation from the curse of the law as lawlessness as such. Julius Schniewind, *Das Evangelium nach Matthäus*, 13th ed. (Göttingen: Vandenhoeck & Ruprecht, 1984), 239.

25. Cf. Romans 13:8–10; James 2:8–12, and the many admonitions in the apostolic letters, e.g., concerning the Sixth Commandment: 1 Corinthians 6–7; concerning the Seventh Commandment: Ephesians 4:28, but also the admonitions for the rich and greedy; concerning the Eighth Commandment and the "sins of the tongue,"

Testament leaves no doubt concerning the conviction that sexual activity, that is, the offering up of one's body to another, should take place only in the marriage between a man and a woman. The thankful reception of the God-given reality of marriage, as well as the rare gift of celibacy, excludes any unlawful, disordered variants of sexuality which are called promiscuity (e.g., Romans 1; 1 Corinthians 6). Like his Lord, Paul harkens back to Genesis 2:24, when he emphasizes the incompatibility of fornication with the life of a Christian who is even joined together with Christ (1 Corinthians 6:13–20). The other theological frontline besides Antinomianism against which the New Testament fights in the realm of the orders is the Gnostic despising of creation, and thus also of marriage as an order of creation, as can be seen very clearly in 1 Timothy 4:1–5:

> Now the Spirit expressly says that in later times some will depart from the faith by devoting themselves to deceitful spirits and teachings of demons, through the insincerity of liars whose consciences are seared, who forbid marriage and require abstinence from foods that God created to be received with thanksgiving by those who believe and know the truth. For everything created by God is good, and nothing is to be rejected if it is received with thanksgiving, for it is made holy by the word of God and prayer.

Also the tables of duty in the letters to the Ephesians, Colossians, and the first letter of Peter,[26] as well as the admonitions in the Pastoral Letters,[27] follow this line of thought in which it is the primeval divine order that shapes human life. The criterion for the manifold human relations in and around the house is the love and self-sacrificial attitude of Christ Himself, which does not do away with the conditions of life, but is lived out within them. Thus, the relations and given conditions of life are seen in the horizon of the First Commandment and the saving work of Christ, which are equally effective and valid for both man and woman, parents

---

e.g., James 3:5–10; Ephesians 4:29. Also the catalogues of virtues and vices can be read as application of the Decalogue, e.g. Galatians 5:20–23; 1 Timothy 1:8–10.

26. Ephesians 5:21–6:9; Colossians 3:18–4:1; 1 Peter 2:18–3:7.

27. Cf. Karl Heinrich Rengstorf, who criticizes the popular conviction that the pastoral letters, "especially in their admonitions concerning marriage and the house, unfortunately do not reach the theological level of the gospel" ("Mann und Frau im Urchristentum," *Arbeitsgemeinschaft für Forschung des Landes Nordrhein-Westfalen, Geisteswissenschaften* 12, 1954: 42. My translation).

and children, and which influence and permeate their respective specific non-interchangeable relations to one another. Especially the passages in the New Testament letters concerning the relationship between man and woman prove to be expositions of the primeval findings from Genesis 1–3, which are of fundamental importance for the biblical view of man in the light of the Gospel of Christ (1 Corinthians 11:7–12; Ephesians 5:22–31; 1 Timothy 2:13–15). Certainly, the interpretation and application of these passages has been burdened by manifold misuses in the course of history. Nevertheless, we should let holy writ conclude her own word before immediately turning away from it due to modern-day allergies against irritating words such as "obedience," "head," or "subordination."

A close look at Ephesians 5:22–31, for instance, makes it clear that both husband and wife are to approach their respective opposite in a specific manner that finds its rule in how Christ and the Church relate to one another. As the Church is subject to Christ as her head, so the wives are to be subject to their husbands. As Christ offered Himself up for the Church, so the husbands are to love their wives. The wives are to be submissive; the husbands are to offer up or sacrifice their lives. Obviously, there are different nuances here, which denote the fact that man and woman, husband and wife, take positions that are not interchangeable. Nevertheless, if we ponder these words, we will find it hard to discern which is more difficult and offensive: submission or the sacrifice of one's life?

Those who only find intolerable offenses here carelessly miss all the divine promises and blessings that are included. For in this passage the marriage between man and woman receives its highest imaginable theological honor and sanctification when the apostle declares it to be a mirror and reflection of Christ's unification with His Church. Christ's rule and dominion (headship) over His Church is a rule of love and mercy. It seems that both the misuse of this text as a justification of male tyranny, as well as its suspension due to an emancipative female impulse, is grounded in the very same mistake—namely, that the readers on both sides refuse to read the text all the way to the end. To put it in stark terms, male chauvinists and ardent feminists have in common that they only read up to the words: "For the husband is the head of the wife." Here the male chauvinist gloats and the ardent feminist indignantly turns away. But only if they both read on will they be able to discover the benefits with which God in Christ here blesses those men and women who try to live their lives together in the light of this Word.

Much like Jesus in the Gospels, Paul in Ephesians goes back to God's order in creation and to the Decalogue when he discusses the relationships between the genders and the generations. In Ephesians 5:31, he cites Genesis 2:24; in Ephesians 6:2–3, he points to the Fourth Commandment as the first commandment that includes a promise. In the same letter when he also discusses the relationship between lords and slaves, he does not argue on the basis of the Old Testament. Obviously, as can be seen also in the letter to Philemon, slavery, unlike marriage and family, is not anchored in the order of creation and thus is not part of the natural law (Philemon 10–19). Concerning marriage and family, however, it is obvious that the praise and high esteem for these orders and relations between husbands and wives, parents and children, as it is expressed despite the negative consequences after the fall in Psalms 127, 128, and others, is explicitly repeated and affirmed also in the New Testament.

In the Letter to the Ephesians can one discover that marriage with its divine purpose of passing on life in the Scriptures is not only relevant in the realm of the theology of creation, but also in the realm of ecclesiology. Many Bible passages depict the marriage between husband and wife as a reflection of the relationship between God and His chosen people (Jeremiah 2:2; 3:1; Hosea 1–3; Ephesians 5:21–33). Just as marriage is an image of God's faithfulness toward His people, so fornication is an image of the unfaithfulness of human beings, including God's people. Just as marriage and faithfulness toward God fall under God's promises, so fornication as well as apostasy fall under God's wrath and judgment. In the New Testament, these motifs are all repeated in a Christological context. The wedding feast and the relation between bridegroom and bride are most important motifs both in the parables of Jesus and in the Book of Revelation. Both describe the life of the Church Militant and Triumphant. These motifs are taken up in many of our best Lutheran hymns.

Concerning the institution of rule or authority as image taken from the realm of creation for the sake of amplifying the effects of Christ's salvation, one can point to the New Testament's proclamation of Christ as the true divine king of His people, as the Good Shepherd of His flock, who rules and multiplies His kinship (e.g., Isaiah 53:10) through the

Word. Christ's and His believers' war against evil demands spiritual weapons (2 Corinthians 10:4; Ephesians 6:11–17), but it nevertheless is a war analogous to the battles of earthly rulers. Thus in the end, Christ alone and all those who believe in Him are able to fulfill what the Creator had assigned for mankind from the beginning (Genesis 1:28): to live as free kings, not be enslaved to creation, but rule over it in love according to His good orders.

The orders of creation serve not only the preservation of the world, but also the work of the Holy Spirit in the mission of the Church; they even serve as images and parables for the proclamation and faithful perception of the Gospel. Aspects from the theology of creation, soteriology, and pneumatology are intertwined. The triune God works through the orders of creation in a reliable, perceivable, and trustworthy manner in His world and for the sake of His world (and His Church!). He will do so until the Last Day arises, when this world with its orders, including marriage (Matthew 22:30), will pass for the sake of a better world in which no sun will be needed anymore, for God Himself will be their sun and rule them from eternity to eternity (Revelation 22:5).

Natural Law and
Later Lutheran Tradition

6

FRIEDRICH JULIUS STAHL:
A Lutheran's Rejection
of Natural Law

Jacob Corzine

Among the Lutherans opposed to the union of German Lutheran and Reformed churches in the mid-nineteenth century was Friedrich Julius Stahl. Unlike the fathers of The Lutheran Church—Missouri Synod, Stahl did not immigrate to the United States. Instead, Stahl spent his career as a politically conservative professor of law and a political advisor to King Friedrich Wilhelm IV of Prussia. Although Stahl was not a theologian by profession, his work concerning Lutheranism and natural law is still valuable.[1] Stahl's concentration on the legal realm allows him

---

1. Stahl was not the only jurist of churchly significance during the confessional revival. Jobst Schöne provides another example in *Kirche und Kirchenregiment im Wirken und Denken Georg Philipp Eduard Huschkes* (Berlin: Lutherisches Verlagshaus, 1969).

to clarify the boundaries of natural law, something he treats in nearly every one of his major works. Before examining Stahl's work on natural law, this essay will introduce his life and the character of his writings.

FRIEDRICH JULIUS STAHL (1802–1861)

Stahl was born to Jewish parents just a few years after the French Revolution. Later, while attending a humanist *Gymnasium*[2] in Munich, he converted to Christianity. However, this conversion was not yet to the theological position of Lutheran confessionalism that he would come to espouse. That came later, during his time studying law at the Friedrich-Alexander University in Erlangen. There he came under the influence of theology professor and reformed preacher, Christian Krafft.[3] While in Erlangen, Stahl heard lectures by the philosopher Friedrich Schelling for the first time;[4] later, during the first years of his professorship in Munich, Stahl would hear Schelling's lectures again. Stahl explicitly declares his reliance on Schelling, which will become apparent in this essay. Schelling

---

2.   A *Gymnasium* education is that which immediately preceded university study.

3.   Erlangen theologians would later suggest that Krafft had influenced their decision to break with rationalistic theology. However, Holsten Fagerberg does not number Stahl among them. Fagerberg divides the Lutheran Confessional movement into followers of Hengstenberg (Berlin); followers of Harless (Erlangen); and those associated with Stahl. Although Fagerberg hesitates to divide too sharply, he sees Kliefoth, Vilmar and, to an extent, Loehe, as dependent upon Stahl. Because of Stahl's activity in nineteenth-century Lutheran debates about the ministry, Fagerberg identifies Kliefoth, Vilmar, and Loehe with Stahl. Stahl's vocal opposition to the Prussian Union fits neatly into Fagerberg's description. See Holsten Fagerberg, *Bekenntnis, Kirche und Amt in der deutschen konfessionellen Theologie des 19. Jahrhunderts* (Uppsala: Almqvist & Wiksells, 1952), 83–84.

4.   Gerhard Masur goes to some lengths to emphasize this in his biography of Stahl. See Gerhard Masur, *Friedrich Julius Stahl: Geschichte seines Lebens. Aufstieg und Entfaltung. 1802–1840* (Berlin: E. S. Mittler & Sohn, 1930), 63–66, 102–7. However, both Schelling and Stahl were hesitant about overemphasizing their connection. Steffen Dietzsch, *Friedrich Wilhelm Joseph Schelling*, (Leipzig: Urania-Verlag, 1978), 92, notes this from Schelling's perspective. In Friedrich Julius Stahl, *Geschichte der Rechtsphilosophie*, vol. I of *die Philosophie des Rechts*, 5. Ed. (Tübingen: Akademische Verlagsbuchhandlung von J. C. B. Mohr, 1878), XVII, annotation (hereafter: Stahl, *Geschichte*), Stahl clarifies his position with regard to Schelling as follows: "What I have received from Schelling, to which have confessed and still do confess, is merely his polemic against what is 'rational' ('negative') and his placing, in opposition to that, the 'historical' ('positive') principle; and no one will call that a whole philosophical system."

criticized Rationalism for its refusal to allow freedom to play a formative role along with reason. In Stahl's work, this freedom is emphasized
in historical development, because history is the place where freedom
comes to expression. Stahl's legal system emphasizes not only divine and
human freedom, but also the central place of historical development for
the legitimacy of government.

The theme of historical continuity for the divine legitimacy of human
government is central in Stahl's work.[5] Stahl fought aggressively against
the antithesis of this legitimacy, revolution. Stahl's work placed him
in the thick of contemporary politics in his day. Not only did he have
the events of the French Revolution to consider, but also those of the
Prussian Revolution of 1848, which occurred while he was a professor in
Berlin.[6] Stahl's rejection of revolution is derived from his denial of both
Rationalism and the sort of natural law doctrine it teaches. For Stahl,
these two inevitably led to revolution. His analysis finds revolution built
on two distinctly rationalist presuppositions: natural law and the sovereignty of the people. Both of these he is unable to accept.

Stahl regarded revolution as "the greatest sin in the political realm."[7]
This perspective is evident in a few of the major elements of Stahl's
thought. By claiming that revolution is a political sin, Stahl was not suggesting that a government, standing in the stream of historical continuity
(thus, divinely sanctioned), could be without sin.[8] A divinely sanctioned
government is just as able to sin against its subjects, other nations, or
God, as a revolution. Because of this ability, even legitimate government is a proper subject for reform. The superlative "greatest" has to
do, rather, with God's sanctioning. According to Stahl, revolution rejects
God's sanctioning of legitimate government. Revolution intends to erect
a human order upon the foundation of reason to replace the given divine

---

5. Gottfried Hütter, *Die Beurteilung der Menschenrechte bei Richard Rothe und Friedrich
    Julius Stahl* (Frankfurt: Peter Lang, 1976), 101–3.
6. According to Christopher Clark, Stahl was important for helping Friedrich Wil-
    helm IV of Prussia come to terms with the revolution of 1848 and find a way
    forward, positively receiving some of its results. Christopher Clark, *Preußen: Auf-
    stieg und Niedergang, 1600–1947,* trans. Richard Barth, Norbert Juraschitz, Thomas
    Pfeiffer (Munich: Pantheon, 2008), 576.
7. Friedrich Julius Stahl, *Was ist die Revolution: ein Vortrag auf Veranstaltung des Evan-
    gelischen Vereins für kirchliche Zwecke am 8. März 1852 gehalten* (Berlin: Verlag von
    Wilhelm Schultze, 1852), 10.
8. Hütter, *Die Beurteilung der Menschenrechte bei Richard Rothe und Friedrich Julius Stahl,*
    116–18, makes this clear in his excursus over the right to protest in Stahl's work.

order. Thus, revolution elevates reason to the place of God. This is the basis both of Stahl's critique of Rationalism, in which reason seeks to take God's place, and of Stahl's political teaching, which suggests that historical continuity ensures divine sanction.

Stahl observed that natural law had failed as a philosophical basis for political theory. Stahl's observation guides the outline of this essay. First, I focus on his evaluation of natural law, both internally and as the foundation of a political system. Ultimately, Stahl critiques both the existence of a reason-based natural law, as well as the legitimacy of the revolutionary political consequences drawn on the basis of it. Next, I sketch Stahl's political system, which excluded Rationalism and its natural law theory. To conclude, I consider the meaning of Stahl's rejection of natural law, both in terms of its theological implications and its relationship to other natural law theories.[9]

STAHL'S CRITIQUE OF NATURAL LAW

In the first volume of his *Philosophie des Rechts*, Stahl begins to analyze the historical development of natural law in the modern era. There he defines rationalist natural law:

> The question, "How can I recognize what is just and what is unjust?" presupposes the higher question: "By what means does a just thing or an unjust thing exist, what effects this difference, what is the source by which all things that should be, should be?" The answer to the second question is that which is decisive for

---

9.   In this essay, "natural law" is the English translation of the German word *Natur-recht*. *Recht*, however, does not always correspond to "law." Frequently, *Recht* refers to the entire system of statutes and laws that, apart from those in authority, comprises government. *Gesetz,* rather than *Recht,* usually refers to an individual law. Although somewhat unwieldy, *Recht* here is translated "legal system." *Recht* can also refer to personal rights to receive certain goods; thus *Menschenrechte* are "human rights." The United States Constitution, for example, assures *das Recht* ("the right") to a trial by jury. This sort of *Recht* is translated as "right." This poses an important question: Is natural law a system of laws (*Gesetze*) or of rights (*Rechte*)? This question will be considered within Stahl's legal system. Similar to what is found in theological literature, Stahl will ask, What is *gerecht?* The adjective *gerecht* is often translated with "righteous" or "just," which it is how it is translated in this essay. "Law," "legal," "right" (noun), and "just" (adjective) can be traced back to the German *das Recht* (noun) and *recht* (adjective).

every form of Ethics.—Philosophy, which only recognizes what follows from reason, can seek this source of the Ethos nowhere else than in reason. Natural law consists in this.[10]

Not every answer to these two questions constitutes, according to Stahl, a form of natural law. Rather, it is the answer of philosophy, which by its nature allows only what reason determines to be necessary to exist. Where the answer to the second question is "human reason," the ethos that results is natural law. The answer to the first question, then, is that one can recognize, by his reason alone, whether a thing is just or unjust. Reason can provide criteria by which one can make such a judgment.

Of course, this definition of natural law is time-bound. Stahl's reference to philosophy is intentionally limited to the modern era, and specifically, to what he perceives to be rationalist. He considers Hugo Grotius (1583–1645) as the founder of this theory of natural law; Stahl traces its development through to his own day via Hobbes, Pufendorf, Thomasius, Wolf, Kant, and Fichte.[11] Stahl's focus on the development of natural law is telling. He argues that these philosophers did not develop the theory anew, but rather they fleshed out the theory until it reached its culmination, its "final form."[12] Stahl's denial of natural law applies specifically to the matured theory of these men.

According to Stahl, these philosophers presume a natural state of man, existing prior to his civil state, and apart from the influence of any laws. In this state, man's individuality is recognized by his "nature or reason."[13] From this it is deduced that the man must have both external and internal freedom. Internal freedom enables man to make decisions based on reason and apart from external influences. Human morality is based on internal freedom. External freedom, which relates to natural

---

10. Stahl, *Geschichte*, 111. All English translations are mine.

11. Stahl sees Fichte as offering a critique of Kant's position. Fichte's foundation in the "free I" is, for Stahl, simply an alternative to Kant's grounding natural law in logically necessary assertions. Stahl's presentation is based on Kant, whose work he perceives as having prevailed despite Fichte's efforts. Stahl, *Geschichte*, 246–47.

    Kaufmann suggests that Stahl does not do full justice to these philosophers, particularly Kant and Fichte, by calling them rationalists. However, Kaufmann notes that Stahl's deduction of rationalist tendencies in their thinking, particularly in the area of natural law, is accurate. Erich Kaufmann, *Studien zur Staatslehre des monarchischen Prinzipes* (Leipzig: O. Brandstetter, 1906), 68.

12. Stahl, *Geschichte*, 246. See also Hütter, *Die Beurteilung der Menschenrechte bei Richard Rothe und Friedrich Julius Stahl*, 85.

13. Stahl, *Geschichte*, 247.

law, enables man to act in the world according to reason. This external freedom is the rationalist foundation for the legal realm.

Because it has no inherent boundaries, the external freedom of one person has the potential to constrain that of another. By logical necessity and on account of the law of no contradiction, this leads to the postulation of the "maxim of coexistence." Each person must sufficiently limit his own freedom so that he does not impose it on another. This is the foundational principle of rationalistic natural law. As such, according to Stahl, all other legal principles are deduced from the maxim of coexistence. The maxim of coexistence objectively expresses what is subjectively referred to as the original right of man (*Urrecht des Menschen*). This is the right to exercise one's freedom up to the boundary necessary to preserve the freedom of others. Stahl expresses it this way: "the right to be duty-bound to others in no other manner than that in which they could be made duty-bound to him."[14]

In rationalist philosophy, the maxim of coexistence, along with its subjective expression in the original right of man, comprises the sole legal principle from which all natural law is derived. This is done by submitting the different human relationships to the sole legal principle. A categorization of rights, naturally held by all people in the context of their coexistence, emerges. First among those rights are inherent rights (*angeborene Rechte*), which are deduced out of the mutual noninjury of the person. These rights include bodily existence, free spatial movement, and honor. Out of these flow property rights: the rights to exert one's will over an earthly object without interference.

This understanding of natural law stipulates only one other institution: the contract. The contract is a binding document in which one agrees to limit one's freedom. The contract requires that all parties to the contract are willing and uncoerced. Natural law neither provides for nor restricts the content of the contract. Every other institution, whether marriage, family, employment, and—of particular importance, the state—comes into being by purely contractual means. Here the state plays a unique role. Although the state's structure is not stipulated by natural law, but only by contract, its existence is nevertheless necessary. The state is the means by which the maxim of coexistence as sole legal principle is upheld. That is to say, the contractual agreement of many

---

14. Stahl, *Geschichte*, 248.

people is necessary, given the circumstance in which an unwilling person would be forced to fulfill the maxim of coexistence.[15]

For Stahl, the causal connection between natural law and the state is important. He constructs a foundation of the state and state institutions upon a different foundation than that of the rationalistic understanding of natural law. This has wide-ranging implications, because according to rationalistic natural law, marriage (a contract) may have a limited duration or it may be polygamous or incestuous. Similarly, lacking a contract, parents have no obligation to raise their children.[16] Stahl summarizes what he calls "natural law" or "reason law," which he consequently rejects:

> Its typical task is the deduction of a legal system and state from the nature or reason of the [individual] man. Its characteristic teaching is, first, the limitation of both the enforceable laws and the purpose of the state for the protection of the rights of the individual man, and second, the denial of all self-instituted authority and exclusive founding of authority in the consent and mandate of the subjects. A legal system and a state exist, therefore, only through individual freedom, and only toward its ends.[17]

STAHL'S CRITIQUE OF RATIONALISTIC NATURAL LAW

Stahl's main argument against natural law is his rejection of the rationalist presupposition of a natural state of man. On this basis, he critiques the logical derivation of natural law. On the other hand, the presumption of absolute freedom provided by this natural state leads to results that

---

15. Stahl, *Geschichte,* 250–51.

16. Stahl offers further distinctions between his presentation of a natural law theory and other theories. In particular, Stahl finds Kant's approach to these matters to be unique, given Kant's overall theory. Kant argues that (1) sexual intercourse is limited to marriage, so that the marriage partner is not used only as a means to an end, and (2) parents have a duty to raise their children, since, lacking a contract, children's freedom is externally limited. This would violate the maxim of coexistence. Stahl, *Geschichte,* 250.

17. Stahl, *Geschichte,* 252.

Stahl considers unreal, or ahistorical, enabling him to challenge natural law not only in its foundations, but also in its conclusions.

The development of natural law is rooted in the anthropological consideration of the individual in his natural state. In this state, man is detached from all other individuals and is not a member of a community. Stahl rejects this as contrary to man's nature. For Stahl, man has never been apart from his historical surroundings. Man is born into a family, but his existence immediately extends to the community in which that family lives, and thus to some form of social order. Man is born into a family and society that have a "binding moral and order." Since this is the case, the "natural state" of man presumed by natural law is at best a product of the imagination. In fact, Stahl contends that such a state of man is unimaginable. Only God, who is His own beginning, or an animal, which is unaware of its relation to other beings, can be imagined in this ahistorical, nonrelational state; but never man.[18]

Next, Stahl observes that natural law has as its goal a legal system and the state; he questions whether it is meaningful to try to develop this on the basis of the nature of the individual. Rights, laws, and the state are meaningful only within the context of community. Further, Stahl finds that a system of natural law that only shields an individual's freedom from other individuals is inadequate. Freedom also needs to be shielded against the community. This can only be achieved with a legal system and state that also have actual ethical content.[19]

Finally, Stahl questions the "silent contract" that attempts to legitimize the state based on the theory that citizens agree to the limitation of their freedom for the sake of preserving the maxim of coexistence. For Stahl, such a silent, state-forming contract is nowhere to be found. It has never been signed, and thus does not exist. Stahl argues that this agreement never occurs. He prefers not to postulate man's freedom as something absolute and yet tempered by a silent contract, but instead man's freedom as something tempered already in his original state. This natural limitation is, again, conditioned by the historical situation in which man finds himself. As a created being, man is subject to the authorities and

18. Friedrich Julius Stahl, *Die gegenwärtigen Parteien in Staat und Kirche: Neunundzwanzig akademische Vorlesungen* (Berlin:Verlag von Wilhelm Hertz, 1863), 20.

19. Stahl, *Parteien*, 22.

moral order present in that place and time, where and when God created him.[20] This, for Stahl, is natural.

Stahl critiques natural law at its foundation and accuses it of not representing what is natural. He understands man not as an independent being, but as God's creation living within a specific human history. Rationalistic natural law presumes the absolute freedom of the individual and attempts to preserve this freedom in a communal context. Because Stahl does not consider man other than in his historical context, he denies that the individual ever has had absolute freedom. Absolute freedom can neither be the foundation of a legal system and the state nor held up as their ultimate goal.

In the introduction, I quoted Stahl referring to revolution as the "greatest sin in the political realm." I now have enough background to describe how this critique relates to natural law. Stahl regards man, on account of creation, never as a mere individual, but always as a person within a larger community. This observation is a theological one, rooted in his understanding of the world and human history as created and directed by God. Stahl sees revolution as rationalistic natural law translated into actual political action, which overthrows the created and directed order in this world. Revolution is sin, not because it seeks to change or reform the reigning political order, but because it rejects the divine origin of the historically present community. Revolution prefers to establish a community based solely on the deductions of human reason—on natural law. To do so is to put man's reason in the place of God. It is for this reason that revolution is a sin against the First Commandment and the "greatest sin in the political realm."

STAHL'S ALTERNATIVE MEANS OF RECOGNIZING WHAT IS JUST OR UNJUST

The principle and measure of the legal system, that which gives its commandments their content, are the thoughts and commandments of God's world-ordering, thus not, as in the case of morality, the idea of the perfected personality, but rather the idea of the perfected communal state, of the perfected structuring

---

20. Stahl, *Parteien*, 22.

of social relations, i.e., the divine plan of the moral world, *the world-economical ideas.*[21]

The distinction between the "idea of the perfected personality," which pertains to the realm of morality, and the "idea of the perfected communal state," which pertains to the legal realm, lies at the foundation of Stahl's definition of a legal system. A legal system has to do with those institutions that are present between men, because of God's free counsel, rather than for the sake of the individual as a consequence of his being.[22] Stahl's quote shows that these institutions founded in the free counsel of God are to be distinguished from the "idea of the perfected personality," which Stahl indeed finds rooted in God's holiness. This is the essence of the foundational distinction in Stahl's legal teaching between morality and the legal system. Morality has to do with the forming and perfecting of the person, and reflects in its content and precepts the holiness of God. These qualities, "love, righteousness, truthfulness, etc.," are "the eternal good." Although these qualities inform it,[23] they do not alone provide the foundation for a legal teaching, because a legal system has to do with the "communal state," with "social relations." Since these are not part of God's holiness, they cannot be deduced from it.[24] Stahl says of the institutions of the communal state, which are created by the free counsel of God, that they contain "world-economic ideas." In each of the institutions, the respective world-economic idea strives to be perfected.

The world-economic ideas, as the object of the legal system, are divided by Stahl into four categories. The first category is "the preservation of individual existence," to which he ascribes "integrity and freedom of the person, protection in the acquiring and use of a means of subsistence." He sometimes summarizes this idea with the concept of personal property. The second category is "the propagation of the human race," which is the institution of the family. The third category is "the whole existence as a race," which Stahl divides into two sub-categories: first, community, estate, and corporation, having to do with those activities of individual entities which help the whole; and second, the state

---

21. Friedrich Julius Stahl, *Rechts- und Staatslehre auf der Grundlage christlicher Weltan- schauung,* vol. II/1 of *Die Philosophie des Rechts,* 5th ed. (Tübingen: Akademische Verlagsbuchhandlung von J. C. B. Mohrj, 1878), 203.
22. Stahl, *Rechts- und Staatslehre auf der Grundlage christlicher Weltanschauung,* 93.
23. Stahl, *Rechts- und Staatslehre auf der Grundlage christlicher Weltanschauung,* 93.
24. Stahl, *Rechts- und Staatslehre auf der Grundlage christlicher Weltanschauung,* 93.

and community of states, having to do with the intentional ruling of the human race. Finally, the last category is "the communal connection to God," intended to reconcile humanity to God and to glorify God through humanity, which for Stahl is the church.[25]

Each of the world-economic ideas is, in a manner of speaking, a goal for its respective institution—a state of perfection to strive toward. Stahl is explicit at this point in his reference to Aristotle's *telos,* which he is careful to distinguish from the German word *Zweck*: the goal of each institution is not external, but internal to it. The institution is not a means to an end; rather, within each divinely given—and, therefore, not expendable—institution, there is a *telos,* the world-economic idea, which represents the completion and perfection of that institution. Stahl sees the concept of *telos* transferred from Aristotle into Christianity in the form of (1) the God-given purpose for relations in life and (2) the God-given vocations of men.[26]

At this stage, a number of differences between Stahl's theory and that of rationalistic natural law have become clear. First, natural law is deduced from a posited natural state of absolutely free man apart from all societal relationships. In contrast to this, Stahl considers these societal relationships to be historical reality inseparable from divine creation; because of them, he denies the absolute freedom of man in any state. On the basis of this initial proposition, natural law develops as the effort to preserve the free natural state as much as possible once man is placed into the civil state, that is, into society. Stahl's conception also has a goal, or rather, each of the world-economic ideas is a *telos.* The purpose of the legal system in Stahl's system is to achieve these goals, each of which represents moral perfection in the corresponding institution.

Even so, a legal system, according to Stahl, does not provide all the tools necessary to reach these goals. It serves instead, in a manner of speaking, to guarantee a space in which the community can strive toward their achievement. In other words, the legal system provides each of the divine institutions with the positive historical realization of their proper boundaries, inside of which the individual is forced by the state

---

25. Stahl, *Rechts- und Staatslehre auf der Grundlage christlicher Weltanschauung,* 197–98.
26. Stahl, *Rechts- und Staatslehre auf der Grundlage christlicher Weltanschauung,* 204. Hütter remarks that this interpretation of Aristotle was already common in the Christianity of the Middle Ages. Hütter, *Die Beurteilung der Menschenrechte bei Richard Rothe und Friedrich Julius Stahl,* 115.

to remain, but it does not force the individual to any action within these institutions beyond observation of the boundaries. Stahl considers the legal system to be the negative side of striving toward the *telos*, which has as its immediate goal not the achievement of the *telos*, but its preservation. The positive side of striving toward the *telos*, which encourages the best action within the institutions, belongs to the realm of morality and the individual conscience.[27]

Unrelated to this use of the terms *positive* and *negative*, Stahl refers to his entire concept of a legal system as "positive" in another way. In the first place, as has been shown, this stands in opposition to the attempt derived from rationalist natural law theory to deduce a legal system from reason alone, apart from the events of history (among which Stahl includes God's creation). Stahl emphasizes the exercise of a freedom of choice not bound by logical necessity, which lies at the foundation of human society. "Positive" is, in this sense, to be understood as the opposite of "logically necessitated." Stahl extends the concept further, though, employing it to show how the particular legal system in the here and now in any given nation, is contingent, rather than divinely, eternally, or reasonably prescribed. In fact, it will be shown that, for Stahl, the positive legal system maintains its legitimacy, even if it is contrary to reason or divine prescription.

Stahl does not hold the state, as the institution that administers the legal system, responsible for the individual's fulfillment of God's commandments. This fulfillment remains outside of the realm of civil government. He leaves it, rather, to the individual conscience. If this individual fulfillment were the only concern, there would be no need for a legal system, indeed for a state, at all. Stahl gives two reasons why this is not the case and why the human community has the duty to establish a legal system for the preservation of God's ordering of the world. First, the majority of people would, without it, not act according to their conscience, and even though some individuals would, the whole would be overcome by the "destructive might of the evil-minded." Second, Stahl maintains that even if all the individuals would behave morally, the human community would still be subject to the expectation to fulfill God's commandments as a unified communal entity. Toward the achievement of these two ends, Stahl posits the necessity of a legal system that

---

27. Stahl, *Rechts- und Staatslehre auf der Grundlage christlicher Weltanschauung*, 205.

seeks to preserve and promote the divine order by means of the wisdom of the persons in authority. Put simply, the plan and goal are provided by God, but it is left to men to provide the rules for execution. These rules are what Stahl calls a "positive legal system."[28]

The legal system is positive, that is, historical according to its content, because that content consists, in its final form, of humanly instituted laws. It is positive according to its validity, since its binding nature is due only mediately to the divine order, but immediately to its place as the accepted human order. In other words, this validity is not miraculously bestowed, but a result of God's working through human history.[29] It is on the basis of this positive character that Stahl makes this impressive claim:

> Corresponding to this independence, the legal system can even enter into opposition to God's world-ordering which it is supposed to serve; the human community, called to give, according to freedom, concrete form to the thoughts of the legal system, can turn those thoughts into their opposite, order what was unjust and unreasonable, and also thus fashioned at odds with God, the legal system retains its binding character.[30]

In the next paragraph, Stahl continues: " 'Legal system' and 'positive legal system' mean the same thing. There is no other legal system than the positive one."[31] This statement is the key to understanding how Stahl's claim can be legitimate. He has narrowed his definition to contain only the human order put in place for the sake of preserving the divine order in the society. This order, because it is humanly inhabited and ordered, is unable to be perfect. But it retains its authority as the only legitimate public order because it is instituted and sanctified by God.[32] A few points may be highlighted from Stahl's explanation of this position.

First, a legal system contrary to God's Word does not disqualify the requirements of God's law for the individual. The realm of morality and the conscience remains fully intact, regardless of what human order is in place. Second, by preserving the realm of morality and the conscience, Stahl provides a basis for refusing obedience to the positive legal system.

---

28. Stahl, *Rechts- und Staatslehre auf der Grundlage christlicher Weltanschauung*, 192–93.
29. Stahl, *Rechts- und Staatslehre auf der Grundlage christlicher Weltanschauung*, 221.
30. Stahl, *Rechts- und Staatslehre auf der Grundlage christlicher Weltanschauung*, 221.
31. Stahl, *Rechts- und Staatslehre auf der Grundlage christlicher Weltanschauung*, 221.
32. Stahl, *Rechts- und Staatslehre auf der Grundlage christlicher Weltanschauung*, 223.

This basis, however, is not in the realm of the positive legal system, but entirely in the realm of morality; thus, the refusal is to be answered for, by the conscience, before God.[33] Third, if the positive legal system is to be declared invalid, then on what basis is that decision made? A return to the term "natural law," with a new definition, should demonstrate how Stahl also in this way argues for the legitimacy of every positive legal system, even one contrary to God's Word.

In positing the right of a government to freely establish the legal system as it sees fit, Stahl is not denying, but much more presuming its duty to have that legal system "correspond . . . to the higher law . . . which it has in the thoughts and commands of God's world-ordering."[34] Still, these thoughts and commands are not equivalent to the positive legal system, but oppose that against which it is measured. Stahl calls these thoughts and commands "something divinely commanded, just, and reasonable."[35] On this account, both reason and revelation can make demands of a positive legal system, but neither is able to stand in its place. In the immediate context of these statements, Stahl denies that these thoughts and commands constitute natural law. A few pages later, he allows them to be referred to as such, but then specifically to demonstrate what he has already asserted, that they have "neither the necessary concreteness (precision), nor the binding power of a legal system."[36] Stahl proceeds by considering the situations where a citizen, the government, or a judge, would decide and act on the basis of such a "natural law." The citizen who stands against the positive legal system, alone or in a group, on the basis of a natural law, is guilty of revolution, that is, of raising himself over God's order. While Stahl asserts that the government may not wield natural law, he does not explain this assertion. Still, one can surmise that in so doing, it would either change the positive legal system, thus in effect continuing to work only according to a positive legal system, though perhaps another; or that it would render the established positive legal system invalid, thus falling short of its duty of providing a legal system to its subjects for the sake of order. Finally, a judge is neither permitted to rule according to natural law in opposition to the positive legal system, nor by way of natural law to supplement the positive legal

---

33. Stahl, *Rechts- und Staatslehre auf der Grundlage christlicher Weltanschauung*, 224.

34. Stahl, *Rechts- und Staatslehre auf der Grundlage christlicher Weltanschauung*, 218.

35. Stahl, *Rechts- und Staatslehre auf der Grundlage christlicher Weltanschauung*, 218.

36. Stahl, *Rechts- und Staatslehre auf der Grundlage christlicher Weltanschauung*, 221.

system, since every citizen has the right to be subjected to the rulings of no other standards than those of the positive legal system.[37]

Even apart from individual morality and conscience, Stahl finds it necessary to have a means of recognizing what is just and unjust, in order to to ensure righteousness in a society.[38] This is necessary so that evil not rule, and so that God's will for the community is fulfilled. This means is informed by the divine institutions of property, family, state, and Church, and the world-economic ideas positively instituted by God in His divine freedom. The content of this means, however, takes the form of laws prescribed by man, positively, in his freedom. These laws, the legal system, may take different forms at different places and times, but are always to be measured against divinely revealed world-economic ideas. They are always valid as the divinely sanctioned order for human society.

Stahl's Denial of Natural Law: Relevant in a Natural Law Discussion?

By questioning assumptions about man's natural state, Stahl challenges the rationalist concept of natural law not only on the basis of its own internal consistency. He also questions it on the basis of his broader critique of Rationalism, which he perceives as antithetical to Christianity. Rationalism, for Stahl, is rooted in the rationalistic deification of reason. Certainly, though, Stahl's critique does not apply to all concepts of natural law, and neither is it intended to do so. One need perhaps look no further than Stahl himself to find an example to the contrary. Ernst Troeltsch argues that Stahl's legal theory can be traced in almost every point back to Luther's prerationalistic understanding of natural law.[39]

Given his insistence on a positive historical context, it is no surprise that Stahl himself was aware that his philosophical work was executed within the context of Germany and Europe in the nineteenth century.

---

37. Stahl, *Rechts- und Staatslehre auf der Grundlage christlicher Weltanschauung*, 222–23.
38. Stahl, *Rechts- und Staatslehre auf der Grundlage christlicher Weltanschauung*, 208–10.
39. Ernst Troeltsch, *Die Soziallehren der christlichen Kirchen und Gruppen,* vol. 2 (Tübingen: Morh, 1912), reprint (Tübingen: Mohr Siebeck, 1994), 536. Troeltsch suggests that concepts such as the divine institution of the government, the divine institutions rooted in divine will rather than divine essence, and the independence of government from divine revelation, are not only present in Stahl but also in Luther.

On this account, Stahl is able to speak far more favorably of the American Revolution than of the French Revolution, although he recognizes a relationship between the two.[40] Thus, it would be improper to conclude Stahl denied everything that might have been called "natural law" since his time. It will be helpful to determine the basis of his denial then which, theologically driven, ought to still have value today, in a different time and place. This conclusion will attempt to do exactly that, and thereby also to shed light on the theological considerations, rarely explicitly dealt with in Stahl's *Philosophie des Rechts*, which nevertheless attend these decisions.

The following principles in particular are evident in Stahl's denial of natural law, which provide criteria for evaluating other theories than just the rationalist one Stahl had in mind.

First, the word *natural* in "natural law," so long as it is intended to make reference to a natural, original state of man, apart from his coexistence with others, is impermissible. In this scenario, "natural" describes a purer source of judging what is just or unjust than that which God sanctifies in history, a source which is sought, in fact, entirely apart from God. Stahl denies that such a source exists, a denial rooted in his belief in God as a personal being. This stands in sharp contrast to rationalist philosophy and its understanding of natural law. Stahl rejects elevating any sort of spirit of humanity or principle of reason to a place where it can be called "god," to which an individual could have recourse over and against the authority of the historical state.

Further, for Stahl, God is not only personal but also the Creator of the world, who remains providentially active in history. It is through this preservation of God's activity in human history that Stahl comes to assert that the given, changing, and temporal institutions of human government are nevertheless divinely instituted. A Christian understanding of natural law is thereby preserved, but boundaries are given to its application. It cannot be used in the legal realm as a criterion for answering the question of what is just or unjust, which was posed earlier in this essay. In the legal realm, this belongs to the laws of the state. Individual recourse to natural law against the laws of the state belongs to the realm of morality, and must be reckoned by the individual conscience against the Fourth Commandment.

---

40. Stahl, *Parteien*, 189–207.

This separation of legal and moral realms has one further consequence. Just as there is no recourse to a higher authority that is called natural law in the legal realm, so also there is no recourse to human authority in the moral realm. For Stahl, if the means of recognizing what is just and unjust given in human authority begins to speak in the realm of morality, that is, to interfere with an individual person and his conscience before God, it has overstepped its bounds and is no longer in the realm of political legality, which has to do with an individual in the community. What has been referred to through this essay as the "realm of morality," into which "natural law" would in this case falsely step, could also be called the realm of justification. Such confusion of realms leads to a confusion of Law and Gospel.

The duty to follow the laws of human government belongs, again, in the realm of the Fourth Commandment. Where a legal system steps over this line, suggesting that its subjects have a moral duty to follow its laws other than that associated with this commandment, it usurps the authority of God's law, either attempting to mediate between God and the sinner by easing the severity of God's law—which leads to the sinner's mistaken self-justification; or attempting to supplement God's eternal law—which is destructive to the Gospel of Jesus Christ, since His active obedience was to *God's* law, not human statutes. Both situations call to mind the Pharisees in the Gospels and the papacy in the sixteenth century. Likewise, both situations disregard the reality that God's own law will be the criterion in the final judgment.

A study of Stahl's work shows how natural law can be connected to the central doctrines of creation, the distinction between Law and Gospel, and justification. His treatment of the rationalistic understanding of natural law on the basis of these truths is helpful today in three ways. First, it serves as a warning against allowing natural law theories to slip toward the rationalist error, by suggesting a new *sola: sola ratione*—by reason alone, which would make reason stand in the place of God. Second, it shows that recourse to a Christian understanding of natural law cannot remain in the legal realm, but in fact, that it engages the moral realm. Finally, it shows the boundaries of human government, which prevent it from entering into the realm of morality, except by its God-given path, as the authority He has given for the sake of our life in a community.

7

AFTER BARTH:

Three Lutheran Appraisals
of Natural Law

John T. Pless

INTRODUCTION

Karl Barth's rejection of natural revelation and with it the category of natural law would set the stage for a variety of Lutheran responses in the twentieth century that continue to shape approaches to ethics today. Recent debates on morality as well as ecumenical conversations have stirred contemporary Lutherans such as Carl Braaten and Antti Raunio[1]

---

1. See Carl Braaten, "Natural Law in Theology and Ethics" in *The Two Cities of God: The Church's Responsibility for the Earthly City*, eds. Carl Braaten and Robert Jenson (Grand Rapids: Eerdmans, 1997), 42–58; also see the second edition of Braaten's

to suggest a retrieval of natural law. Others, often claiming to have the theoretical support of such middle twentieth century theologians as Werner Elert (1885–1954), Helmut Thielicke (1908–1986), and Gustaf Wingren (1910–2000), reject any place for natural law in the evangelical ethic.[2] This essay describes how these three Lutheran theologians, quite varied in method and approach, respond to Barth and address the question of natural law, each in his own way. Following this review of their responses to Barth, we will be equipped to assess and evaluate their part in the shaping of contemporary Lutheran approaches to ethics and the place of some form of natural law theory within an authentically Lutheran theological ethic.

Werner Elert

"The Law is nothing else than the necessary form of the Gospel, whose content is grace"[3] was the salvo fired by Barth against the classical Lutheran position. For Barth, "The very fact that God speaks to us, that, under all circumstances, is, in itself grace."[4] One of the most vocal critics of Barth's encapsulation of the Law in the Gospel and his reversal

---

Principles of Lutheran Theology (Minneapolis: Fortress, 2007) where Braaten writes, "The fear of normlessness and its nihilistic effects on the field of human rights has sparked a revival of interest in the classical notion of natural law" (156); also see Antti Raunio, "Natural Law and Faith: The Forgotten Foundations of Ethics in Luther's Theology" in *Union with Christ: The New Finnish Interpretation of Luther,* eds. Carl Braaten and Robert Jenson (Grand Rapids: Eerdmans, 1998), 96–124. For the place of natural law in Luther's thinking, see Johannes Heckel, *Lex Charitatis: A Juristic Disquistion on Law in the Theology of Martin Luther,* trans. Gottfried Krodel (Grand Rapids: Eerdmans, 2010).

2.   Certainly other Lutheran theologians of the period also could merit attention, particularly Paul Althaus, *The Ethics of Martin Luther,* trans. Robert Schultz (Philadelphia: Fortress, 1972); Walter Künneth, *Politik Zwischen Dämon und Golt; Eine Christliche Ethik des Politischen* (Berlin: Lutherisches Verlagshaus, 1954); Regin Prenter, *Creation and Redemption,* trans. Theodor I. Jensen (Philadephia: Fortress, 1967); and Edmund Schlink, "Das theologisches Problem des Naturrechts" in *Viva Vox Evangelii. Eine Festschrift für Landesbischof D. Hans Meiser zum siebzigsten Geburstag am 16. Februar 1951,* ed. Lutherisches Kirchenamt in Hannover (Munich, 1951); *The Theology of the Lutheran Confessions,* trans. Herbert J.A. Bouman (Philadelphia: Fortress, 1961), 49–52, 240.

3.   Karl Barth, "Gospel and Law" in *Community, State, and Church: Three Essays,* ed. Will Herberg (New York: Doubleday Anchor, 1960), 80.

4.   Barth, "Gospel and Law," 80.

of Luther's sequence of Law and Gospel was Werner Elert of Erlangen. His theological critique of the *Barmen Declaration* at this very point would make Elert a target of sometimes vicious attacks and slanderous attempts to identify him with the ideology of national socialism.[5] For Elert, the critical starting point for genuine evangelical theology is the radical distinction of the two revelations of God, the revelation of His wrath through the Law and the revelation of His grace in the Gospel.

Elert takes up the question of natural law in the locus of "The Law of God" (Chapter 2) in his *Christian Ethos*, written after World War II. In a fashion reminiscent of Luther's 1525 treatise "How Christians Should Regard Moses," Elert argues that the giving of the Decalogue to Israel does not mean that Gentiles "lived outside the order of necessity, or that the principle of *lex semper accusat* were not applicable to them, or that they had no need to protect their communal life by a social use of the law. On the contrary, the conviction that all this applies equally to non-Christians and non-Jews is the reason for the doctrine of the natural law whose validity is as extensive as human existence itself, as far as that existence is ordered by law and by nature (*legaliter et naturaliter*)."[6] This conviction, Elert asserts, cannot be given up out of a fear that it conflicts with a particular notion of revelation.

Natural law has political ramifications. Here Elert examines what he sees as the paradoxical situation "in which ruler and subject are bound by the same order which one experiences as right, the other as injustice."[7] The positivistic theory that the lawgiver is the party in power and therefore has the right to create law is challenged by an appeal to morality. The distinction between right and wrong is not interpreted by legality, but by morality. Elert observes how the clash between "two systems of law," one identified as moral law and the other as prevailing legal practice, takes place: For the legal positivist, existing legislation can never be illegal. For those who make the appeal to morality, natural law is invoked as the criterion by which existing legal codes are to be evaluated. *Right* is defined

---

5. Here see Lowell Green, *Lutherans against Hitler: The Untold Story* (St. Louis: Concordia, 2007), 239–49; Lowell Green, *The Erlangen School of Theology* (Fort Wayne, IN: Lutheran Legacy Press, 2010), 241–57; and Matthew Becker, "Werner Elert in Retrospect," *Lutheran Quarterly* (Winter 2006), 265–71.

6. Werner Elert, *The Christian Ethos,* trans. Carl J. Schindler (Philadelphia: Fortress, 1957), 70.

7. Elert, *The Christian Ethos,* 70.

by established legal definitions or by an appeal to that which is moral in itself:

> It is termed "natural law" because its opposite is felt to be "unnatural," a perversion of human nature and the relationship that ought to exist between human beings. In this connection natural law means practically the same as natural rights (*jus naturalis*). Such a development is inevitable when in the course of history an indigenous, native code of law is replaced by alien jurisprudence and learned jurists take the places of lay judges. The protagonists of every great revolutionary movement have justified their abolition or modification of the existing legal order by an appeal to the ideal right which transcends all legal orders and social institutions. The peasants in Luther's time invoked the "natural law," the French revolutionaries the "rights of men," Karl Marx the inevitable operation of the law of economics. But even the party in power is constantly forced to modify the existing law in order to forestall revolutionary unrest by fostering "progressive" legislation.[8]

Politically, an appeal to some notion of natural law appears inescapable.

Surveying the history of dogma, it is evident that Christian theologians have found it necessary to give attention to the place and significance of natural law. Elert observes that the Church Fathers could see examples of natural law in Greek classical literature and in Roman civil code. Here Elert cites a line of reasoning that runs through Clement of Alexandria, Theophilus, Thomas Aquinas, and Philip Melanchthon as reflected in Article XXIII of the Apology of the Augsburg Confession, where celibacy conflicts with "divine and natural law" (Ap XXIII 6) and contradicts that which is confirmed by the jurists who "have said wisely and correctly that the union of male and female belongs to natural right" (Ap XXIII 9). More common, according to Elert, is the appeal of the patristic writers to the Stoic claim that *natural* means those human characteristics that distinguish the human being from animals, especially the ability to exercise reason. Elert observes that this theme becomes settled Catholic teaching, accepted by Luther and used as axiomatic for theoretical jurisprudence in the Enlightenment.

---

8.   Elert, *The Christian Ethos*, 71.

Three reasons account for the existence of a theological teaching on natural law, according to Elert. First, "It can be used to find some common ground with non-Christians from which an appeal to their conscience can be launched."[9] Elert offers no objection to this approach. Second, natural law can be used as a beginning point for the confirmation of God's revelation. This, Elert says, is theologically problematic, although he does not engage his objections as this discussion belongs in the domain of dogmatics, not ethics.[10] Third, natural law bears a relationship to matters of the Christian ethos.

In taking up this third point, Elert poses the question "Can the natural law require more of us than the dedication of our entire existence to the service of God and neighbor?"[11] Like the Decalogue, the *lex naturalis* is always accusing. Natural law does not provide a sphere where human beings can live without guilt. While natural law serves to curb chaos among human beings, regulating behavior and protecting orders established by the creative will and governing work of God, it cannot provide justification for sinners. Natural law, Elert argues, cannot be reduced to a formulaic principle nor into a system. Rather, natural law is expressed in prohibitions that "remind us that all created orders of God are subject to human interference and destruction."[12] Evil exists as a creaturely reality in which creatures are not only victims, but perpetrators. Quoting Schiller, the German poet, that it is "the nature of the evil deed to go on creating new evil,"[13] Elert observes that the reign of sin has its own laws. Sin begets sin and so the "laws of a good creation are perverted to serve evil."[14]

Elert faults Aquinas and the Thomistic tradition for delivering a picture of natural law as an order of harmony without friction that does not take into account "another law" (Romans 7:23) that is at work in creation; hence, he concludes:

> In the perennial conflict between the positive law of secular sovereigns and the natural law to whom the victims of injustice

---

9. Elert, *The Christian Ethos,* 72.

10. Elert does address this in his *Structure of Lutheranism,* trans. Walter Hansen (St. Louis: Concordia, 1962), 41–43, 49–58.

11. Elert, *The Christian Ethos,* 72.

12. Elert, *The Christian Ethos,* 74.

13. Elert, *The Christian Ethos,* 75.

14. Elert, *The Christian Ethos,* 76.

appeal, theological ethics cannot take sides so easily as well-meaning individuals expect. The natural law is not a coherent system in which all parts fit together without friction. It also contains the *law* of sin, the *law* of the demonic within the same creaturely reality. It may well be the task of positive legislation to erect a protecting wall *against* nature, i.e. against a demonized nature with its "natural" determinism.[15]

It is in the light of natural law that Elert treats natural orders as the work of the Creator locating human beings in relationship to each other and creation itself. The commands and prohibitions of the Decalogue presuppose and protect these orders. Elert discusses the significance of the natural orders for ethics; he distinguishes between the laws of nature that are rigid and without exception, such as the biological fact that male and female are needed to produce offspring. "We are subject to these laws and we cannot change them or set them aside. We can use them or misuse them."[16] This datum is not irrelevant for ethics. But according to Elert, the more immediate concern of ethics is with the question of right and wrong, which means that the individual is confronted with the regulative activity of the Creator. God does not establish marriage with the Sixth Commandment, but prohibits the breaking of the marital bond. The Creator places human beings in particular orders; law binds them to the creation: "By means of creation, man is placed into the world; by means of *nomos,* he is held secure in it."[17] Yet the security provided by natural law can provide only external security in this life. In the end, Elert writes, "the same natural law which secures our earthly life also ensure[s] the inevitability of our death."[18]

For Elert, ethics is not about establishing rules for life based on the Decalogue or discovering a system of natural law that is immanent in the universe. Rather, "the Christian ethos conceives itself as the divine evaluation of the human quality."[19]

Elert does not exclude natural law from theological ethics, but identifies its potency not with the establishment of morality or a dimly under-

---

15. Elert, *The Christian Ethos,* 76.
16. Elert, *The Christian Ethos,* 78.
17. Werner Elert, *Law and Gospel,* trans. Edward Schroeder (Philadelphia: Fortress, 1967), 14.
18. Elert, *Law and Gospel,* 15.
19. Elert, *The Christian Ethos,* 7.

stood ethic that is polished and restored by grace, but with its energy to restrain and convict, to judge and deliver God's own retribution not merely to a morally errant creature, but to a sinful human being defined by unbelief.

HELMUT THIELICKE

Though Helmut Thielicke would find Elert problematic, describing him as an "arch-Lutheran,"[20] he would share in certain aspects of Elert's critical rejection of Barth. Like Elert, Thielicke would reject Barth's collapse of the Law into the Gospel. Unlike Elert, Thielicke would conclude, "Natural law and the Decalogue in fact belong to completely different worlds."[21] Thielicke has his own approach to the question of natural law, set within the context of his recognition of the "two aeons" as defining spheres for theological ethics.

Thielicke grants that fallen humanity knows something of the imperative of the law, yet is unable to grasp this imperative as the law of God. Man might know the law, but because he does not know the Giver of the law, man is blind to the purpose and outcome of the law's work. "Natural man" says Thielicke, "knows the imperative, and one may regard this knowledge as a recollection of the Law of God."[22]

Writing after the Second World War, Thielicke notes that the question of natural law was raised in a particularly urgent way by the Nuremberg trials as the prosecution appealed to moral standards as basic axioms of humanity not to be overturned by governmental edicts. It is assumed that a fundamental morality exists that ultimately binds humanity together in spite of differing religions and worldviews. The sovereignty of the state is limited by basic rights of the individual that are inviolate: "Accordingly there must necessarily be certain fundamental orders of life whose decisive characteristic is that they are obligatory for all, for if they were not obligatory the world would be delivered over to chaos."[23] This order is

---

20. Helmut Thielicke, *Notes From a Wayfarer,* trans. David Law (New York: Paragon House, 1995), 74; Also see John T. Pless, "Helmut Thielicke," *Lutheran Quarterly* (Winter 2009), 440–41.

21. Helmut Thielicke, *Theological Ethics, Volume I: Foundations,* trans. William Lazareth (Philadelphia: Fortress, 1966), 444.

22. Thielicke, *Theological Ethics,* 1:383.

23. Thielicke, *Theological Ethics,* 1:387.

not derived from empirical knowledge or theoretical analysis, "but from a perception of ultimate ethical obligations, those which strike us with the force of an imperative the moment we encounter them."[24] This order is experienced not with the intellect, but with the conscience, yet in such a way that the conscience is challenged.

For Thielicke, two essential features distinguish natural law. First, natural law implies an order of being that is foundational for every imperative. Second, this order possesses universality; it is recognizable by all. This presses the question of the meaning of "nature" in natural law. Nature includes more than those elements that are biological; it includes a personal aspect. "Nature thus embraces everything this-worldly, including all the orders of this world, and that means the orders that are bound to matter."[25] Natural law is grounded in the essence of humanity—who man is from his origin and the goal toward which his life is directed. Thus, Thielicke notes that natural law, as it is conceived in the Aristotelian-Thomistic system, is the law that belongs to mankind not merely by his biological make up, but by virtue of what he is essentially—a creature made in the *imago Dei*. Hence, natural law is binding on all people, for it is independent of all exterior influences, including positive law. "Indeed, so far from being influenced by these laws it is itself normative for them. It is grounded in the relatively undisturbed likeness between creator and creature."[26] Because natural law is accessible to all, it establishes a norm to which all are, by nature, accountable. Natural law is so called because it is immanent in the world of nature, being expressed in the operative forces at work in the cosmos, and is embraced by theoretical and practical reason.

Theologically, Thielicke observes that this understanding of natural law raises the question of how human beings are to understand this ordering of creation. Already Thielicke is anticipating a basic difference between Roman Catholic and Reformation approaches. But before he moves into a lengthy treatment of these differences, Thielicke suggests that we can make inquiry of natural law on the basis of two presuppositions. The first is the capacity for historical observation and reflection. The second is an expanding vision beyond our own geographical horizons that allows us to compare moral standards and codes of behavior.

---

24. Thielicke, *Theological Ethics*, 1:387.
25. Thielicke, *Theological Ethics*, 1:389.
26. Thielicke, *Theological Ethics*, 1:392.

According to Thielicke, this allows us to know that certain things ought not be, but we cannot say with certainty what specific conditions should positively prevail. From the position of the fallen nature of life in this aeon, we cannot work our way back by way of negation to what should be.

Thus, Thielicke sees the basic difference between Roman Catholic and Lutheran understandings of natural law resting in contrasting theological evaluations of sin: "For the possibility or impossibility of working back to the eternal order depends upon the understanding of sin, upon the degree to which we think the being of the world is altered and impaired by the rent of the Fall. If sin involves only a kind of subtraction from original perfection, as in Thomistic thinking, and if there is thus a kind of continuing analogy between the two states, then that working back is quite possible; it is not difficult to reconstruct the order of natural law."[27] For the Thomistic tradition, an order of being exists that is accessible to human reason after the fall.

Thielicke suggests that a Lutheran response to natural law begins not with the character of this law, but with the impotency of fallen reason to comprehend what this good is. Life in this aeon, this old creation now dominated by sin, is incompatible with the will of God and incapable of producing good from within itself. Natural law, then, functions to restrain and prohibit. As such, Thielicke says, it must be recognized, noting that even Karl Barth observed that civil community has no option but to think and act "on the basis of this allegedly natural law."[28]

The conceptuality of natural law has consequences for Thielicke. First, natural law has significance only as an "emergency order," which in the strict sense is dissolved by the new creation. Second, natural law is never an "order of salvation," but always an "order of protection," restraining evil rather than establishing good. Third, natural law does not function for the ethical restoration of human beings. Rather, "it simply contains a veto of certain structures of society and its orders which are to be described as objectified forms of lawlessness and wrong."[29]

Secular appeal is made to natural law to ground concepts of human dignity, freedom, and justice. Here, Thielicke says that "the church's task

---

27. Thielicke, *Theological Ethics*, 1:398.
28. Thielicke, *Theological Ethics*, 1:430.
29. Thielicke, *Theological Ethics*, 1:447.

is not to destroy this secular appeal to natural law."[30] Instead, the preaching of the Church proclaims

> that which natural law has in view but in respect of which it entertains illusions. The church has to preach the patience of God with the fallen world, as this patience is expressed in his covenants with Israel and in the new covenant with the Christian church and the whole world, as well as in the commandments which have been given in connection with these covenants. Hence the Christian must act on very different grounds from those of the natural law. He acts in obedience to the commandments of God. He acts in the knowledge that even those actions which conform to the ultimate norms perceptible in this aeon must stand under forgiveness, and that these perceptible norms are not identical with the divine commandments, or more precisely, with the "true" will (the *voluntas propria*) of God."[31]

In this way, Thielicke maintains the need for natural law in the present age without attempting to attribute any kind of transformative or restorative significance to natural law.

GUSTAF WINGREN

Gustaf Wingren[32] is best known for his work with the theology of creation and the doctrine of vocation. Both of these topics press the question of natural law. Wingren's own theological development was shaped by sharp conflict with Barth. Fundamentally, Wingren believed that Barth was so much in reaction to the anthropology of nineteenth-century liberalism that he allowed its framework to determine his approach. Humankind's problem is a lack of knowledge of God. In revelation, God now gives the knowledge of His grace. God's law is then seen as a part of this one revelation. Wingren, by way of contrast, argues that what man lacks is not knowledge, but redemption. Human beings know from

30. Thielicke, *Theological Ethics*, 1:431.
31. Thielicke, *Theological Ethics*, 1:431–32.
32. For a helpful historical study of Wingren's theology, see Mary Elizabeth Anderson, *Gustaf Wingren and the Swedish Luther Renaissance* (New York: Peter Lang, 2006).

creation the demands that are made upon them. The law for Wingren is not informational but accusatory, as it relentlessly works within creation.

Wingren does not take up the question of natural law per se in his early and celebrated work, *Luther on Vocation.* Wingren wrote his book to challenge the central assertion of his fellow-Swedish Lutheran Einar Billing's book, *Our Calling,* that the calling is a matter of Gospel, not Law. Wingren instead defends the claim that "vocation falls within the kingdom of the law,"[33] for it has to do with life in creation. Recognizing that the Christian simultaneously lives his life "with the Spirit in the paradise of grace and peace, and with the flesh in the world of toil and cross,"[34] Wingren cites Luther's Galatians commentary: "So as the law holds sway in the flesh, the promise rules most graciously in the conscience. When you have thus recognized the proper sphere of each, you walk most securely with the promise in heaven and the law on earth, with the Spirit of grace and peace in Paradise and in the body of works and the cross on earth."[35] Here Wingren isolates two themes that will become dominant in the remainder of his book: the distinction between the life of the body and that of the conscience and vocation as the place of the cross.

As vocation is earthly, it is the location of cross and suffering. Crosses are not to be sought after; they are inevitably present: "In one's vocation there is a cross—for prince, husband, father, daughter, for everyone—and on this cross the old human nature is to be crucified."[36] The cross has a twofold purpose. It is God's instrumentality for putting the old Adam to death, and it provides occasion for service to the neighbor. What Wingren describes as "hard, legalistic character of vocation"[37] is the cross that puts to death the sinner with his notions of autonomy and self-sufficiency. In this sense, the cross drives to despair. "Vocation is the place where God himself lets the cross take form."[38] Here the old Adam is put to death and a new man is raised up by the absolution to live before God in righteousness. The new creature is not extracted from creation;

---

33. Gustaf Wingren, *Luther on Vocation,* trans. Carl C. Rasmussen (Philadelphia: Muhlenberg, 1957), 26.

34. Wingren, *Luther on Vocation,* 26.

35. Wingren, *Luther on Vocation,* 26.

36. Wingren, *Luther on Vocation,* 29.

37. Wingren, *Luther on Vocation,* 66.

38. Wingren, *Luther on Vocation,* 54.

he or she continues to live on earth in anticipation of the resurrection. The new life remains hidden under the cross and suffering as it is active in love to the neighbor. Luther's understanding of the hidden nature of the Christian's life guards against a triumphalistic notion of sanctification. In this way, Wingren sees creation and eschatology held together in Luther's doctrine of vocation.

Located as it is on earth, vocation is within space and time. For Wingren, this means that human beings are bound to the earth by God's law, living as creatures between life and death.[39] Much of the remainder of Wingren's career was spent in drawing out the implications of the doctrine of creation, or "creation faith,"[40] for Christian theology. We may observe the roots of his later work in *Luther on Vocation*. Given a place in creation, human beings are given life in and through the stations they occupy. It is also through these temporal stations that human beings are daily bread to one another, to paraphrase Luther, for these stations are so ordered that the neighbor is served: "It is only before God, i.e., in heaven, that the individual stands alone. In the earthly realm man always stands *in relation*, always bound to another."[41] Thus, vocation is a place of tension for Wingren. It is the tension between time and eternity, earth and heaven. According to Wingren, this tension evokes prayer that is an expression of the First Commandment in the midst of vocation. This tension may not be resolved in seeking a model to emulate even in Christ. "Christ is not to be imitated by us, but rather to be accepted in faith, because Christ also had his special office for the salvation of man, an office which no one else has."[42]

Instead, the Christian is directed to the office that he or she has in space and time for the good of the neighbor. We have observed that

39. See Gustaf Wingren, *Creation and Law*, trans. Ross Mackenzie (Philadelphia: Muhlenberg, 1961), 45–82. Again Wingren argues this point over and against Barth. He sees in Barth a fundamental mistake of holding that humanity's primary problem is lack of knowledge about God. Wingren, with Luther, asserts that humanity's problem is not ignorance of God, but guilt before God. See the summation of the theological conflict between Barth and Wingren in Gerhard Forde, *The Law-Gospel Debate: An Interpretation of Its Historical Development* (Minneapolis: Augsburg, 1969), 159–61.

40. See Gustaf Wingren, *Credo: The Christian View of Faith and Life*, trans. Edgar M. Carlson (Minneapolis: Augsburg, 1981), 37–57; Wingren, *The Flight from Creation* (Minneapolis: Augsburg, 1971).

41. Wingren, *Luther on Vocation*, 5.

42. Wingren, *Luther on Vocation*, 172.

for Wingren, vocation does have a hard and legalistic character given its nomological setting as law that is essential in creation. However, that does not mean that vocation can be reduced to a legalism of principles for behavior. Wingren writes, "The sign of a right ethics is not found in a certain fixed outward behavior, but in the ability to meet, in calmness and faith, whatever may come."[43] Explicit in his renunciation of legalism, Wingren writes, "Legalism is a continual flight from God's command. Faith is a way toward understanding God's command."[44] Such faith gives birth to love that is open to the need of the neighbor: "What love of my neighbor will ask of me next year, I cannot know this year. . . . Precisely for the neighbor's sake, one ought to be free to what becomes necessary, free from the vows (the law), to obey the command."[45]

The tensions implicit in vocation will not be resolved until the resurrection. Vocation finds its consummation eschatologically. Then the earthly realm and the sway of the law will be forever past. Until then, "The old man must bear vocation's cross as long as life on earth lasts and the battle against the devil continues. As long as he continues in his earthly vocation, there can be no end to the struggle. After death comes a new kingdom free from the cross; heaven has taken the place of earth, God has conquered the devil, and man has been raised from the dead. Then man's struggle is at an end."[46] In the meantime, the Law and the Gospel remain: "The gospel acts in man's conscience, and extinguishes sin; wherefore the new man has no sin. The law acts in the body, and there it does not at once efface sin, but drives sin out slowly. The old man thus retains his sin till the death of the body, and in the meantime he is disciplined by the law, cross, and suffering. Law and gospel both come from God, and for God the two are one, a single reality. For man, however, the two cannot even appear to be in harmony until the old man is annihilated, that is, not at any time in this life, but only after the death of the body."[47] Hidden under the cross of vocation, the life of the believer is lived by faith in Christ's promises and in the hope that anticipates the new heaven and earth. The law remains until the final day.

---

43. Wingren, *Luther on Vocation*, 181.
44. Wingren, *Luther on Vocation*, 200.
45. Wingren, *Luther on Vocation*, 201.
46. Wingren, *Luther on Vocation*, 250–51.
47. Wingren, *Luther on Vocation*, 239.

A more explicit discussion of natural law is found in Wingren's later writings, *Creation and Law* and *The Flight from Creation*. In *Creation and Law*, Wingren seeks to defend the thesis that "There is no contradiction between this natural order and the idea that Christ has a new command to give man."[48] Paradoxically, this new command is as old as creation and as new as the salvation brought by Christ. For Wingren, creation is both the means by which God bestows His gifts and, at the same time, a force that is "prompting man in his external relationships in the same direction as the command of love."[49] The corrupted nature of the old Adam fights against this prompting, enslaving man to his acquisitive greed so that he is not free to give as God intended. God's sovereignty over humanity's sinfulness is demonstrated in and through natural law.

Writing against N. H. Søe, who understood natural law as an expression of some power or capacity in man, Wingren argues that because the demand of natural law is from outside of man, it cannot be reduced to a minimal requirement or interpreted as lacking universality. Instead, natural law makes a maximum demand in that it does more than merely prohibit; it calls for faith. Hence, Wingren writes, "In Romans 1 Paul shows that God's revelation in Creation is the primary basis for the demand of *faith* and not simply for refraining from heinous offences, or for adopting an attitude of regard for one's neighbour. The unrecognized demand, which is addressed to men by the very fact of their living in the world, is a demand for faith and trust in God, and so also a demand to put away 'idols' (i.e., the worship of the creature rather than the Creator, Romans 1:19ff, 23, 25) and to love their fellow men (Romans 1:30ff)."[50] The demand of natural law for faith is unrecognized and unformulated; it can only be seen for what it truly is in light of the fulfillment brought about in the Incarnation. It is there that the demand of creation and the commandment of love meet.

In *Creation and Law*, Wingren also takes up the connection between Old Testament law rendered obsolete in Christ and the continuing significance of the law. He writes, "If we reject the concept of natural law, then the Law of the Old Testament becomes an insoluble problem."[51] Wingren argues that the point of connection is found in creation, which

48. Wingren, *Creation and Law*, 42.
49. Wingren, *Creation and Law*, 43.
50. Wingren, *Creation and Law*, 60.
51. Wingren, *Creation and Law*, 124.

precedes redemption. But this does not mean that creation is assigned to the past. Rather, creation itself has a dynamic aspect as God continues to uphold and sustain His creation. It is in this context that we may speak of natural law, thus avoiding the Barthian inversion of "Gospel/Law," which ultimately gives the Gospel a "legalistic twist."[52]

Wingren revisits his treatment of "creation and law" in *The Flight from Creation*, which may best be understood as an attempt to recover a robust understanding of creation over against the negation of the doctrine he sees both in Kierkegaard and Barth. This is a challenge in light of the misapplication of the "creation orders" (*Schöpfung*) in the time prior to the Second World War in Germany and an allergic reaction to anything that appears to be in the proximity of a Roman Catholic understanding of natural law invoked to buttress traditional social ethics.

Wingren seeks to distance his proposals for a creation theology from the cultural wars in Sweden: "I have been urged several times to take part but so far I have refused to be enrolled as a soldier in the war which morality is waging against immorality in Sweden."[53] At this point, Wingren sees neither a return of an "orders theology" or the embrace of a "theology of revolution" as a viable ethic. Following Løgstrup, Wingren posits natural law as a "natural ethos" as the givens of "trust, charity, and general humanity without which life cannot be lived."[54] These elemental human qualities are givens for existence in creation. It is in this sense that Wingren sees a convergence between the law given in creation and the new commandment given in Christ: "The idea of a universal ethos, a 'natural law' is not difficult to combine with the idea that the church has a specific, a *unique* word to preach. On the contrary, these two points go together very well."[55]

RECEPTION IN LATE TWENTIETH AND EARLY TWENTY-FIRST CENTURIES

Elert, Thielicke, and Wingren each in their own distinct way would play a part in various trajectories within contemporary Lutheran ethical

---

52. Wingren, *Creation and Law*, 126.
53. Wingren, *The Flight from Creation*, 26.
54. Wingren, *The Flight from Creation*, 70.
55. Wingren, *The Flight from Creation*, 69.

reflection. Edward Schroeder,[56] Walter Bouman,[57] and others associated with the party in The Lutheran Church—Missouri Synod whose work would be defined by the events leading to Seminex would serve as primary filters for Elert in the United States. Friend and foe alike associated Elert with this movement, pointing to his alleged rejection of the "third use of the law." Unfortunately, Elert was most often read through the lens of these interpreters. Thus, David Yeago points to Elert as representative of Antinomian Lutheranism.[58]

As we have observed, Elert is critical of the Thomistic understanding of natural law, not because it is heteronomous, but because it does not reckon sufficiently with the disruption brought into creation by sin. Creation, then, is not seen under the radical judgment of its Creator, but in terms of its potential for perfection through a reorientation toward God, the highest good. Thus, ethics becomes a *mimesis* of a pattern that is perceptible to human reason. Grace restores nature. Like Luther, Elert can and does speak of the place of natural law in ethics when it comes to the *usus politicus*. But it remains a law that continues to accuse the conscience. The conscience does not find peace through conformity to natural law, but in the absolution that frees the believer not to ignore or set aside God's ordering of creation but to live within these orders under God's grace in Christ. It is hard to see how some of Elert's interpreters could use his theology to promote an approach to sexual ethics that would free the believer to transcend the creaturely realities of being male or female in light of Elert's affirmation: "Creation places man into the world, *nomos* binds him to the world. In the first place, nomological existence under law means only that we, like all other creatures, are subject to the orderly rule of God and that we do not live in a world of chaos and arbitrariness."[59]

Thielicke, more than either Elert or Wingren, gives substantial and, in many ways, comprehensive attention to the question of natural law, devoting over seventy-five pages explicitly to the topic in the first volume

---

56. See Edward Schroeder, "The Relationship between Dogmatics and Ethics in the Thought of Elert, Barth, and Troelstch," *Concordia Theological Monthly* (December 1965): 744–71.
57. See Walter Bouman, "The Concept of 'Law' in the Lutheran Tradition," *Word & World* (Fall 1983): 413–22.
58. David Yeago, "Gnosticism, Antinomianism and Reformation Theology," *Pro Ecclesia* (Winter 1993): 37–49.
59. Elert, *The Christian Ethos,* 51.

of his *Theological Ethics* and integrating it into a discussion of various issues throughout the project. Because we continue to live within the eschatological overlap between the old and new aeons, natural law must not be dismissed, even though in "borderline" situations, Christians may find themselves caught in moral dilemmas that are insoluble. Christians are given more than natural law in that they have the promise of Christ's Spirit to strengthen them in trusting His righteousness alone and serving the neighbor in love within ambivalence of life in a fallen world. Thus for Thielicke, Christian ethics cannot be reduced to a system of casuistry, but must remain an eschatological ethic standing under both God's judgment and His grace.[60]

Thielicke distances his approach from "situation ethics" in that God's law is not subject to arbitrary and subjective definitions of love. The commandments of God carry definitive content. Thus, Thielicke sees the Decalogue as going beyond nonhistorical natural law in that it both occupies a specific place in salvation history and addresses the fallen man who is in revolt against the Creator.[61]

Gustaf Wingren is in many ways an enigma. On the one hand, he is insistent that vocation, hence ethics, remain grounded in creation. In a time when any talk of natural law and creation orders was suspect, Wingren insisted that Christian theology can ill-afford to allow itself a "flight from creation." Wingren is critical of his older colleague, Anders Nygren, for not allowing natural law to have a place in the fundamental motifs of *agape, eros,* and *nomos.*[62] Yet Wingren himself is unable to articulate what constitutes natural law: "A theological concept such as 'natural law' really cries out for a purely philosophical analysis. The task is there waiting but I pass it by. My excuse is that, despite many years of searching, I have found no philosopher, neither analytical nor existential, whom I could take over directly. I am not capable myself of constructing a philosophy from the very foundations."[63] Wingren would have significant influence on the development of Gerhard Forde's theology,[64] yet Forde demonstrates a precision in discussing both the content and func-

---

60. For more on Thielicke's approach to ethics, see Pless, "Helmut Thielicke," 448–51.

61. *Theological Ethics, Vol. I,* 442.

62. See Anderson, *Gustaf Wingren and the Swedish Luther Renaissance,* 79.

63. Wingren, *The Flight from Creation,* 29.

64. See James Nestingen, "Examining Sources: Influences on Gerhard Forde's Theology" in *By Faith Alone: Essays in Honor of Gerhard O. Forde,* eds. Joseph Burgess and Marc Kolden (Grand Rapids: Eerdmans, 2004), 10–21.

tion of the law that is lacking in Wingren.[65] Given Wingren's pronounced move toward a more liberal and tolerant position on social ethics especially in the 1970s and beyond,[66] it is hard to imagine that he would endorse Forde's conservative stance on homosexuality.

Today's renewed interest in natural law goes beyond the work done by Elert, Thielicke, and Wingren in the last century.[67] Current attempts to reclaim natural law are fueled by those with both ecumenical agendas and ethical concerns.[68] As we have seen, representative Lutheran responses to Barth raise as many, if not more, questions than they provide answers. Yet these questions are well worth exploration and engagement, especially in light of recent work being done on Luther's understanding of the three estates and their function in creation.[69]

65. See, for example, Gerhard Forde, "Law and Sexual Behavior," *Lutheran Quarterly* (Spring 1995): 3–22. Also note my article that contrasts Edward Schroeder's Antinomian approach to homosexuality with that of Forde. In this article, I maintain that Schroeder distorts Elert's understanding of Law and Gospel. See John T. Pless, "Using and Misusing Luther on Homosexuality," *Lutheran Forum* (Winter 2004): 24–30.

66. See Carl Axel Aurelius, "Gustaf Wingren (1910–2000)" in *Theologische Realenzykolpädie,* 36 (Berlin: Walter de Gruyter, 2004), 110–14.

67. See, for example, *A Preserving Grace,* ed. Michael Cromartie (Grand Rapids: Eerdmans, 1997) for an anthology of articles by Roman Catholic, Reformed, and Lutheran authors.

68. Mark C. Mattes has rightly raised some cautions here. See Mark C. Mattes, "The Thomistic Turn in Evangelical Catholic Ethics," *Lutheran Quarterly* (Spring 2002): 65–100.

69. See especially Oswald Bayer, "Luther's Ethics as Pastoral Care," *Lutheran Quarterly* (Summer 1990): 125–42; Oswald Bayer, "Nature and Institution: Luther's Doctrine of the Three Orders," *Lutheran Quarterly* (Summer 1998): 125–59; Knut Alfvåg, "Christians in Society: Luther's Teaching on the Two Governments and the Three Estates," *Logia* (Reformation, 2005): 15–20; Hans Schaeffer, *Createdness and Ethics: The Doctrine of Creation and Theological Ethics in the Theology of Colin E. Gunton and Oswald Bayer* (Berlin: Walter de Gruyter, 2006), 101–89; and Nathan Yoder, "The Order of Marriage and the Lord of the Orders," *Lutheran Forum* (Summer 2009): 42–45.

8

Natural Law, Human Sexuality, and Forde's "Acid Test"

"The acid test for any method is its practical consequences."[1]

Robert C. Baker

Introduction

In one sense, Lutherans have been debating the place of the law since the Reformation. In another sense, however, this debate was revived during the nineteenth-century Luther Renaissance. Law, and natural law as a subset of law, received a treatment unlike what had been systematized and accepted during the period of Lutheran Orthodoxy (ca. 1580–1730).

---

1. Gerhard O. Forde, "Law and Gospel as the Methodological Principle of Theology," in *Theological Perspectives: A Discussion of Contemporary Issues in Lutheran Theology* (Decorah, IA: Luther College Press, 1967), 68.

Why do I make such a claim? Because without noting the underlying
shifts in philosophical and theological approach, especially the interscho-
lastic rivalries by those claiming legitimacy as "confessional Lutherans,"
specifically the Erlangen and repristination schools of that movement,
one might misunderstand claims about the law made within the broader
Lutheran tradition today. This has repercussions not only for the law generally understood, but also for natural law, the "third use" of the law, civil
law, and so on. Hence, it is always fitting to analyze the philosophical and
theological methods of Lutheran theologians as well as possible practical
consequences of their methods. For this reason, I examine the method
proposed by Gerhard O. Forde (1927–2005) in an attempt to determine
its consequences on the development of his sexual ethics.

I have chosen Forde for a number of reasons. First, Forde is a well-
respected twentieth-century American Lutheran theologian and scholar;
he enjoys a widely appreciative ecumenical and international audience,
including members of my own denomination, The Lutheran Church—
Missouri Synod. Second, though certainly unique in his own right, Forde
is a post-Barthian heir of the Erlangen school. Third, Forde's writings
convey a sense that he genuinely sought to confront what he perceived as
threats to the Gospel of Jesus Christ, threats he sought to address through
faithful pastoral care centered upon preaching. Fourth, and perhaps most
important, Forde warned against encroaching changes in sexual mores.
He did this by specifically addressing the attempt to legitimize same-sex
behavior[2] within his church body, the Evangelical Lutheran Church of
America, of which I am a former member.

Before going further, I would like to make three important points.
First, while Forde's thinking matured and became more nuanced over
time, as I would expect from any thoughtful and careful theologian, I
assume that his early key insights were consistent over the breadth of
his career. Second, I see Forde as a twentieth-century, post-Barthian
representative of a particular school of theology, *not* as the harbinger of
change regarding sexual morality. I look at the method and possible con-

---

2.   "Same-sex behavior" avoids the post-Freudian/Kinseyan way of objectifying per-
     sons primarily in terms of their sexual desire. It also sidesteps *moral reductionism*
     (see footnote 3), which inherently limits sexual sin to illicit activity specifically
     involving the human genitalia. For a brief but fine summary of the development
     of the modern concept of "sexual orientation," see Roland D. Martinson, "Sexual
     Orientation: The History and Significance of an Idea," in *Word and World,* vol. xiv,
     no. 3 (St. Paul: Luther Seminary, 1994), 239–45.

sequences of the method, not the man. Third, inasmuch as a method reflects reductionism,[3] the consequences of that method, including morality, will be reductionistic. In the following, I survey a number of Forde's works, including "Law and Gospel as the Methodological Principle of Theology," which Forde delivered while serving at Luther College in Decorah, Iowa, and Forde's major contribution, *The Law-Gospel Debate: An Interpretation of Its Historical Development*. I also briefly explore themes in Forde's "Lex semper accusat?" and "Luther's Ethics." Finally, I look at two of Forde's essays in which he addresses sexual behavior. The first of these is "Human Sexuality, Romans Chapter One"; the second is "Law and Sexual Behavior." These and other works by Forde have been cited as indicative of Forde's approval of a traditional sexual ethic.[4]

EPISTEMOLOGICAL CRISIS: HOW DO YOU KNOW?

LAW AND GOSPEL AS THE METHODOLOGICAL PRINCIPLE

I first take a look at Forde's methodology. In "Law and Gospel as the Methodological Principle of Theology," he sets out to relieve contemporary Lutheran theology, burdened by historical and scientific developments as well as biblical criticism, from an epistemological *angst*. For Forde, the way to resolve the tension is to answer the question "How do you know?" Within the Lutheran tradition, he finds and contrasts two radically different ways of providing an answer: the "verbal inspiration

---

3.   By reductionism, I mean the theory that complex ideas or concepts can be broken down into essential components and understood solely on the basis of those components. Both liberalism and fundamentalism are reductionistic in that they seek to interpret and convey the complexity of Christianity in smaller, understandable concepts: pious deeds (liberalism) or certain key doctrines (fundamentalism). In contrast, Orthodox Lutheranism accounts for and systematizes all biblical doctrine in a comprehensive way. For the now classical treatment of "Law-Gospel Reductionism," see John Warwick Montgomery, *Crisis in Lutheran Theology: The Validity and Relevance of Historic Lutherism vs. Its Contemporary Rivals*, vols. 1 and 2 (Grand Rapids: Baker, 1967).

4.   See, for example, Albert Mohler, "*Ex Libris*—The Preached God," September 18, 2007, available at www.albertmohler.com/2007/09/18/ex-libris-the-preached-god/ (accessed November 14, 2010); and John T. Pless, "Using and Misusing Luther on Homosexuality," *Lutheran Forum* (Winter 2004): 24–30.

method" and the "Law-Gospel method." While conceding that both were present in early Lutheranism, Forde suggests that the superior Law-Gospel method accords better with Scripture.[5] In the verbal inspiration method, faith must answer "How do you know?" by an *a priori* claim identifying the Word of God with Scripture.[6] However, Forde suggests that the verbal inspiration method is particularly disadvantaged. First, Scripture itself does not demand that it be accepted as the Word of God. Second, the verbal inspiration method is unable to answer the challenges proposed by scientific advancements and historical-critical research of the Scriptures in a successful way. For Forde, verbal inspiration is based on human theorizing about the nature of God's Word. Because it is based on human logic that can be broken, the verbal inspiration method is bound to collapse.[7]

As an alternative, Forde proposes the Law-Gospel method, which he suggests best represents Lutheran theology.[8] For Forde, Law and Gospel are experienced in Christian preaching. People cannot be convinced of the truth of Christianity through the mere doctrine of verbal inspiration. Rather, Law and Gospel must be properly divided, proclaimed, and experienced. While Forde's emphasis on the preached Word is to be commended, it likewise highlights his apparent bias of practice over

5. Forde, "Law and Gospel as the Methodological Principle of Theology," 52.
6. Forde, "Law and Gospel as the Methodological Principle of Theology," 52. Forde notes that this *a priori* view was shared by Francis A. O. Pieper (*Christian Dogmatics*, vol. 1, p. 238), Johannes A. Quendstedt (quoted in *Christian Dogmatics*), and Johann W. Baier (quoted from H. Schmid, *The Doctrinal Theology of the Evangelical Lutheran Church*, 39). See also Forde's qualitative difference between the Word of God and man's word, p. 64. Here Forde identifies himself with a key feature of Erlangen theology: an appeal to Luther while avoiding the contributions of Lutheran Orthodoxy. Forde later claims that the Church's acceptance of natural law theory skewed the doctrine of eschatology, as well as influenced the Church toward "Antinomianism." See Gerhard O. Forde, "Justification and This World," in *Christian Dogmatics,* eds. Carl E. Braaten and Robert W. Jenson, vol. 2 (Philadelphia: Fortress Press, 1984), 447 and 448, respectively.
7. Forde, "Law and Gospel as the Methodological Principle of Theology," 56–57. Forde will later suggest that the doctrine of scriptural inerrancy led to a "dogmatic absolutism" in Lutheranism. See "Radical Lutheranism," in *A More Radical Gospel,* eds. Mark C. Mattes and Steven D. Paulson, Lutheran Quarterly Books (Grand Rapids: Eerdmans), 2004), 7. First published as "Radical Lutheranism: Lutheran Identity in America," *Lutheran Quarterly* 1 (1987), 5–18.
8. Forde, "Law and Gospel as the Methodological Principle of Theology," 59.

theory, preaching over dogma, and experience over systemization.[9] Close examination reveals a reductionistic tendency that inheres in his works. For Forde, contemporary Lutheran theology seeks to reclaim Law and Gospel in the Church's life; it "seeks to restore this practical insight to its proper place and raise it to the level of the method which governs our theology as a whole."[10] Forde does not explain how the elevation of one systematic category[11]—in this case, Law and Gospel as experienced by the believer—can successfully serve the entire rich buffet of biblical theology. Neither does he offer insights into how this "governing method" will affect other biblical doctrines. Forde also does not explain how this "raising" cannot otherwise be construed as an establishment of dogma.

In contrast to the verbal inspiration method, Forde proposes a Law-Gospel method that rejects an *a priori* understanding of God's Word. "I cannot start with *my ideas* of what the Word of God is or what it would have to be and then try to make the scripture fit this idea."[12] For Forde, the Word of God is not a rational proposition to be believed; it is an "event."[13] Here, I find evidence of clear existentialist themes. Forde

9. In a style more common in yesteryear, Forde writes: "It is extremely interesting in the contemporary debate that those who constantly accuse today's theologians of intellectualism are themselves usually the ones who have unwittingly taken the intellectualistic side of the argument," 60. See also Forde's portrayal of "theological books" and "theological wordplay" in *The Preached God: Proclamation in Word and Sacrament,* eds. Mark C. Mattes and Steven D. Paulson (Grand Rapids: Eerdmans, 2007), 216 and 224, respectively.

10. Forde, "Law and Gospel as the Methodological Principle of Theology," 60.

11. By systematic category, I simply mean the theological shorthand theologians generally use to categorize complex doctrines. When systematic categories, which are themselves very helpful, are used to "trump" key Bible passages (thus becoming what I call übervalues), they truncate Christian doctrine. While the genesis of such an approach was earlier, I call this method of theologizing "The Twentieth Century Project." In his 1884 *Lehrverhandlung,* Francis A. O. Pieper engaged the "New Theology" of Hofmann and Luthardt, representatives of the Erlangen school, who suggested that theology could be approached like any other science. They claimed to be building a theology based on the "totality of Scripture." Pieper wrote, "In reality the matter is this: The single expressly-written word which, in the opinion of the theological architect, doesn't fit so well into the structure, is either totally discarded or at least is modified so that it fits into the whole. One calls this 'good theological mediation'." Deutsche ev.-luth. Synode von Missouri, Ohio, u. a. Staaten, Neunzehnter Synodal-Bericht der allgemeinen Deutschen Evangelisch-Lutherischen Synode von Missouri, Ohio, u. a. Staaten versammelt als vierte Delegaten-Synode in St. Louis, Missouri, im Jahre 1884 (St. Louis: Lutherischer Concordia-Verlag, 1884), 164. The English translation is mine.

12. Forde, "Law and Gospel as the Methodological Principle of Theology," 60.

13. Forde, "Law and Gospel as the Methodological Principle of Theology," 60.

appeals to Luther to verify his claim. For Luther, God's Word is certainly living and active, but it is very unlike the words of men.[14] In fact, Forde seems to attempt to drive a wedge between Luther and verbal inspiration. For Forde, when God's Word is preached, two results occur: Hearers are judged and are redeemed, hence Luther's emphasis on Law and Gospel. "The Word of God as law attacks me in my security and as gospel convinces me of grace, and I become convinced that this Word is the *Word of God* only in and through this experience."[15] For Forde, the Word of God is not the Bible, God's words written in human language on a page. Rather, the Word of God is in the experience of the hearer of Law and Gospel. Thus, the question "How do you know?" is answered through the experience of faith.[16]

To affirm his view of God's law, Forde again invokes Luther. Just as the Gospel does not refer merely to the promises, the Law does not merely mean the laws recorded in the Bible.[17] Forde does not suggest what Christians would call a traditional view of natural law—that a remnant of God's divine will still resides in the human heart even after the fall and is accessible by human reason. Rather, for Forde, and like the Gospel, the Law relates to human experience. "Law for [Luther] means a way of hearing the Word of God."[18] Virtually anything in life—be it a thunderstorm, the rustling of a leaf on a dark night, or even the words "Jesus died for your sins"—can be law.[19] Likewise, the Gospel, which "is not merely a set of words which man's reason can apprehend,"[20] is accessible only through faith. In contrast to the existential anguish of the Law, the Gospel "is a whole new way of hearing; it is an entire new dimension of life; it is a word which is full of promise, which makes all of life blossom with good news."[21] In the end, the crisis brought about by the law, which

---

14. Forde, "Law and Gospel as the Methodological Principle of Theology," 60.
15. Forde, "Law and Gospel as the Methodological Principle of Theology," 61.
16. Forde, "Law and Gospel as the Methodological Principle of Theology," 61.
17. Forde, "Law and Gospel as the Methodological Principle of Theology," 62.
18. Forde, "Law and Gospel as the Methodological Principle of Theology," 62.
19. Forde, "Law and Gospel as the Methodological Principle of Theology," 62. Forde notes Luther's fondness of the "rustling leaf" (Leviticus 26:36, NIV). See *Law-Gospel Debate*, 177, and "Justification and This World," in *Christian Dogmatics*, eds. Carl E. Braaten and Robert W. Jenson (Philadelphia: Fortress Press, 1984), 2:418. See also Luther, AE 1:170–74; 3:8; 7:328.
20. Forde, "Law and Gospel as the Methodological Principle of Theology," 63.
21. Forde, "Law and Gospel as the Methodological Principle of Theology," 63.

destroys all self-confidence, is resolved through the experience of faith. Forde's Law-Gospel method pertains to the nature of faith, the question for the basis of faith, and preaching.[22] God's Word is the experience of Law and Gospel in the heart of the believer. Forde offers his Law-Gospel method as part of the fight "for the restoration of the gospel."[23]

The Law-Gospel Debate

Having answered "How do we know?" Forde fleshes out his Law-Gospel methodology in *The Law-Gospel Debate*.[24] Although appearing two generations after Karl Barth's 1935 essay, "Gospel and Law," *The Law-Gospel Debate* situates Forde's review some one hundred years earlier in Johann C. K. von Hofmann's (1810–77) attack on the confessional orthodox Lutheran interpretation of the vicarious satisfaction of Christ. This attack was part of Hofmann's *Heilsgeschichte* theology,[25] which militated against the "biblicistic" orthodoxy of Ernst Wilhelm Hengstenberg (1802–69).[26] According to Forde, one of Hofmann's chief doctrinal aims was to reconstruct the doctrine of the atonement.[27] Hofmann argued against the traditional view that the law of God resided in God's eternal will and which man, by the use of his reason and to an extent even after the fall, could understand. Hofmann portrayed Luther as affirming his claim. In fact, as Forde relates through a footnote, the atonement controversy marked the beginning of the nineteenth-century Luther Renaissance. For the first time, Luther was pitted against the orthodox Lutherans.[28] Heretofore, Lutheran theologians had taught that Christ

22. Forde, "Law and Gospel as the Methodological Principle of Theology," 67–68.

23. Forde, "Law and Gospel as the Methodological Principle of Theology," 67.

24. Scott R. Murray provides an excellent treatment of Forde's dependence upon and departures from Erlangen theology in *Law, Life, and the Living God: The Third Use of the Law in Modern American Lutheranism* (St. Louis: Concordia, 2002). See esp. pp. 123–30.

25. Forde, *The Law-Gospel Debate* (Minneapolis: Augsburg, 1969), 3. In the first footnote, Forde claims the mantle of "orthodoxy" for those views, presumably similar to Forde's, on Law, Gospel, and the atonement, *not* the views of sixteenth and seventeenth century "orthodox Lutheran" theologians. This is not an atypical move for proponents of the Erlangen school, which tends to pair traditional words with radically different content.

26. Forde, *Law-Gospel Debate*, 11.

27. Forde, *Law-Gospel Debate*, 36.

28. Forde's quotation of Hirsch bears repeating: "For the first time a theologian sets Luther against Lutherism on a basic problem. This assertion of Hofmann's be-

atoned for man's sins vicariously by becoming our substitute on the cross. By rejecting that teaching, Hofmann incurred the wrath of Hengstenberg and the repristinationist school of confessional orthodox Lutheranism.

Forde suggests that orthodox Lutherans spoke their doctrine of justification in forensic terms. Justification is primarily seen in the terms of law, of God rendering a verdict in man's favor for the sake of Christ. Forde notes that for the orthodox, the "law is, therefore, an eternal, objective order, a *lex aeterna* which sets forth the ideal to which human life must attain in order to find favor with God."[29] The orthodox identified God's law with the eternal law, which "echoed"[30] the "natural law" residing in man's heart. The natural law is accessible by human reason even after the fall, providing a point of contact for man and God's divine will.[31] Forde recognized that, in a move not made by Anselm, the orthodox also included within their system Christ's active obedience to the law as man's substitute.[32] The results of the orthodox view of law greatly influenced the rest of their theology. While it made their approach rationally coherent,[33] it also tended relegated faith to a mere act of cognition.[34] The orthodox approach to the law also required the belief in scriptural infallibility in order to fill the breach between divine revelation and the reception and validation of Law and Gospel.[35] That approach led to a split between the "objectivism" of Orthodoxy and the "subjectivism" of Pietism.[36]

---

came the starting point for the entire Luther research of the nineteenth- and twentieth-centuries. Emmanuel Hirsch, *Geschichte der neueren Evangelischen Theologie*, vol. V (Gütersloh: C. Bertelsmann Verlag, 1954), 427." Quoted in Forde, footnote 48, p. 64. Claude Welch maintains that Hofmann appealed to Luther to support Hofmann's denial of Christ's vicarious satisfaction: "Hofmann's defense of his orthodoxy by appealing to Luther against the 'orthodox' in this important area was the real beginning of modern Luther research. . . . To drive a wedge between Luther and Lutheranism at such a crucial point was to necessitate a thorough reconsideration of Luther's Lutheranism." See *Protestant Thought in the Nineteenth Century*, vol. 1, 1799–1870 (Eugene, OR: Wipf and Stock Publishers, 1972), 225.

29. Forde, *Law-Gospel Debate*, 4.
30. In his later work, Forde will describe this "echo" as a "mimetic copy." See footnote 57.
31. Forde, *Law-Gospel Debate*, 5.
32. Forde, *Law-Gospel Debate*, 5.
33. Forde, *Law-Gospel Debate*, 5.
34. Forde, *Law-Gospel Debate*, 7.
35. Forde, *Law-Gospel Debate*, 7.
36. Forde, *Law-Gospel Debate*, 8. The "objective" and "subjective" categories of being ultimately derived from Wilhelm M. L. de Wette's *Lehrbuch der christlichen Dogmatik*

Following a brief review of Lutheran orthodoxy and an extended treatment of Hofmann's *Heilsgeschichte* approach, and while noting deficiencies, Forde assays Hofmann's positive contributions. Among Hofmann's emphases are the consideration to think theologically given the current situation, the rejection of legalism, the consideration of divine love (in contrast to the orthodox Lutheran emphasis on divine law), and the consideration of the atonement as God's victory of divine love.[37] Most of all, however, Forde appreciates Hofmann's focus on man's "new humanity in Christ."[38] This sets the stage for Forde's later emphasis on eschatology realized in the personal Law-Gospel event. Through Hofmann, Forde suggests, "eschatology is no longer just the 'doctrine of the last things' as it was for orthodoxy, but it now permeates the entire system."[39] Forde also notes his dependence upon Finnish theologian Lauri Haikola (1917–87). "Haikola finds that the major difference between Luther and later orthodoxy lies precisely in the understanding of law. In later Lutheran orthodoxy, law was understood as an eternal objective order, a *lex aeterna,* which described the ideal to which human life must aspire. Law in this sense was defined as an objective scheme of demands and prohibitions, which must be fulfilled. Since law was understood in this way, it was quite easy to conceive of the atonement as a substitutionary fulfillment, provided one did not press the logic too far."[40]

For Forde, Haikola's interpretation of Luther was that Luther denied law in the terms of an objective legal order. Although Luther used the term *lex aeterna,* as did later orthodox Lutherans, Haikola's Luther meant something else by it. For Haikola, man possesses knowledge of the law only insofar as it is appropriate for his actual situation, whether that situation is pre- or post-fall.[41] Following Haikola, Forde denies that man can know God's will in the form of eternal or first principles that are accessible by human reason. "Rather, man must learn to know God's will anew in each situation."[42] Here, following Swedish theologian Gustaf Wingren (1910–2000), Forde begins to construct an ethic that will seek to link

---

in ihrer historischen Entwicklung dargestellt (Berlin: n.p., 1813), 1:1–18. I am grateful to my colleague Charles P. Schaum for this citation.

37.   Forde, *Law-Gospel Debate,* 77.
38.   Forde, *Law-Gospel Debate,* 77.
39.   Forde, *Law-Gospel Debate,* 77.
40.   Forde, *Law-Gospel Debate,* 176.
41.   Forde, *Law-Gospel Debate,* 176.
42.   Forde, *Law-Gospel Debate,* 177.

what man eventually does within creation. The content of the law "will depend upon the concrete situation in creation at any given time; man cannot have it in the form of eternal principles in advance of any concrete situation."[43] Thus, the suggestion is made that Luther did not identify the law with any moral propositions, whether the Decalogue, natural law, and so on.[44] Given the denial of *lex aeterna* and an objective external content to the law, the "third use of the law" must also be rejected. The *lex aeterna* and the law's third use go "hand-in-hand."[45]

LEX SEMPER ACCUSAT?

In "*Lex semper accusat?* Nineteeth-Century Roots of Our Current Dilemma" and in an apparent attempt to address the contemporary scene, Forde reflects on the theological use of the law.[46] Taking Melanchthon's *lex semper accusat* ("law always accuses"[47]) as his point of departure, Forde considers whether the reformers were correct in attempting to devise a positive use of the law for the civil sphere. Although Forde does not name them, I assume that here he means the theologians of the period of Lutheran Orthodoxy, those who ascribed to the *lex aeterna*, natural law, and the third use of the law.[48] These reformers understood law "as a force, backed by the power of the state as God's representative in civil matters to restrain evil and preserve human society."[49] Forde surveys Enlightenment and post-Enlightenment philosophical and theological approaches, including those of Kant, Schleiermacher, and Hegel. Noting

---

43. Forde, *Law-Gospel Debate*, 177. For Forde, Law does not exist *a priori*.
44. Forde, *Law-Gospel Debate*, 177.
45. Forde, *Law-Gospel Debate*, 180.
46. Gerhard O. Forde, "*Lex semper accusat?* Nineteenth-Century Roots of Our Current Dilemma," in *A More Radical Gospel: Essays on Eschatology, Authority, Atonement, and Ecumenism*, eds. Mark C. Mattes and Steven D. Paulson, Lutheran Quarterly Books (Grand Rapids: Eerdmans, 2004), 33–49. Originally published as "*Lex semper accusat*," *dialog* 9/4 (Autumn 1970): 265–74.
47. Among several places where Melanchthon uses this phrase is in the Apology, see Ap IV 136 [257]; XII 34.
48. This seems to be confirmed by Forde's footnote, which specifically mentions that some reformers also spoke of the law in its third use. See footnote 2, p. 35. Forde will later suggest that his presentation of law likewise was Luther's view. See "Fake Theology: Reflections on Antinomianism Past and Present," in *The Preached God: Proclamation in Word and Sacrament*, eds. Mark C. Mattes and Steven D. Paulson, Lutheran Quarterly Books (Grand Rapids: Eerdmans, 2007), 222.
49. Forde, *Lex semper accusat?* 34–35.

the rejection of liberalism following the postwar crises of existentialism, Forde wonders if going back to the beginning, to Hegel and his followers, might result in the discovery of what went wrong.[50]

Forde rejects the possibility, hinted at by Hegel but developed more thoroughly by the "young Hegelians," that man himself can negate the law; this is impossible from a Christian point of view.[51] For Forde, the only solution to the Law is Christ; it is only in the Gospel of Christ that such a negation of the Law has occurred.[52] Ultimately, Forde is unable to find a positive use of the law in the civil sphere, due to Christ's negation of it. Faith is the only source of positive action. "Faith opens up an entirely new sphere of possibility and action, *this* world bounded by the end."[53] Hence, when the reformers spoke about the law in its "civil use," Forde believes they were speaking only about whether individual acts could be considered good in this life, not whether they measured up to an eternal moral absolute.[54] Liberated from an external, objective standard or moral absolute independent of personal experience, the Christian "can take care of this world"; she can, as Luther suggested, write her own Decalogue "to fit the times."[55]

Luther's "Ethics"

In "Luther's 'Ethics,' " Forde firmly situates himself within the theological approach of the Erlangen school, and particularly within the approach of twentieth-century, post-Barthian theological heirs of that school, by focusing almost exclusively on Luther's early writings. Forde suggests a paucity of evidence supporting a positive portrayal by Luther of the complete medieval ethical tradition that Luther had inherited. Here Forde is correct. In Luther's early works such as *Against Scholastic Theology* (1517) and *Lectures on Romans* (1515), Aristotle, especially in view of his *Ethics*, is definitely a black hat. Forde notes that the early Luther rails against the prevailing *ad modum Aristotelis* thinking, proposing instead

---

50. Forde, *Lex semper accusat?*, 46.
51. Forde, *Lex semper accusat?*, 47. Another name for "young Hegelians" (*junge Hegelianer*) is "neo-Hegelians."
52. Forde, *Lex semper accusat?*, 47.
53. Forde, *Lex semper accusat?*, 48.
54. Forde, *Lex semper accusat?*, 48.
55. Forde, *Lex semper accusat?*, 49. See AE 34:112. For Luther's view on the relationship between Mosaic law, the New Testament, and natural law, see AE 35:165.

the *ad modum scripturae* thinking.[56] But in this discussion, Forde notes the reason for such railing by the reformer and his simultaneous appeal to Scripture. The appropriation by medieval Scholastics of Aristotle was problematic because that appropriation suggested man's goodness *coram Deo* ("before God") is achieved, in part, by virtue of his good works, once he is set upon a path of practicing the virtues. Luther was entirely correct in suggesting that "good works do not make a person good, but a good person does good works."[57] What makes a person "good," and subsequently his works "good," is faith. But the requirement of faith for such goodness does not make good works *unnecessary* for those who lack faith.

Forde, looking to Luther in *Freedom of the Christian* (1520), again finds that creation is the proper sphere of ethical action. But for the purposes of this essay, Forde's comments about Luther's philosophical position, and how Forde's interpretation of that position affected his views on natural law, is most telling: "For Luther, the law is natural to humans. It is written on the heart. He was, it could be said, a kind of 'natural law' ethicist. But he was a nominalist, not a realist."[58] Forde's interpretation of Luther as a nominalist squares well with fundamental assumptions Forde made in the development of his theological method. One implicit assumption within that method is that Luther made a clean break with the moderate realist position of medieval theology that held a place for positive use of law including natural law and the law in its third use. But Forde rejects any interpretation of law as "a mimetic copy" of God's

56. Gerhard O. Forde, "Luther's 'Ethics,'" in *A More Radical Gospel: Essays on Eschatology, Authority, Atonement, and Ecumenism,* eds. Mark C. Mattes and Steven D. Paulson, Lutheran Quarterly Books (Grand Rapids: Eerdmans, 2004), 139–40.

57. AE 31:361. Quoted in Forde, "Luther's 'Ethics,'" 141.

58. Forde, "Luther's 'Ethics,'" 154. A discussion of the legitimacy of Forde's claim, as well as to which variety of nominalism Forde thinks Luther adhered, goes well beyond the scope of this essay. For a contrasting view, see the Reformed theologian John T. McNeill, "Natural Law in the Thought of Luther," *Church History,* vol. 10, no. 3 (September 1941), 211–27. McNeill agrees with French Protestant theologian Eugene Ehrhardt, who suggests that Luther parted ways with nominalism when it came to natural law. For a helpful introduction to nominalism along with English translations of primary sources, see *Five Texts on the Mediaeval Problem of Universals: Prophyry, Boethius, Abelard, Duns Scotus, Ockham,* trans. and ed. Paul Vincent Spade (Indianapolis: Hackett, 1994). Perhaps a fair assessment of Luther's philosophical approach is best summarized by E. G. Schwiebert: "Although Luther was trained as a 'Modernist,' following Occam, Biel, d'Ailly, and others, he was far too critical and original in his thinking to be bound by the thoughts of any one man or school." *Luther and His Times: The Reformation from a New Perspective* (St. Louis: Concordia, 1950), 156.

eternal law.[59] Rather, "the law is simply a statement of what created life should naturally be."[60]

LAW AND SEXUAL BEHAVIOR

HUMAN SEXUALITY AND ROMANS, CHAPTER ONE

Having explored the method, I now examine two essays in which Forde addresses human sexual behavior. In the first, "Human Sexuality and Romans, Chapter One," Forde recasts and builds upon the dichotomous "verbal inspiration method" and the "Law-Gospel method" of biblical interpretation that he developed in "Law and Gospel as the Methodological Principle of Theology." This restatement is necessary in order to address human sexuality. In "Human Sexuality," Forde recognizes that the most universal method of Bible interpretation is where "the exegete as 'subject' opposes the text as the 'object' to be interpreted."[61] Forde finds this approach to be subjective and arbitrary because it ultimately relies on an external authority, whether the pope for Roman Catholics or scriptural inerrancy for Protestants, in order to arrive at the proper interpretation.[62] While he confesses that it is more "unwieldy," Forde's second model is the "Law-Gospel method" now recast as the "Reformational model" in which Scripture interprets Scripture. In this model the roles of exegete and Scripture are reversed: the exegete does not interpret the Scripture; the Scripture interprets the exegete.[63] "The scriptural word, that is, finds, exposes, and establishes the very being of the hearer, that is, as creature, as guilty sinner, as justified, obligated, called to serve, etc."[64]

Assuming a consistency with his earlier work, Forde does not mean here that the Holy Spirit uses the propositional Word of Scripture—the

---

59. Forde, "Luther's 'Ethics,'" 154.
60. Forde, "Luther's 'Ethics,'" 155.
61. Gerhard O. Forde, "Human Sexuality and Romans, Chapter One," in *The Preached God: Proclamation in Word and Sacrament,* eds. Mark C. Mattes and Steven D. Paulson (Grand Rapids: Eerdmans, 2007), 205. Originally appeared as "Normative Character of Scripture for Matters of Faith and Life: Human Sexuality in Light of Romans 1:16–32," *Word and World* 14 (1995): 305–14.
62. Forde, "Human Sexuality and Romans, Chapter One," 205.
63. Forde, "Human Sexuality and Romans, Chapter One," 206.
64. Forde, "Human Sexuality and Romans, Chapter One," 206.

written words of the Bible—to find, expose, and establish the hearer. The Word of God, for Forde, does not exist *a priori,* but is experienced by the hearer as *an event.* In Forde's scheme, all external *a priori* authorities— not just propositional truth derived from the Bible—must be rejected.[65] This includes tradition, a magisterial teaching office, scholarly consensus, declarations on inerrancy, and so on. In "Human Sexuality," Forde suggests that these are mere attempts "to substitute collective for individual subjectivism."[66] For Forde, Scripture interpreting Scripture is nonpropositional; it does not mean using clear Scripture passages to interpret less clear passages. That would be treating Scripture propositionally, which would militate against Scripture's purpose and authority. The authority of God's Word lies in what it does to us, in its ability to give us new life.[67] Ultimately, for Forde, the authority of God's Word lies in its functionality.

Given that the Bible speaks—often explicitly—about human sexual behavior, how are Christians to proceed with that topic? Forde suggests that the focus should not be on the meaning of the words in Scripture, per se, but on how we are delivered from the experience of what those words might suggest. Here Forde appeals to hearers being "exegeted" by the Scripture. "The question that arises is not so much 'What do these words mean?' That is painfully obvious, I should think. The question is rather, 'Who shall deliver us?' 'How can the voice of the law be stilled?' And the only answer to that, if one is to honor the normative claim of Scripture, is Christ."[68] Here Forde suggests that the Gospel norms Scripture. Such a reductionistic move is not unanticipated given Forde's theological system. "Christ is the end of the law that those who have faith may be justified. That being the case, the Christian understanding of the normative character of Scripture as law 'resonates,' to use an image from

---

65. Forde's heritage in the American Lutheran Church (ALC) doubtlessly fits with this position, given the Iowa Synod's contribution to the ALC tradition that valid deductions based on Scripture (*Vernunftfolgerungen*) cannot provide authoritative proof. This position grew out of the Election Controversy (*Gnadenwahlstreit*) in the Synodical Conference. See George John Fritschel, *Die Schriftlehre von der Gnadenwal* (Chicago: Wartburg, 1906).

66. Forde, "Human Sexuality and Romans, Chapter One," 207.

67. Forde, "Human Sexuality and Romans, Chapter One," 207.

68. Forde, "Human Sexuality and Romans, Chapter One," 207.

chemistry, between two poles."[69] For Forde, those two poles are derived from Romans 10:4 and Romans 3:21.[70]

In the context of human sexuality, Forde maintains that human sexuality doesn't concern salvation so much as it concerns law and what Scripture says about the law.[71] Here Forde's two "poles," that Christ is both *telos* and *finis* of the law, come into play.[72] The law cannot be imposed on the believer, whether derived from the Scriptures or even if it is a divine command.[73] The first pole, Christ as the law's *telos*, suggests that those who are accused by the law when reading or hearing the first chapter of Romans will find their only remedy in Christ.[74] The second pole, Christ as the Law's *finis*, suggests how, according to Paul, the law's true authority is established. "Indeed, I think Paul can be read in these early chapters of Romans to be saying that now that Christ has come, we all have no excuse for not heeding the law, whoever we are."[75]

What is the nexus between the Bible and human sexuality? Forde offers two answers. Because Christ is the end of the law, isolated Bible passages appealed to directly and legalistically cannot be decisive.[76] For Forde, propositional truths derived from Bible passages cannot be used to condemn sexual immorality. Mere proof-texting is forbidden. That is not to suggest, however, that such texts have no value. This establishes Forde's second point. Such passages should be considered and are relevant insofar

---

69. Forde, "Human Sexuality and Romans, Chapter One," 207.

70. For a contrasting interpretation of Romans 10:4, see Martin Chemnitz in *Loci Theologici III*, Chemnitz's Works, vol. 8, trans. J. A. O. Preus (St. Louis: Concordia, 1989, 2008), 1251. See also Chemnitz's discussion of the Decalogue's ongoing accusational and instructional work in the life of the believer, 1251.

71. In contrast, see Matthew 19:3–12; 1 Corinthians 6:9–11; Revelation 22:7–21.

72. For perhaps the fullest treatment of the two "poles," see Forde's "Radical Lutheranism," in *A More Radical Gospel: Essays on Eschatology, Authority, Atonement, and Ecumenism,* eds. Mark C. Mattes and Steven D. Paulson, Lutheran Quarterly Books (Grand Rapids: Eerdmans, 2004), 3–16. Originally published originally as "Radical Lutheranism: Lutheran Identity in America," *Lutheran Quarterly* 1 (1987): 5–18. In the introduction, the editors suggest that Forde's treatment of the law "utterly changes our understanding of authority in the church," and that his treatment of the Gospel "gives a peculiar, new authority attributed especially to the Holy Spirit who creates anew, out of nothing," xvii.

73. Forde, "Human Sexuality and Romans, Chapter One," 208. This doesn't seem to square with Forde's earlier assertion of Luther's nominalism.

74. Forde, "Human Sexuality and Romans, Chapter One," 208.

75. Forde, "Human Sexuality and Romans, Chapter One," 209.

76. Forde, "Human Sexuality and Romans, Chapter One," 209.

as they put the law to its proper, accusational, or theological use.[77] In other words, if the primary use of law is to accuse, then anything that can accuse us—even Scripture passages—must be accepted. Here again Forde establishes the law's authority vis-à-vis its function. However, what he offers with the right, he takes away with the left, albeit hesitantly. Forde would prefer not to contend about Scripture passages specifically condemning same-sex behavior.[78] Law might be found in those Scripture passages dealing with sexual immorality only indirectly; we should look for those passages as a way to honor Scripture.[79]

But those indirect Bible passages do not seem to be enough from which to construct a sexual ethic. Forde looks for other sources of law, this time, law in its civil use. Here Forde invokes the spirit of natural law. "Mention of natural law, of course, conjures up all sorts of ghosts out of the ethical abyss which we need not contend with at the moment. By natural law, Luther just meant that which nature and common sense enjoin to care for human community."[80] This "natural common sense" and "care for human community" approach fits within the theological framework that Forde already established. But is it sufficient? Perhaps not. Paul's first chapter of Romans requires us also to look at even more biblical doctrines touching upon anthropology, creation, marriage, family, as well as Church tradition.[81] However, in this quest Forde is not looking for an independent source of authority; he is looking for anything that might help us arrive at and affirm his conclusion.

LAW AND SEXUAL BEHAVIOR

Forde addresses sexual behavior in a second essay, "Law and Sexual Behavior." While "Human Sexuality and Romans, Chapter One" treats sexual ethics primarily from the theological use of the law, this second essay treats sexual ethics more from the civil use of the law. It is consistent with Forde's understanding of the law.[82] In an interesting turn, Forde focuses on the law's relationship to sexual behavior in the civil sphere

77. Forde, "Human Sexuality and Romans, Chapter One," 209.
78. Forde, "Human Sexuality and Romans, Chapter One," 210.
79. Forde, "Human Sexuality and Romans, Chapter One," 210.
80. Forde, "Human Sexuality and Romans, Chapter One," 210.
81. Forde, "Human Sexuality and Romans, Chapter One," 211.
82. Forde, "Law and Sexual Behavior," *Lutheran Quarterly*, 9, no. 1 (Spring 1995): 3.

in order to address encroaching secular arguments for changing sexual ethics within the Church. First, Forde notes that the civil or political use of the law in the Lutheran tradition focuses on outward behavior, not on the amorphous categories of "orientation" or "sexuality." Second, Forde suggests that claims about such categories are inconclusive and not germane to a discussion about law. "Our question is about how we are called to behave in our sexual relations with others under law, particularly in its civil use, whatever our 'orientations.' "[83] In bypassing "orientation" and "sexuality," Forde aligns himself with the traditional condemnation of illicit sexual *behavior* without identifying persons with their sexual *feelings*, the latter being a product of nineteenth- and twentieth-century psychology and sociology.

Yet Forde is clear, even within the discussion of sexual behavior vis-à-vis the civil realm, that Christ is the end of the law. For Forde, the human tendency to become "Antinomian" is evident not only when the law is experienced theologically but also when it is exercised in the civil sphere. Forde insists that sinful human nature will attempt "by one means or another to erase, discredit, or change the laws. We become antinomians."[84] That is not to suggest, however, that Forde now recognizes the authority of an external law apart from the conscience of the citizen, whether from God or from a secular judge. In the same way that the hearer of churchly proclamation is struck by law-as-accusation, the citizen is struck by law-as-accusation. "Law is authoritative ultimately not because it is written in law books or even in the Bible, but rather because it is written 'in the heart.' "[85] Thus, in the civil sphere the law's authority still resides in its ability to accuse the citizen of improper behavior. The

83. Forde, "Law and Sexual Behavior," 4.
84. Forde, "Law and Sexual Behavior," 5. By "Antinomians," Forde means those who, like the orthodox Lutherans, find a positive use for the law, whether natural law, law in its third use, and so on. Unfortunately, Forde charges such persons, who include the authors and subscribers to the Formula of Concord, with heresy. See "Fake Theology: Reflections on Antinomianism Past and Present," in *The Preached God: Proclamation in Word and Sacrament,* eds. Mark C. Mattes and Steven D. Paulson (Grand Rapids: Eerdmans, 2007), 214, 217, 223, 224.
85. Forde, "Law and Sexual Behavior," 5. By "natural law," Forde does not mean that God's will revealed in nature and accessible to human reason is the basis of the authority of civil law. Rather, what is "written in the heart" is the ability of the human conscience to be accused by the law, regardless from whence such an accusation comes, or the ability to respond appropriately in any given situation. In Forde's theological framework, the law cannot be *a priori* and propositional, even in the civil sphere. It must be experiential or situational.

functionality of the law and the primacy of the individual's experience as
being accused are preserved.

How is this appropriated in the context of sexual behavior and
society? Here Forde needs to make an additional claim about the civil
use of the law. And he does: The civil law's purpose is to care for God's
creation, a care that is well-suited for the situation.[86] Here we might ask
about the specific content of such a law. If law accuses, then violations
of civil law are those instances in which citizens do not exercise care for
God's creation, or they do so inappropriately, given the situation. Perhaps
recognizing that his proposal presents an insufficient ethic for contemporary society, in which positive law is often determined by popular vote
or judicial whim, Forde offers two qualifications. First, and despite the
teachings about the different uses of the law, whether theological or civil,
Forde argues that the content of the law does not change. The civil use
of the law can neither be a milder form of, nor can it be contrary to,
the theological use of the law.[87] The law must always accuse. Second,
inasmuch as the civil use of the law concerns caring for creation, it also
pertains to human sexuality and the the social order. The law's civil use
encourages socially beneficial sexual relationships and inhibits the negative social consequences of sexual irresponsibility.[88] The Christian tradition, which interprets marriage as an estate, supports this view.[89]

Having proposed a view of the law in the civil realm, and having
affirmed traditional marriage, Forde then treats the uses of the law and
same-sex genital relations.[90] Again, Forde's distinct purpose is to address
how secular arguments favoring same-sex behavior in the civil sphere are
being transported into the Church. Forde makes two observations. First,
the Bible and Christian tradition forbid same-sex genital relations. Forde
rejects any type of argument that would militate against the traditional
definition of marriage or the traditional understanding of sexual intimacy
being reserved for husband and wife. Contemporary psychological and

---

86. Forde, "Law and Sexual Behavior," 7.
87. Forde, "Law and Sexual Behavior," 8.
88. Forde, "Law and Sexual Behavior," 9.
89. Forde, "Law and Sexual Behavior," 10.
90. Forde, "Law and Sexual Behavior," 12–17. Forde's limitation of his discussion to
    illicit genital relations between persons of the same sex is unfortunate. It is also
    morally reductionistic in that it does not account for sexual sins, such as lust, aris-
    ing from the corrupt human heart. See Genesis 8:21; Matthew 15:19; Galatians
    5:19.

sociological understandings of persons primarily in terms of their sexual "orientation" do not apply. Second, Ford rejects the call by those advocating for a reinterpretation of marriage, which reinterpretation would include same-sex genital relationships. The Christian tradition does not permit such a view. Further, Forde fails to find how any social or moral good would come out of such a reinterpretation.[91]

Given a traditional definition of marriage—the one-flesh union of one man and one woman for life—and human sexuality as a subset of traditional marriage, the weakness of Forde's defense should be readily apparent. In today's civil sphere, appeals to tradition such as Forde's fall on deaf ears. In contemporary society, and with the acceptance of contraception, no-fault divorce, abortion, and same-sex marriage, the traditional definition of marriage has faced increasing opposition. Marriage, for many people, no longer is primarily about the procreation and the education of children within a sexually exclusive and lifelong monogamous union of husband and wife. Rather, it is about "love." For many people today, romantic love is not only a constitutive aspect of marriage; it is perhaps the *sole* aspect. Further, Forde's ethic is based in part on an argument of silence—that social or moral goods of reinterpreting marriage and human sexuality have not yet been discovered. This is woefully thin. A counterargument might suggest that such social or moral goods may indeed be discovered and ultimately valued—if traditionalists like Forde would only get out of the way.

The turn that Forde is required to make is in part reflective and in part the result of the reductionism inherent in his theological method. Having severed the law from an objective morality that has an authority independent of and prior to human experience, Forde reduces the civil use of the law to a thin prudential ethic[92] and the "categorical imperative" forbidding using others as a means to an end.[93] Forde's conclusion[94] that the apparent lack of a social or moral good of illicit genital sexual activity

---

91. Forde, "Law and Sexual Behavior," 17.
92. Forde, "Law and Sexual Behavior," 13.
93. Forde, "Law and Sexual Behavior," 15. This squares well with Copleston's interpretation of William of Ockham: "Ockham . . . seems to have thought that men, without revelation, are able to discern a moral law in some sense. In this case they can presumably discern a prudential code or a set of hypothetical imperatives." Frederick Copleston, S. J., *A History of Philosophy*, vol. 3, *Ockham to Suárez* (Mahwah, NJ: Paulist Press, 1953), 108.
94. Forde, "Law and Sexual Behavior," 17.

of persons of the same sex is weak within the civil sphere, and perhaps even weaker still within a church body already well-versed in rejecting the robust, authoritative, objective content of Scripture. Yet while this civil use of the law within the Church is curious, it is not unanticipated. For Forde, the operative law both within the civil sphere and in the Bible is the law "written on the heart." Far from being a summary, the actual "fundamental and ineradicable content" of law is "love and service to the neighbor."[95] Because love and service are not summaries of the law but abstract reductions of its actual content, Forde looks for any law that will work.

CONCLUSION

In addition to Haikola, Wingren, and others, Forde was influenced by Hans Joachim Iwand,[96] as well as popular postwar existentialism that immediately preceded Forde's career. Yet Forde seems particularly indebted to Haikola's "discovery" that Luther rejected the ancient Christian teaching of *lex aeterna*. Although under attack in the latter eighteenth century, "moderate" theologians would still at least offer traditional-sounding language regarding topics such as *lex aeterna* until the twentieth century.[97] For the orthodox, law both reproves *and* teaches; the law is God's unchanging will.[98] God's will is revealed primarily and infallibly through Scripture, but it is also accessible to human reason, although that reason is severly compromised by sin. The irony is that, by acceding to Hofmann's rejection of the substitutionary atonement of Christ, Forde attached himself to an understanding of *lex semper accusat* that apparently Melanchthon never intended.

A strong case can be made that, in his *Loci Communes Theologici* (1521), Melanchthon accepts a moderate realist and not a nominal-

---

95. Forde, "Law and Sexual Behavior," 18.
96. James Arne Nestingen suggests that Iwand (1899–1960) made substantial contributions to Forde's thinking. See "Examining Sources: Influences on Gerhard Forde's Theology," in *By Faith Alone: Essays on Justification in Honor of Gerhard O. Forde,* eds. Joseph A. Burgess and Marc Kolden (Grand Rapids: Eerdmans, 2004), 10–21.
97. See Welch, footnote 27.
98. FC Ep V 2; see also VI 7.

ist view of natural law. Why is this important? Because of Luther's resounding affirmation of this work.[99] In it, Melancthon writes,

> The law of nature, therefore, is a common judgment to which all men give the same consent. This law which God has engraved on the mind of each is suitable for the shaping of morals. For just as there are certain common principles in the theoretical branches of learning, in mathematics, for instance (they might be called "common thoughts" or "a priori principles," such as "The whole is greater than its parts"), so there are certain axioms and a priori principles in the realm of morals; these constitute the ground rules for all human activity. (We must use these terms for pedagogical reasons.) These rules for human activity are rightly called "laws of nature."[100]

Later in his *Commentary on Romans* (1540), Melanchthon suggests that it is the Epicureans and the academicians who try to bury the natural knowledge of God, which includes the natural law.[101] On this note, Melanchthon takes Luther's approach by appealing to Scripture: "Paul testifies that this knowledge is a work of God, found in the mind as light is in the eyes. For 'by nature' really signifies something created by God. Therefore this knowledge is true and divine Law."[102]

Those familiar with the natural law in the Western tradition will recognize Melanchthon's use of moral first principles, an approach with which Luther and confessional orthodox Lutherans would have been familiar. These principles are embedded in the rich Western tradition of natural law doctrine appropriated and used by Luther, Melanchthon, Chemnitz, Gerhard, and other classical theologians of Lutheran orthodoxy. Contemporary Lutheran scholars have observed key theological moves made by twentieth-century, post-Barthian adherents of the Erlangen school. Such observations include an effort to "recover" Luther's

---

99. Luther suggested that theologians should have both a copy of the Scriptures and a copy Melanchthon's *Loci*. "No better book has been written after the Holy Scriptures than Philip's. He expresses himself more concisely than I do when he argues and instructs. I'm garrulous and more rhetorical" (AE 54:440). See also AE 33:16.

100. Philip Melanchthon, *Loci Communes Theologici* (1521), in Library of Christian Classics, vol. xix, Melanchthon and Bucer, ed. Wilhelm Pauck (Philadelphia: Westminster Press, 1964), 50.

101. Philip Melanchthon, *Commentary on Romans* (1540), trans. Fred Kramer (St. Louis: Concordia, 1992), 75.

102. Melanchthon, *Commentary on Romans*, 89.

hermeneutic, a cautious acceptance of historical-biblical criticism, and an openness to ecumenism.[103] To this we could add an alternative account of the natural law and a denial of the law in its third use. In sexual ethics, other contemporary scholars are noting Luther's strong condemnation of every form of unchastity.[104] This treatment is compatible with that of Augustine, Lombard, and medieval confessional manuals, the latter of which relied on Augustine's robust treatment of the sin of *luxuria*.[105] Given the current state of theological disarray, especially as it concerns human sexuality, perhaps it is time to reconsider the usefulness of nineteenth- and twentieth-century theological methods, which reduce systematic treatments to a few controlling categories and offer thin versions of ethics. Perhaps it is also time to reexamine the rich patrimony of biblical and confessional orthodox Lutheran theology, especially as it touches upon natural law, human sexuality, and other pressing issues. Marshaling these resources, we might then research all theological methods using Forde's acid test.[106]

---

103. Erik M. Heen, "The Distinction 'Material/Formal Principles' and Its Use in American Lutheran Theology," *Lutheran Quarterly,* 17, no 3. (Autumn 2003): 341.

104. Albrecht Peters, *Commentary on Luther's Catechism: The Ten Commandments.* Charles P. Schaum, gen. ed., Holger K. Sonntag, trans. (St. Louis: Concordia, 2008), 243.

105. Peters, *Commentary on Luther's Catechism,* 243–44.

106. I wish to thank the Rev. Charles P. Schaum, Mr. J. W. Case, Rev. Dr. Albert B. Collver III, and Dr. Jack Kilcrease for their helpful review and critique of prior drafts of this essay.

9

NATURAL LAW AND THE ELCA

Marianne Howard Yoder and J. Larry Yoder, STS

FROM GOD'S NATURAL LAW TO MAN'S —OR WOMAN'S—OPINIONS[1]

THE LETTER NOT ANSWERED

In the editorial "Blacks Should Be Supportive of Gays' Struggle" (*The Miami Herald*, March 12, 2004), syndicated columnist Leonard Pitts excoriated black clergy and blacks in general for failing to join the new civil rights movement against discrimination on the basis of sexual

---

1.   Editor's note: The authors present a collection of brief essays, written from their perspective and experiences while members of the ELCA.

orientation. Pitts argues that just as the social conservatives of the 1960s used "Bibles to justify bigotry," described "equality" as "unnatural," and invoked "the sanctity of tradition," in their attempts to justify the continuance of discriminatory policies, so too the conservative black community is doing in regards to issues concerning gays. Pitts states, "And we are wrong, just as they were."

When I read Mr. Pitts's article, I was distressed by what I assumed was his lack of understanding of the appropriate and faithful response by black clergy to the comparing of the gay rights movement of today with the civil rights movement led by Martin Luther King, Jr. I felt compelled to respond, and wrote:

> Dear Mr. Pitts,
>
> Congratulations on the Pulitzer. Your attribution of your success to your mother's influence was a wonderful piece. I too am a mother (of three sons) who has attempted to bring out the best in my sons, both as to their vocational pursuits and as to each one's essential being. I have tried to teach my sons always to seek the truth. It is in that vein that I wish to address one of your recent essays, "Blacks Slow to Support This Fight for Equality." [Note: The title of the editorial as it appeared in *The Charlotte Observer* was different from the original *Miami Herald* version.]
>
> I'm certain that you have read Martin King's "Letter from Birmingham Jail."[2] You should read it again. In his letter to clergymen, Dr. King argues that the standard for judging whether or not a human law is a just law is the moral law of God, which is revealed both in the Holy Scriptures and in the natural law of the Creator. Dr. King knew philosophy and theology. His reference to natural law comes down from Aristotle and the Stoics through St. Thomas Aquinas. Natural law as explained by Thomas Aquinas combines both Aristotelian naturalistic teleology (i.e., intended purpose as virtue or excellence) and the Stoic view of Logos within the human being (i.e., reason or conscience as one's connectedness with God). Aquinas explained natural law as the intended purpose of the Creator God within human

---

2.   An electronic copy of the letter, dated April 16, 1963, can be found at http://www.africa.upenn.edu/Articles_Gen/Letter_Birmingham.html (accessed October 11, 2010).

beings such that we are inclined toward our proper acts and ends. In other words, what is right to do is what conforms to the purpose [even of a body part] designed by the Creator. Sexual morality, according to natural law, would involve using one's sexual organs for their intended purpose (i.e., the purpose of the Creator/Designer). Aquinas further explained that God restates His law in the Decalogue of Moses (the Ten Commandments), just in case human beings are unsure as to what the natural law prescribes.

Dr. King was a man of faith. Indeed, when you read the words of his speeches, sermons, etc., it becomes clear that the civil rights movement had at its heart the religious faith of the courageous men and women who marched and demonstrated throughout the South and elsewhere. Their religious convictions gave them the strength to persevere, and the religious convictions of many of the rest of us led us to the discernment that our racially discriminatory laws were unjust. Have you noticed that in addition to black church leaders, also missing from the fight for gay marriage is the Catholic Church? Those two groups were out front in the civil rights marches and protests of the 1960s. It was because of their Christian faith that they were there then, . . . and it is because of their faith that they now oppose the demands of the gay, lesbian, bisexual, and transgender coalition.

It is no surprise that religious leaders in the black community "bristle at the comparison" of the gay rights movement to the civil rights movement. The black pastors and laity are being true not only to the teachings of their God as revealed both in the Holy Scriptures and in the natural law, but also to what they know was an authentic push for civil rights, an acknowledgement of and the demand for certain universal human rights which apply to all societies because they conform to a law above the laws which human societies make for themselves. However the debate continues, and regardless of the outcome, the black religious community should not be chastised for remaining true to the teachings of their faith.

Marianne Howard Yoder
April 28, 2004

I did not receive a response to my letter.

In his editorial, Pitts failed to acknowledge what was foundational for the civil rights movement of the 1960s: the way one can know whether a human law is a just law is by evaluating the law in terms of God's moral law. If a human law conforms to God's moral law, says Dr. King, then the law is just. If a human law fails to conform to God's moral law, then the law is unjust. More specifically, Dr. King states in his letter, "To put it in the terms of St. Thomas Aquinas: An unjust law is a human law that is not rooted in eternal law and natural law." Dr. King, following Aquinas, cites the Creator God as setting in place—throughout the universe and within human beings—His standards for human conduct, standards by which we are not only able to judge the justice or injustice of our man-made laws, but also the rightness or wrongness of our personal actions and relationships.—MHY

Natural Law Theory:
The Stoics, Aristotle, and Aquinas

Aristotle (384–322 BC) understood that human beings, unlike animals, are uniquely rational, and that rationality leads one to discern her *telos* or end—her intended purpose. The happiest persons are those who fulfill their intended purpose of being rational—of being controlled by reason. Reason leads one to make purposeful choices toward the fulfillment of one's potential. To be virtuous—to be excellent—is a matter of fulfilling one's intended purpose, both in lifelong pursuit of the goal of a good life (i.e., the life of reason) and in the habitual practice of virtuous living (i.e., achieving equilibrium or balance—and thereby moral virtue—by learning to control through practice the excesses and deficiencies of one's character).

The Stoics, represented for example by Epictetus (AD 55–135), understood that a human being has a conscience—or soul—and that it is through the conscience that mankind is connected to the Divine, the *Logos* (the cosmic intelligence that governs the universe from within). In fact, the Stoic view is *pantheistic* [from Greek: *pan* (all) *theos* (god)]; that is, everything in the universe is a part of God. As a comparison, think of the universe and everything in it as a patchwork quilt. We are all stitched onto—or connected to—the quilt that is God. Our ability to think or reason makes us aware of the God within us. Our connection to God is through the rational part of our being: our reason, our mind—our soul.

St. Thomas Aquinas (1225–1274) combined Aristotle's assertion of virtue as excellence as intended purpose with the Stoics' understanding of conscience as one's connectedness to the Divine in the formulation of his natural law theory. Aquinas names the One who has created the human with a conscience and has put within her the design that is the blueprint for His intended purpose. It is God the Creator who has made us in such a way that His law is already written within us.

For Aquinas there are four types of law: eternal, natural, divine, and human. Eternal law is the law that God the Creator has set in motion in the universe. Natural law is the law of the Creator within the human being so that we understand our natural ends—God's intended purpose. Divine law is the Decalogue, the Ten Commandments given to Moses—the laws instructing us regarding our relationship to God and our relationships with each other, laws specifically written out, just in case we fail to discern the natural law placed within us by the Creator God. Human laws are the rules we agree to among ourselves so that community life is conducted with respect and fairness.—MHY

Law(s) of Nature: No God Intended

Natural law theory is sometimes misunderstood as equivalent to what certain empiricist thinkers describe as the law(s) of nature or natural desires. For empiricists, the physical, material world of matter is the only realm for knowledge. Only the body and its sensory responses provides direction for our actions, our behavior.

According to Thomas Hobbes (1588–1679), atoms within the human body rotate in two opposing directions. When the atoms move in one direction, we are drawn toward things or activities—the things we want to have or to do. When the atoms move in the opposite direction, we are pushed back away from things or activities—the things we don't want to have or to do. The things we are attracted toward are our "desires"; the things we find repulsive, Hobbes calls "aversions." In a word, we act according to our bodily impulses.

Hobbes's view is entirely materialistic. There is nothing beyond the empirical world of matter in which we find ourselves. Reality can be known only through the senses. What exists, what we can know, we know by seeing, hearing, touching, tasting, or smelling. Hobbes's view allows no possibility for knowledge of a spiritual or metaphysical realm. God cannot be known because He cannot be seen, heard, touched, tasted, or smelled. Only human sensory experience can convey knowledge.

David Hume (1711–1776) expanded Hobbes's empirical view to include moral knowledge through feelings or emotions. Hume's theory recognizes our gut-level feelings of physical pleasure or nausea while observing or participating in certain activities. These natural emotional responses, says Hume, lead us to approve or disapprove of the actions experienced. Hume's view is, therefore, a cognitivist (knowledge based) theory concerning moral knowledge in that one can know what is right to do or wrong to do based upon physical feelings or emotional responses.

The laws of nature of the empiricist thinkers are based entirely upon human bodily existence within the physical world as described by the natural sciences. Reason as one's connectedness with God cannot be known. The laws of nature of the empiricists have no Creator, and, therefore, no Creator's purpose to be discovered. There is no law above human law. Rules or laws relating to human conduct are the social contracts or agreements made between persons (Hobbes), and emotions are the source for moral knowledge (Hume).—MHY

Positivism and Emotivism: The Denial of Moral Knowledge

While Hume's view acknowledges that there is moral knowledge—knowledge of right and wrong behavior—and that the source of this knowledge is emotional response, the theory called "emotivism" is a noncognitivist view (i.e., moral knowledge cannot be known). Emotive expressions, according to emotivism, are merely emotive expressions; they have no factual content; they convey no knowledge. Emotivism is best understood in its relationship to logical positivism.

Positivism was an attempt by certain thinkers, prominent among them A. J. Ayer (1910–1989), to put philosophy on a solid foundation: that of analyzing language. Positivists restricted knowledge, restricted what can be known, to what can be verified. In other words, a sentence is true if one can prove it to be true. A statement of fact, for example, may be verified, may be proven true or false through investigation—through experience, through the senses. "Susan is wearing a blue shirt" may be verified by looking at Susan. If she is wearing a blue shirt, then the sentence is true; if she is not wearing a blue shirt, then the sentence is false. Another type of statement that can be verified is a definition, a tautology—a statement in which the subject and the predicate are equivalents; that is, they convey the same information. "A circle is round" is known to be true even without looking! It is known to be true simply by analyzing the structure and meaning of the words in the sentence. "A circle" and "is round" convey the same information. By definition, a circle cannot be otherwise than round.

By reducing what can be known—what is true—to verifiable empirical or analytic statements, the positivists have eliminated ethical ("Murder is wrong"), aesthetic ("The sky is beautiful"), and religious ("Christ died for our sins") statements from what they consider to be meaningful discourse. Because a statement such as "Murder is wrong" cannot be verified by the senses (i.e., there is no so-called fact that a person can see, touch, hear, taste, or smell that corresponds exactly to the word "wrong"), or through analysis of sentence structure show equivalency in meaning for the words *murder* and *wrong*, the sentence conveys no knowledge.

The problem, of course, in demanding empirical or analytical verification in order to ascertain what is true or false is that any knowledge above or beyond human direct or vicarious experience is precluded. Ethical statements are reduced to descriptions of the behavior of individuals (psychology) or of social customs and structures (sociology or anthropology). Normative sentences, those statements that direct us as to what we "ought" or "should" do, are, according to positivists, literally meaningless—unless, of course, the one writing or speaking is expressing strong emotion, which indicates emotive meaning. All statements, unless verifiable, are equally meaningless (i.e., they convey no knowledge).

Metaphysical knowledge—knowledge above or beyond human experience—cannot be known. Scientific knowledge gained from physical experiment and analysis reigns as the only truth. We no longer have the ability to speak about what people should do or what God might want them to do. We are left with descriptions and our own self-centered condition. "You cannot go from *is* to *ought*," say the empiricists; "you cannot know what you cannot prove," say the positivists. "But," say the emotivists, "when you feel strongly about something, you shouldn't ignore your feeling(s)!"

Finally, there is no longer a still, small voice; there is no Creator of the universe; there is no natural law; there is no universal law to take us beyond the self. We are left with our egalitarian opinions, our changeable feelings, and our rules to be voted on. God, help us!—MHY

REFLECTIONS ON THE CHURCH'S ABANDONMENT OF GOD'S MORAL LAW

THE SPEECH NOT MADE

On Wednesday, August 19, 2009, at the ELCA assembly in Minneapolis, I stood for a long time at the microphone waiting for a time to speak. I had stood aside for persons who wanted to speak against amendments. It was nearly my turn: the lines of those speaking "for" were long, and those of us wishing to speak "against" were relatively short.

Then the young man in front of me "called for the question." I was dumbfounded; I couldn't fathom why someone against the social statement would wish to end the debate. The delegates voted to close debate, and I returned to my seat. At first, I couldn't sit down; I wanted to leave the hall. My husband gently persuaded me into my seat, and I sat quietly and prayed. The woman sitting to my right put a caring arm around me, and I sobbed silently.

The Holy Spirit did not call me to be a pastor. I was called, I believe, to be a moral philosopher, an ethicist. The skills and knowledge I have gained in my study of the history of ethical theory have led me to discern that the ELCA's *A Social Statement on Human Sexuality: Gift and Trust*[3] is seriously flawed. That Wednesday afternoon, I felt called to speak a word in behalf of the Lord. My two-minute speech would have been as follows:

---

3.   Evangelical Lutheran Church in America, *A Social Statement on Human Sexuality: Gift and Trust*. This statement, as amended, was adopted by a two-thirds majority at the ELCA's eleventh biennial Churchwide Assembly, August 19, 2009. Available online at http://www.elca.org/What-We-Believe/Social-Issues/Social-Statements/JTF-Human-Sexuality.aspx (accessed November 2, 2010).

1. The Human Sexuality social statement is seriously flawed in its interpretation of God's grace. It interprets Luther's "only by grace, through faith" as God's unconditional love toward us, which we, in turn, pour out upon our neighbors.

2. Let me suggest that Luther (following Augustine) taught that God's grace comes to us through no effort on our part, that we have the free will to "turn away from God," and that the faith part of "only by grace, through faith" is our ongoing relationship with God, provided we don't turn away from Him.

3. It is our faith relationship with God that enables not one, but two responses:

   > That we love the Lord our God with all our heart, soul, and mind; and

   > That we love our neighbor as ourselves.

4. Luther's teaching on grace is not only a theology of the cross; it is also an ethic of the cross. The vertical dimension of the cross is symbolic of God's unconditional love and our ongoing relationship with Him. The horizontal dimension of the cross is the love of neighbor, each for the other.

5. Luther's ethic is a both/and ethic: both love of God and love of neighbor. The social statement before us gives much attention to the "loving our neighbor" part, but very little emphasis on the "loving God" part. What is left out entirely is St. John's instruction (1 John 5:3) that "this is the love of God, that we keep His commandments."

6. Luther's ethic is not just a Gospel ethic. It is a Law and Gospel ethic: love of God (that is, to love God is to keep His commandments) and love of neighbor. The social statement on human sexuality fails to emphasize the keeping—as best we can, enabled through grace—of God's moral law (that is, loving the Lord our God with heart, soul, and mind: conforming our wills to God's will).

7. The social statement is seriously flawed. I urge that you vote against it.

If a motion had not been made to reduce the length of speeches from three to two minutes, my three-minute version would have included a comparison of God's grace to sunshine coming down on us (Luther following Augustine following Plato) and the example—if time permitted—of the unconditional love of a parent for her child. I would have explained that my love for my sons is unconditional (that is, there is nothing any one of the three of them could do that would cause me not to love him), but that if they love me in return, they will strive to live lives that will honor me. Note that the living of his life so that it honors his mother is done freely in response to the unconditional love of the mother; living in such a way as to honor his mother is done not in order to earn his mother's love, but rather because his mother loves him no matter what he does!

If I had had the time for a full lecture, I could have explained more about Plato's "Analogy of the Sun," more about Augustine's interpretation of Plato's Good as God, more of Augustine's progressive steps from belief to understanding to mystical vision and how these compare to Plato's educational progress toward the Good—both made possible by the Good enabling the soul to know what can be known (Plato) and grace enabling our faith relationship with God through belief and understanding (Augustine). I could have reminded our Lutheran brothers and sisters that Luther knew both philosophy and theology and used knowledge and God-given reason to come to the truth of "only by grace, through faith." But the reality of Minneapolis was that I had two minutes at the most—and then not even that!

It is my opinion that what happened in Minneapolis in August 2009 was the result of the work of a powerful political machine. The advocates had been working for at least twenty years to accomplish their goals. When the work of the first task force (early 1990s) did not yield their desired outcome because of overwhelming negative response from ELCA church members, the revisionists saw to it that there would be a second task force. When the Orlando assembly did not ratify the changes recommended by that task force, the sexuality study was already in place. Political maneuvering yielded the changes in ministerial policies as recommendations requiring only simple majority votes. Community organizing—synodical-level organizing—gave them the rest.

Those of us whose consciences are captive to the Word of God made good arguments based on sound biblical principles all the way through.

For example:

- The Holy Spirit would not do a new thing against His own teaching or against the teaching of God the Father or against the teaching of God the Son—the three are one, and They cohere!

- The issue of same-sex blessing as in marriage and the rostering of practicing homosexuals is not a justice issue. Dr. Martin Luther King, Jr., in "Letter from Birmingham Jail" states, unequivocally, that the way we can know whether a human law is a just law is by whether it conforms to the moral law of God.

- The numerous ceremonial laws of custom that are no longer thought to be relevant (for example, "You shall not wear cloth of wool and linen mixed together" in Deuteronomy 22:11) are not equivalent to God's moral law, which does not change.

The outcome in Minneapolis finally boiled down to emotion and its legitimizing foundation, the self. Each time there was lengthy debate those on the side of the tradition had the better arguments, but the revisionists have always had the advantage of emotional appeal, which evokes sympathetic response. It's hard to argue persuasively for coherence and scriptural authority when the speaker before or after is telling his heart-rending story of exclusion and hurt feelings. In the end, it didn't matter! Those whose consciences were bound (to their own moral autonomy) had the votes!

My academic discipline is profoundly rational. I can make persuasive, substantive arguments, pro or con, on almost any controversial topic. Philosophers are critical thinkers. We look for coherence and substance in the arguments that are made by our colleagues. We can see when coherence is lacking between theory and practice, between founding principles and actions. The social statement implementing resolutions, and the recommendations on ministry policies do not cohere with the teachings of the Holy Scriptures and the Lutheran Confessions. We are no longer a church with integrity if our policies and actions do not follow from—do not cohere with—our founding documents: God's revelation to us in the Holy Scriptures and the witness of the saints across the centuries, the witness of the catholic faith. Our church bears the name of Martin Luther. Luther stated his standard for coherence at Worms: "Unless I can be persuaded by plain reason and the Holy Scriptures. . . ." In the case of the Minneapolis assembly, critical thinking and adherence to the Holy Scriptures did not prevail. The appeals of the emotivists carried the day.

We have come to a time when the logical positivists and the emotivists are telling us that "right" and "wrong" are merely terms of expression sometimes tied to strong feelings, that the only factual statements about ethical concerns are the ones that reveal statistically the opinions of people or their votes. Emotivism is the prevailing ethical understanding in our culture today, and perhaps the majority of people in our democratic society think that is as it should be, even though emotivism is a path to radical subjectivism. But in the Church? How can it be a church that says God's moral law is only a matter of perspectival truth, only a matter of perspective as in "my opinion" being opposed to "your opinion," or "my bound conscience" being opposed to "your bound conscience"?

Those whose consciences are bound to the Word of God have been set free from the bondage of a "church" whose leaders sought to stifle and marginalize those holding fast to the Holy Scriptures. We gained unambiguous clarity in Minneapolis: the ELCA is no longer a Law-and-Gospel church; the ELCA is no longer the church of Luther.

Martin Luther was a Law and Gospel theologian and ethicist. The eternal law of the Creator/Designer, the natural law within human beings leading them toward their God-given natural inclinations and purposes, and the divine law (the Decalogue given to Moses, the Great Commandment, and the New Commandment of our Lord) were all included in his teaching. Luther emphasized that it is because God loves us, because we are in a faith relationship with Him, that we strive, enabled by grace, to live our lives in conformity to His will. When we fail, we repent and are forgiven, redeemed by the precious blood of Christ, our Savior. A church that ignores God's revealed law is not Lutheran. Luther taught that it is the Law and our inability to keep it that drives us to Christ—to the Gospel—in the first place. Without the Law, there is no need for redemption.

Luther and his followers understood that the church of the Reformation is always in the process of reforming. With God's help, we continue the reforming, back to who (and Whose) we are: a Law and Gospel church of those who are at the same time saint and sinner, ever penitent . . . thankful to God, Who in His abounding and steadfast love, saved us by the cross of Christ and calls us to the two-directional life of loving Him and loving one another.—MHY

Early ELCA Sexuality Discussions

My journey within the Evangelical Lutheran Church in America (ELCA) misadventures in sexuality began with the initial sexuality task force, to which I was appointed after the task force "discovered" at its first gathering that it did not have in its number a "conserving voice." At the time, I considered myself rather more "moderate" than "conservative," by the definitions of those days. But I came soon enough to understand how the center had already shifted.

The first meeting that I attended was in Chicago in a former monastery. Each participant was invited to prepare a paper, in advance, to address the topic. The one that was read aloud argued that human sexual relations ought to be assessed—measured, evaluated—by "quality rather than by kind." In the discussion, I responded that I had no quarrel with "quality" as to "loving, caring, committed, and just." But there are some "kinds" of human sexual relations that are simply out of bounds as to the Christian faith: adultery, incest, pedophilia, and bestiality, to name a few (but not to name the sort the author wanted to include). The author acknowledged the exclusions, but insisted on "quality over kind" in the assessment.

At the refreshment break, another member of the task force, an ELCA staff person, came to me and said, "We need to talk." I said okay, and we agreed to talk at supper. We sat opposite each other in the cellar of the monastery, talking first about what we had in common: both of us had sons who had played Little League baseball the previous summer. Then she asked, "Where do we begin?" I figured I would aim high and straight: "Give me faithfulness in marriage and chastity outside marriage." This is the biblical norm, based upon God's commandments as well as resident in natural law. She replied, "I consider marriage a patriarchal invention of power designed to subjugate women."

"*A patriarchal invention of power designed to subjugate women!*" On those grounds, one just as easily could argue that marriage is an invention of women, designed to curb the male libido by exchanging access for exclusivity. But invoking an uncharitable read of George Bernard Shaw would be just as illegitimate as invoking Karl Marx. As a matter of both fact and faith, the Holy Scriptures declare marriage to be "a holy estate, ordained of God . . . to be held in honor by all . . . it becometh those who enter therein to weigh with reverent minds what the Word of God teacheth concerning it."[4] "The LORD God said, 'It is not good that the man should be alone. I will make him an help meet for him.' . . . 'For this cause shall a man leave father and mother, and shall cleave to his wife: and they twain shall be one flesh. Wherefore they are no more twain, but one flesh.' What therefore God hath joined together, let not man put asunder" (Genesis 2:18; Matthew 19:5–6, KJV). Needless to say, the conversation ended without agreement.

Already in the early 1990s, not five years after the "birth" of the ELCA, revisionist thinking was already resident—if not dominant—in the staff of "churchwide" offices. The notion that marriage is a "human construct" presupposes that cultural and religious norms are "emergent," rather than reflective of natural law, or God's revealed law.

The *archē,* the first principle, of the ELCA is power. As for the church staffer—herself with a doctorate in social ethics—her invocation of the "patriarchal invention of power" is consistent with the "first principle" of the ELCA: power, and who has it. What is reflected here is the utter disregard for the notion of natural law, which served as a prelude to the overt rejection of the declared moral law of God—the Decalogue, the "Great Commandment," and the "New Commandment." What is here, rather, is an overt embrace of the "social construction of reality"—like language, morality and ethics are human constructs—not anteceded or informed by what Thomas Aquinas referred to as eternal law, or natural law, and not informed or interdicted by God's revealed law in the Holy Scriptures.—JLY

THE STATE OF CONTEMPORARY HUMANITY: *HOMO AUTONOMOUS* (A REFLECTION ON CHRIST THE KING)

The distance between Dante (c. 1265–1321) toward the end of the Medieval period, and Machiavelli (c. 1469–1527) in the middle of the Renaissance is two centuries and several light years, the former measured in time and the latter in philosophical difference. For Dante, what counts is the reign of Christ eternally. The pilgrimage of life is informed negatively by agonies of the inferno, positively by the beatific vision—the former to be avoided in terror, the latter passionately sought. For Machiavelli, the political is the proper arena for allegiance, with the eternal deferred, the

---

4.   Board of Publication, Lutheran Church in America, *Service Book and Hymnal* (Minneapolis: Augsburg Publishing House, 1958), 270.

reign of Christ put aside in pursuit of power according to an accurate-if-cynical understanding of human nature. If the prince is cunning, even cruel, his actions are in the proper service of power. The kingdom of this world is the kingdom that counts. Leave to God the affairs of God.

The allegiance of postmodern man is neither to God nor to the state, but to himself. Some trace this to Luther, with his stand at Worms, unwilling and unable to concede to church or empire any recanting of his views, God help him. It is the *individual* who decides whether to submit to the authority of the state and the church in matters of conscience and faith. The political and the ecclesial alike come under the scrutiny and judgment of the reflecting and asserting *individual*. If Luther is responsible for this framing of individual autonomy, it is a charge more serious than that of his later anti-Semitism giving aid and comfort to Hitler. But Luther's conscience was *captive to the Word of God*. In his freedom he is subject to no man, but at the same time he is responsible servant to all. Luther's liberation is not <u>from</u> *Christus Rex* but <u>for and by</u> Christ the King. Luther's respect for the state is as the left hand of God, ordained for civil order. Luther was a theological revolutionary, but a political conservative. He consistently rejected, even railed against, political appropriation of his newly asserted freedom, as rediscovered in the writing of Paul.

One may also trace the problem of individual autonomy to Jefferson and his co-signatories, denying both divine right and inherited privilege to kings and emperors. Government, they insisted, in their innovation of the grand American experiment, "derives its just authority from the consent of the governed." Governments are both the creation and concession of the people, rather than an institution by divine mandate to the legacy of kings. It appears to have been only a small move to shift the conferral of "just authority to govern us" from the political to the theological: We will concede to God *only what we deem appropriate. We* will determine the content of right and wrong, rather than to be governed by the intrinsic divine authority of God.

The shift in allegiance from submission to divine authority toward a humanity otherwise "uncommanded by other than self and self choices"[5] may have been a small move, but it was some time coming after Jefferson. For him, the endowment of the people with "unalienable rights, among

---

5.   Russell Hittinger, who teaches at the University of Tulsa, coined the term "uncommanded man," and has written extensively concerning the asserted moral autonomy of contemporary humanity.

them life, liberty, and the pursuit of happiness" is *by nature and nature's God*. A Deist, Jefferson knew only a humanity "endowed by their Creator," not a humanity emergent from primal slime by material cause and evolution only. Jefferson did not acknowledge Christ the King, but neither did he assert *homo autonomous*.

The distance between Luther and Nietzsche, between Jefferson and Derrida, is the disjuncture between freedom and truth, as John Paul II observed.[6] What has facilitated this move from the theoretical and intellectual to the practical and physical in the popular culture is the influence of the mass media and the various accompanying cultural revolutions. If the invention of the printing press enabled Luther's Reformation, the age of instant information has augmented instant gratification and the emancipation of the individual from responsibility either to God or to the state, much less the neighbor. Even parents must now resist the temptation to pursue life according to their own interests at the expense of their children. They can choose not to have children, even after those children are conceived and gestating.

In such a climate of fundamental and radical autonomy, truth is "only perspectival," or primarily a "function of power." The assertion that Christ is King must now sound almost as strange as it did to Pilate, almost as quaint as the sign above the cross. To the faithful, it must be proclaimed that we need radically to examine our allegiance. The tyranny of totalitarianism, defeated in the last century several times at enormous human cost, is no more a threat than the tyranny of radical autonomy. Both deny the lordship of Jesus Christ. The signers of the Barmen Declaration[7] knew it; they asserted that the church is "solely Christ's property, and that it lives and wants to live solely from his comfort and from his direction in the expectation of his appearance, rather than under the subordination of the state." The people in our congregations need to hear it too.

If Christ is King, then I am not. It is as simple as that. The Roman Empire could not understand it and thought it, at first, irrelevant—then dangerous. The danger to my personal control of my allegiances is both

---

6.   *Veritatis Splendor*. Available at http://www/vatican.va/edocs/ENG0222/_IN-DEX.HTM (accessed November 24, 2010).

7.   The declaration, dating from 1934 and authored by Karl Barth, among others, was a statement from the Confessing Church opposing the Nazi-supported, so-called "German-Christian" movement. This movement embraced, among other things, Nazi anti-Semitism. Available at http://www.sacred-texts.com/chr/barmen.htm (accessed October 11, 2010).

radical and destructive. But also salvific. As St. Paul writes, "I have been crucified with Christ. It is no longer I who live, but Christ who lives in me. And the life I now live in the flesh I live by faith in the Son of God, who loved me and gave Himself for me" (Galatians 2:19b–20). The ELCA 2009 Minneapolis vote reflects prominently the moral climate and self-assertions of postmodern autonomous man rather than the teachings of the "one, holy, catholic and apostolic church."—JLY

GRAVITAS OF THE MINNEAPOLIS ELCA VOTES

The content of the votes has been measured in different levels of gravity by various quarters in the church, from celebration in Goodsoil[8] to affirmation and embrace at Higgins Road.[9] Among those who reject the hegemony of autonomous man the yield is reckoned from "error" as least severe to "apostasy" as the most severe. To judge the yield of the votes as "error" is to argue that the recognition of committed, long-term public gay or lesbian unions, though contrary to the teaching of the Scriptures and the Church is, at this "least level" of severity, a circumstance that can be endured in other persons or parishes even if one does not embrace it locally, as an individual or a congregation. On this reading, the ELCA is at that point in error, in its embrace of heterodox teaching and practice. A congregation, or a pastor, or a layperson can continue in fellowship and roster, and simply agree to disagree.[10]

There is about the vote and the policy a reckoning more severe: that the ELCA is, at that point, in heresy, though some disagree. Witness this view, from Pastor Richard Johnson, editor of *Forum Letter*: "Some [have gone] so far as to accuse the ELCA of heresy—a bit over the top, seems to me. Heresy generally involves a specific and overt repudiation of some

---

8. "Goodsoil is a collaboration of organizations working for the full inclusion of lesbian, gay, bisexual, and transgender people and their families in the full ministerial and sacramental life of the Evangelical Lutheran Church in America (ELCA). Goodsoil is comprised entirely of lay and clergy members of the ELCA." See www.goodsoil.org (accessed September 15, 2010).

9. "Higgins Road" refers to the official address of the Evangelical Lutheran Church in America, 8765 W. Higgins Road, Chicago, IL 60631.

10. To rely upon the phenomenon of "bound conscience" is proving to be a fragile option. Fractious indecision, rather than overtly embraced "bound conscience," is rather more the order of the day in parishes otherwise troubled by the decision, but not so much troubled to act on the offense.

key doctrine of Christian faith. What the ELCA has done is serious error, to be sure, but I don't think it rises to the status of heresy."[11]

But, *contra* Pastor Johnson's view, what has occurred is an overt challenge to—and alteration of—the content of the Sixth Commandment. Our Lord Jesus Christ said, "Have ye not read that He which made them at the beginning made them male and female and said, 'For this cause shall a man leave father and his mother, and shall cleave to his wife. And they twain shall become one flesh. Wherefore they are no more twain, but one flesh.' What therefore God hath joined together, let not man put asunder" (Matthew 19:4–6, KJV). Both the "ordained of God" and the "male and female" are normative as to marriage. Adultery consists in sundry violations—actions, thoughts, imaginings, arrangements—of the normative conditions for the exercise of human sexuality: violations apart from marriage (i.e., by those not married). Against marriage (overt adultery). Other than marriage (something not male and female). God made us male and female, and ordained marriage for the purpose of bringing forth and nurturing children, for love and companionship, and for life-long fidelity.

Thus, what precisely occurred in the Minneapolis vote is a direct challenge to both the *content* and the *authority* of the Sixth Commandment. But more than that, the vote, in challenging the content and authority of the Sixth Commandment, challenges also, and more significantly, the First Commandment. That is, it challenges *the authority of God to make any commandments whatsoever*. I argue that such a challenge is an "overt repudiation of a key doctrine of the Christian faith." To "challenge the authority of God" gets at the heart of the matter.

There is more. The Minneapolis vote regarding gay and lesbian clergy assaults all three articles of the Apostles' Creed. It challenges what constitutes—and belongs in—God's good creation. At no point do the Holy Scriptures acknowledge (much less assert) that homosexual relations reside in Genesis 1–2. The debate is precisely that fundamental: that homosexual *behavior* or *relations* are part and parcel of Genesis 3 and beyond. In the Minneapolis vote, the first article of the Creed is challenged by an expansion as to what constitutes God's good creation.

And likewise the second article vis-à-vis the redemption resident in the life, death, and resurrection of our Lord Jesus Christ. If homosexual

---

11. Richard O. Johnson, "At the Foot of the Cross," *Forum Letter*, 38, no. 11 (November 2009): 2.

relationships are part and parcel of life in Christ, then no repentance is needed for the relationship, per se, only for sins otherwise committed in it, or during it, or before it, or after it. What the Church has previously taught, based on the teaching of the Holy Scripture, is that the Church does not bless, or accept, that kind of relationship. One does not need to repent of marriage, only for sins he or she commits within the marriage or apart from the marriage. The Minneapolis move incorporates into the "God blessed" category a relationship not acceptable to Holy Scripture.

Again, the third article is like unto the second: how one lives his or her life in the one, holy, catholic, and apostolic Church is now expanded to include a category of intimate human relationship universally scorned by Holy Scripture in all its manifestations.

The Minneapolis vote challenges specifically the content of the Sixth Commandment and, moreover, the First Commandment—the authority of God to command in such fashion whatsoever, as well as all three articles of the Creed as to creation, redemption, and sanctification. That's not simply heresy (specific and overt repudiation of some key doctrine). The cumulative rejection of Creed and Commandments amounts to apostasy, *an overt repudiation of the faith, while still claiming allegiance to the faith,* believing that the innovation is itself consistent with the received faith. Such is the *gravitas* of the situation.—JLY

THE WAY FORWARD

Luther was obliged to recall the Church to the proclamation of the Gospel. What he saw in Wittenberg was a system and structure that had largely reduced faith to quantifiable observance and empty rituals, distorting the Gospel not so much to a vigorous legalism, but to a piety that concerned itself with purchased indulgences, funded masses, perfunctory prayers. Luther understood natural law as well as the revealed law of God. But he scorned "legalism."

The proclamation of the Gospel in our time presupposes a vigorous preaching of the Law. The law is not obliterated in the new covenant. Adultery is still sin. Honoring one's parents is required. Keeping God's name holy is not perfunctory but mandatory. The Good News is not that the Law is crushed and obliterated. The Good News is that God does not judge us by our achievements within the Law. We are, instead, declared righteous by His grace as a gift, through the redemption that is in Christ Jesus.

We will not begin to understand either the power or the beauty of the Gospel until we understand the requirements, the severity, and the judgment of the Law. We will not understand the requirements and severity of the Law until we come to terms with its Author. The Author of the law is the author of the universe, the Father of all, the Judge of all. "You shall have no other gods," the commandments begin. *Commandments!* The practical atheism of our time makes God remote, even impotent, to the *hoi polloi*, even to ostensible Christians. Luther's appreciation of his *predicament* so far surpasses the *Selbsverstandnis* of most of us so as not even to be in the same universe of humanity. Luther *understood* that his situation before the wrath of God was absolutely untenable. Luther *understood* that the requirements are there, articulated and enforced. Luther knew what he was up against.

So many of us skip to the grace part—what we want to call the whole part, the Word part, the Gospel part—without paying attention to our predicament. We address our predicament with moments of affirmation, seek self-esteem from sources congenial, "compadres" kind. We seem unwilling to tend our soul in any sense other than its aspect as *self*, a modern distortion of soul unknown to Greeks and Hebrews, unaddressed by Jesus—except in terms of what must be *denied*, that is, rejected, along with taking up the cross, in order to follow Him.

It is now fashionable to ignore the power of God. Various proponents of natural theology are re-invoking one or another forms of the teleological argument, which in turn invokes causality, the Uncaused First Cause. Many liberal theologians, including quite a few in the ELCA, have reduced God to metaphor by reducing *talk* about God to metaphor.

The modern paradigm is hardly the subservient medieval peasant, whether of the common or royal variety. Restricting our view to the United States, though as many as 90 percent acknowledge God as "existing," significantly fewer acknowledge Him as Lord. In a culture of plenty, seduction by mammon takes many forms. In a culture of freedom understood as individual rights, the notion of obedience is consigned to enclaves of "primitive religiosity." As noted earlier, a state where just authority is constitutionally declared to be first and only by the consent of the governed, many have made the political paradigm also the moral paradigm: God's will and authority in religion has its origin and its limits, like the state's authority in political affairs, by the *consent of the governed*. The law is, in the main, regarded as positive (that is, of human origin), rather than natural or divine, in origin: a human construct.

In the "church" as in the culture, the paradigm is not obedience but freedom—the freedom, in principle, of the human person from any constraint except what is self-acknowledged and self-consented. Freedom not only to decide what and when to act and say, but also *to define what is sin*. "Reformers" seek to enlighten by now making noble and virtuous the relationships and acts declared by Scripture to be sinful, with the 2009 ELCA vote now exhibit A. Reformation, understood uncritically as "change," is blessed as the proper avenue to "enlighten" in the direction of new cultural understanding.

There is no short answer to a culture with the bit between its teeth, to a church so acculturated as to presume to redefine as "loving, caring, committed, and just" what God in Scripture declares to be sin. "All have sinned and fall short of the glory of God" (Romans 3:23) is invoked to silence voices of prophetic concern. The fallen condition of humanity is understood as warrant to preclude anyone's making legitimate judgment of what someone has consented to as just and loving.

Only the power of God in the Law makes the power of God in the Gospel meaningful. Only the realization of how we are trapped in sin and failure before God can make our understanding of grace any more than "Ho hum. Of course, God forgives us. We deserve it. God don't make no junk." Such a view is the apotheosis of sin, because it amounts to saying that we have no sin.—JLY

10

Natural Law in
an African Context

Carl E. Rockrohr

Natural law is the law under which all people live. This law might be found in the societal norms, religious teachings, and the personal conscience of the individual. The natural law gives guidance to a person on how he should act toward other humans and the Creator. These basic truths of natural law are clearly taught in Romans 1:18–32, 2:12–16, and Acts 17:22–34.

Because the Scriptures teach that natural law is available to all human beings, we should not be surprised to find human ideas of right behavior toward humans and the Creator in many different sorts of societies. The Christian expects that no matter what the culture or historical circumstance, some evidence of natural law will exist in that society. Perhaps, in some cases, consciences will be hardened and people will have gone in the ways prohibited by natural law (Romans 1:24–27). Natural law does not reveal the redeeming and saving nature and work of the true God; instead, it provides a witness to the person of the existence of the Creator and gives some glimpse into the will of the Creator for humans.

Martin Luther judged that an unbeliever following natural law may have a better understanding of God than another who knows the Scriptures, but makes up his own rules and regulations to try to achieve his own righteousness before God.

> To illustrate, let us take a monk. He depicts God to himself as enthroned in His heaven, tailoring cowls, shaving heads, and manufacturing ropes, coarse shirts, and wooden shoes. And then he imagines that whoever clothes himself in these not only merits heaven for himself but can also help others get to heaven. This is blindness beyond all blindness, as must be apparent to all. It is not one whit better than the blindness of the heathen, who worship oxen and calves and cannot be compared to those who seek to keep the Law of Moses or the dictates of the natural law. For what comparison is there between a friar's lousy, shabby jester's cap and cord, plus all his hocus-pocus, and the command to obey father, mother, and government? Even the heathen are superior to this group. They demonstrate a deeper knowledge of the Lord, our God, by their better comprehension of God's Commandments and demands. One might speak of this as sniffing the existence of God without tasting it. The heathen, the philosophers, and all wise people have progressed to a point where they recognize God through the Law. You have already heard, however, what is accomplished by this type of knowledge.[1]

This essay presents one setting of African traditional beliefs to provide opportunity to identify natural law in African beliefs. Such an endeavor is not merely academic; it is an undertaking that appreciates another person as a fellow creature of God to whom is given natural law, just as the Scriptures have said. If indeed the non-Christian person has beliefs and practices that indicate the knowledge of the existence of a Creator, and perhaps even the need for honor and obedience to the Creator, natural law may reveal common points for conversation of revealed Law and Gospel.

---

1.   AE 22:152.

THE NON-CHRISTIAN AS MY NEIGHBOR

Before examples of natural law can be studied, preliminary consideration must be given to the concept of neighbor. My neighbor is a divinely created fellow human being for whom God provides blessings necessary for life in this world. Even evil people receive God's material blessings (Matthew 5:45). The other person should be approached, honored, and considered as one whom God calls my "neighbor." This fundamental biblical category of neighbor might seem too obvious to discuss, but it is often *not* the standard operating procedure of the world (Matthew 20:25) and needs to be emphasized. This section first briefly reviews Jesus' teaching of the concept of neighbor. Second, the classic theory of *animism*, often used in earlier decades (though still around) to understand African religious beliefs, is reviewed and critiqued. This preliminary consideration of the concepts of neighbor and animism prepares the approach to the African setting based on a biblical view discussed in the next section.

The biblical concept of neighbor can be seen from Jesus' discussion with the lawyer in Luke 10:25–37 on how to inherit eternal life. When the lawyer tried to justify himself, Jesus told the story of the Good Samaritan to help the lawyer think through the question, "Who is my neighbor?"

Arthur Just comments that the lawyer would have excluded a Samaritan as neighbor; thus, Jesus' story of the Good Samaritan would have been offensive and shocking to the lawyer. Why?

> Jesus parades a priest and a Levite as models of the indifferent, unmerciful, and loveless. The hearer might expect the third traveler to be a layperson. It is a great surprise that the third traveler is a Samaritan—and he is portrayed as the hero in the story. The last person the lawyer would expect to be held before him as an example of one who fulfills the Law by loving his neighbor as himself is the hated Samaritan![2]

In the Good Samaritan story, the unexpected understanding of neighbor cannot be overlooked. Jesus shows the actions of a despised one loving others to be actions of a neighbor. The Samaritan did not regard

---

2.   Arthur A. Just, *Luke*, Concordia Commentary Series (St. Louis: Concordia, 1996), 2:452.

similarity or difference in race, religion, or culture as a barrier to assisting his neighbor.

Ultimately, Just argues, the story of the Good Samaritan should be interpreted that Christ Himself is the Good Samaritan. The lawyer cannot obtain eternal life by assisting many people here and there. In reality, the lawyer needs the healing that only Christ can give. Christ, then, is the perfect neighbor.[3]

Though the lawyer, or any sinful human, cannot adequately fulfill love toward the neighbor or be a perfect neighbor, Jesus does define the neighbor as the one not necessarily like me. My neighbor may be quite different from me. Reflecting on Jesus' teaching of the neighbor in the story, I suggest that

> Jesus presents the neighbor as the person who is different from me. My neighbor is *not* the one like me. The person who is of a different race, who observes different customs, who holds different values, who believes a different religion, has a different everything!—that person is my neighbor. Neighbor is the infidel. Neighbor is not valued vis-à-vis my own self-identity. My neighbor has been given his own identity and value by God and he must be treated as equally valued in all of creation.[4]

Just's comment that Jesus is the perfect neighbor that sinners need points out another truth Jesus' story gives about the neighbor. My neighbor may be in a better social or economic position than I am. This is most certainly true of Jesus as the holy Son of God who came to save lost sinners. Is this not also true concerning neighbors in the civil realm? Scriptures teach that servanthood among humans does not presume the superiority of one over the other.[5] Certainly, Christ's disciples are not to lord their positions over one another (Matthew 20:20–28). Further, the disciples may also find themselves subject to civil authorities who do not fear and trust God (Mark 10:42). When a disciple brings the Gospel of Christ to his neighbor, the saving message of Christ cannot be silenced

---

3.   Just, *Luke*, 2:454–55.
4.   Carl E. Rockrohr, "Jesus' Sacrifice Death in an African Context" (PhD dissertation, Concordia Seminary, 2008), 107–8.
5.   It has been lamented that too often Christians did not act as servants when they came to Africa. See A. Ngindu Mushete, "An Overview of African Theology," in Rosino Gibellini, *Paths of African Theology* (Maryknoll, NY: Orbis, 1994), 9–10.

(Acts 5:27–32), yet in civil affairs the unbelieving neighbor may be an authority to whom the disciple submits (Matthew 22:15–22).

A final point about the neighbor is that the clear goal of evangelization is that the unbelieving neighbor might become a believing brother or sister in Christ. Physical birth is the origination of human neighborliness. It is the Holy Spirit who gives spiritual birth through the Gospel so that we become brothers and sisters in Christ (John 3:1–8). God desires all neighbors to come to faith in Christ and be His sons and daughters. God's goal is that our neighbors might become our brothers and sisters.

The importance of a focus on the biblical teaching of neighbor becomes evident when one understands how various theories with unbiblical approaches can change one's perception of neighbor and interfere with the understanding of natural law. Edward Burnett Tylor's (1832–1917) theory of animism is a case in point. A brief overview of Tylor and his theory of animism is given here to demonstrate that not every approach of analyzing religious beliefs aligns well with a biblical understanding of neighbor.[6]

E. B. Tylor was an Englishman, brought up in a Quaker household, who educated himself as an amateur geologist. He traveled only once outside of England in 1856 to Mexico, where he studied various cultural and archeological artifacts including remains from the Aztec culture. He was appointed head of the University Museum of Oxford in 1883, became a Reader in Anthropology in 1884, and was Professor of Anthropology from 1896 to 1906. He wrote over 250 essays and four major research books, including the two-volume work *Primitive Culture* in 1871. It was in this study that Tylor developed the theory of animism. That *Primitive Culture* was widely consulted is evidenced by its ten reprints and translations into Russian, German, French, and Polish during Tylor's lifetime.[7]

In volume one of *Primitive Culture*,[8] Tylor analyzed many aspects of culture from all around the world and throughout history. His methodology made the assumption that uniformity existed in the evolutionary development of all human knowledge, societies, religions, technologies,

---

6.   Unless otherwise noted, the following points of Tylor and his analysis on the theory of animism are taken from previous work. See Rockrohr, "Jesus' Sacrifice Death in an African Context."

7.   Jerry D. Moore, *Visions of Culture: An Introduction to Anthropological Theories and Theorists* (Walnut Creek, CA: AltaMira, 1997), 26.

8.   Edward Burnett Tylor, *The Origins of Culture,* vol. 1, *Primitive Culture* (Gloucester, MA: Peter Smith, 1970).

governments, etc. so that data drawn from all cultures and all periods of time could be placed on a scale of gradual development.[9]

In volume two,[10] Tylor focused his study on religious beliefs; it was here he proposed and defined *animism* as the beginning level of religious belief in its evolutionary development.[11] Thus, animism was a sort of universal starting point for the development of what he called Natural Religion and Philosophy of Religion outside of any consideration of supernatural revelation.[12] The data for his theory in *Primitive Culture* was gleaned from reports from missionaries and travelers from around the world that he assembled together like pieces in a complex puzzle of universal religious development.[13] Other pieces of religious beliefs and practices that he fit into his scheme of animism were parts of the Old Testament. For example, he understood simple patriarchal sacrifices as examples of earlier forms of belief that later developed into more complex priestly and sacrificial rites.[14]

Tylor deemed the Old Testament prophets' teaching more developed because it included ethical considerations, while earlier sacrificial practices contained no thought of ethics.[15] Tylor theorized that early forms of animism were "unmoral," without ethics, and not until the later religious developments were teachings of morality found in religious beliefs.[16]

---

9.   Tylor, *The Origins of Culture*, 1. For helpful sources of the background history of anthropological study and thought in Europe, see Margaret T. Hodgen, *Early Anthropology in the Sixteenth and Seventeenth Centuries* (Philadelphia: University of Pennsylvania Press, 1964); Bernard McGrane, *Beyond Anthropology: Society and the Other* (New York: Columbia University Press, 1989). Gillian Bediako's work highlights the interplay between nineteenth-century Old Testament scholarship and the view of Africans and other non-Europeans. Gillian M. Bediako, "Primal Religion and the Bible: William Robertson Smith and His Heritage," *Journal for the Study of the Old Testament*. Supplement Series; 246 (Sheffield: Sheffield Academic Press, 1997).

10.   Edward Burnett Tylor, *Religion in Primitive Culture*, The Library of Religion and Culture, vol. 2 (New York: Harper, 1958).

11.   Tylor, *Religion in Primitive Culture*, 9–10.

12.   Tylor, *Religion in Primitive Culture*, 10–12.

13.   An example of this patchwork methodology can be seen in Tylor, *Religion in Primitive Culture*, 461–95. Tylor brought in evidence from ancient Greek, Roman, and Babylonian sacrifices and compared them with various sacrifices among native American, African, and Asian people. He also considered in his evidence Old Testament sacrifices and contemporary Christian sacrifice rituals.

14.   Tylor, *Religion in Primitive Culture*, 472–73.

15.   Tylor, *Religion in Primitive Culture*, 473.

16.   Tylor, *Religion in Primitive Culture*, 445–46. "Unmoral" is Tylor's term.

The intent of Tylor's theory was not to belittle less religiously developed people, but to show their common humanity.[17] He believed religions were not degenerative but progressive. That is, religions moved progressively from beliefs of many spirits to monotheism. Tylor opposed those in his day who suggested that degeneracy was based upon race. Rather, he theorized that different peoples were at different stages of similar evolutionary development.[18]

Many nineteenth- and twentieth-century anthropologists and theologians have not agreed with Tylor. Notable critiques have been made by anthropologists Franz Boas[19] and E. E. Evans-Pritchard.[20] Tylor's broad generalizations that all cultures and times fit into one grand scheme, and his nineteenth-century assumption that his own view of religion was at the highest level of development from which he could look down and analyze lesser developed people, are not accepted by many later anthropologists. African theologian John Mbiti specifically rejected Tylor's theory of animism as a completely inappropriate view of African religious beliefs in his late twentieth-century standard work, *African Religions and Philosophy*.[21]

Though the theory of animism remains the basis of religious comparison for some missiologists,[22] Tylor's theory of animism distorted both the biblical message and the relationship of neighbor. First, Tylor's theory of animism assumed that the more "primitive" religious beliefs and practices evolve into the more advanced. Thus, primitive concepts, such as sacrifice, are only what he termed "survivals" remaining from primitive forms and should be abolished in current religious beliefs. Tylor said the ethnologist and historian need to assist the theologian with this process of culling older doctrines and rites that are no longer needed.[23] With

---

17. Tylor, *Religion in Primitive Culture*, 1–5.
18. Tylor, *Religion in Primitive Culture*, 441–44.
19. See Jerry D. Moore, *Visions of Culture: An Introduction to Anthropological Theories and Theorists*, 2nd ed. (Walnut Creek, CA: Altamira, 2004), chapter 3, 33–43.
20. E. E. Evans-Pritchard, *Theories of Primitive Religion*, Sir D. Owen Evans Lectures, 1962 (Oxford: Clarendon, 1965).
21. John S. Mbiti, *African Religions and Philosophy*, 2nd rev. and enl. ed. (Oxford; Portsmouth, N.H.: Heinemann, 1990), 6–10. The 1990 edition was the 2nd edition, with the first 1969 edition having been reprinted thirteen times.
22. Gailyn Van Rheenen, *Communicating Christ in Animistic Contexts* (Grand Rapids: Baker, 1991). I comment on the illogic of Van Rheenen's use of Tylor's theory in chapters 3 and 4 of my dissertation.
23. Tylor, *Religion in Primitive Culture*, 536–38.

that theoretical maneuver, the judgment of the theoretician becomes the arbiter of the religious belief and practices both in the neighbor's life and in the Scriptures. At such a point, the theory has taken on the role of decider of ultimate truth, subverting the authority of Scripture.

Second, Tylor's view that religious beliefs are based upon a progressive development obscures the scriptural teaching of shared natural law, which teaches that the Christian and non-Christian may hold some beliefs and practices in common because they are truths given to all people by the Creator. A theory such as animism can override evidence that some things held in common are universal truths and rather call them primitive survivals that should be deleted.[24] Whenever a label is put forward as a rationale to judge certain religious beliefs and practices, it should be considered whether the label is a biblical concept or merely a cultural and theoretical judgment.

This overview of the biblical concept of neighbor and critique of the theory of animism is important for discussion in an African setting. We have seen that it is a basic biblical axiom that any other human being is my neighbor. The Christian is called to "love your neighbor as yourself" (Romans 13:8–10). Such an attitude approaches neighbor as a fellow human being who can be engaged in theological dialogue. Scriptural teaching may judge many parts of the neighbor's beliefs as ungodly, but at the same time there may be points of agreement in natural law. A discussion with the neighbor may reveal whether this is the case. I believe such a discussion with the individual neighbor to find out his or her specific beliefs is in accord with love for neighbor. It is incongruous for missiologists and missionaries who do love neighbor, and who also do not hold to the progressive view of religious development, to use universal theories that prejudge the neighbor and assign religious beliefs to the neighbor without even talking to the person. Some have suggested that the term "animism" is just a general term about beliefs in spirits without the baggage of Tylor's theory of the evolution of religions. This suggestion lacks logic, for it has been noted that in a broad use of the term animism, Christians are animists.[25]

---

24. This is the perspective of John Shelby Spong, *Why Christianity Must Change or Die: A Bishop Speaks to Believers in Exile: A New Reformation of the Church's Faith and Practice*, 1st ed. (San Francisco: Harper, 1998).

25. Paul G. Hiebert, R. Daniel Shaw, and Tite Tienou, *Understanding Folk Religion: A Christian Response to Popular Beliefs and Practices* (Grand Rapids: Baker, 1999), 17, footnote 3.

The biblical teaching of neighbor can help weed out the use of unbiblical categories about my neighbor. How do we approach and dialogue with a fellow human being whom God calls my neighbor? The foregoing review and critique of the theory of animism is meant not only to critique any current use of the theory, but to explore its broader implications. When we dialogue with and study the beliefs of our unbelieving neighbor, do the methods and theories we use represent our own faith? Is the person being honored as a fellow creature of God, with courtesies and respect shown across cultures and languages? Cultural assumptions and misunderstandings will abound, but will the attitude and approach be humble, listening and caring for the neighbor's body and soul?

SOME BELIEFS OF AN AFRICAN NEIGHBOR

In 2000, I conducted dissertation research in Ghana, West Africa.[26] Working with host pastors and lay members of the Evangelical Lutheran Church of Ghana (ELCG), many of whom I had known while a missionary,[27] I conducted interviews in six tribal areas of Ghana. The goal was to research not only some beliefs of traditional African sacrifices but also to test out an approach of cross-cultural systematic theology called the "Four Voices."[28] Instead of relying on a universal theory such as animism to quantify what an African non-Christian believes, the approach relies upon theological dialogue from four sources: the Scriptures, the Lutheran Confessions, the African traditional practitioner, and the African Christian.[29]

---

26. This was funded in part by an overseas study grant awarded through the Graduate School of Concordia Seminary, St. Louis.
27. I served as a missionary with LCMS World Mission 1992–1998 under the auspices of the ELCG. The primary work was with the Konkomba people of northern Ghana, though the work involved many different tribes.
28. Rockrohr, "Jesus' Sacrifice Death in an African Context," 115–30.
29. In 1972, John Mbiti proposed "four pillars" for doing Christology in Africa that accord very closely to my approach of the four voices. John S. Mbiti, "Some African Concepts of Christology," in *Christ and the Younger Churches: Theological Contributions from Asia, Africa and Latin America*, ed. Georg F. Vicedom and Jose Miguez Bonino, *Theological Collections*, 15 (London: S.P.C.K., 1972). I read this article after we returned from Ghana in 1998, but I no longer know if I read it before or after I developed the "Four Voices" idea. For an in-depth explanation of the "Four Voices," see Rockrohr, "Jesus' Sacrifice Death in an African Context," 115–30. Another proposal for a fourfold approach was given by E. W. Fashole-Luke, "The

188 Carl E. Rockrohr

The approach consisted of three interviews held in each of the six tribal areas. The main interview would be conducted with a person who practiced traditional blood sacrifices, the African Traditional Practitioner (ATP). I would first interview the area host (a Christian pastor or layperson) regarding what the host expected to hear and learn during the interview with the ATP. This was the preparatory interview. The main interview was then conducted with the ATP with the host present. Finally, I interviewed the host again in a debriefing interview that allowed for reflection and clarification of any points in question. The preparatory and debriefing interviews were done in English, while the main interview was conducted in the local tribal language with a translator.

The following excerpts are from the main interview in the Konkomba area. The excerpts illustrate evidence of natural law and opportunities for that shared common knowledge to provide a bridge for further theological dialogue. The interviews are dense with linguistic, theological, cultural, and sociological details. It is not possible here to delve into all of these details, but a few comments after each excerpt will help the reader to observe and reflect upon what one African neighbor believes about the existence of the Creator and the will of that Creator. What knowledge of natural law does this man share with the Christian?

Quest for African Christian Theologies," in *Mission Trends No. 3: Third World Theologies*, ed. Gerald H. Anderson and Thomas F. Stransky (New York: Paulist Press, 1976). See Rockrohr, "Jesus' Sacrifice Death in an African Context," 116–18.

Interview with Traditional Konkomba Believer[30]

Excerpt 1:

Rockrohr: So, we have read through the agreement and agreed for our interview and at this time I will begin with the questions. The first topic we will talk about is the blood sacrifices that he makes. And so the first question is: what are the different sacrifices he makes, what different kinds of sacrifices does he make?

ATP: They have so many different kinds of blood sacrifices. First, he said something about land god. Land god: if you go to a soothsayer and then he predicted to you, "Go and makes sacrifice to the land god," you have to do that so that the Lord God will bless you. And also, they have something called "*kuulog,*" the bag, the bag from the animal. So sometimes the soothsayer will tell you "Go and makes sacrifice to *kuulog* so that you get blessings."[31]

Comment: This excerpt was toward the beginning of the interview. The ATP was asked to share as much or as little as he wished. He chose to talk about a sacrifice to the land god and to the *kuulog* (bag). Immediately, the belief in a high God was brought into the conversation. The translator was a Konkomba Christian, knowledgeable in both traditional Konkomba beliefs and practices as well as Christian beliefs and practices.

Excerpt 2:

Rockrohr: So . . . He is answering this but maybe he wants to . . . I don't know.[32] To whom is the sacrifice given? And we are

---

30. The following excerpts are from the interview with a Konkomba man from the village of Gbindiri conducted on July 17, 2000. The complete interview is available in Rockrohr, "Jesus' Sacrifice Death in an African Context," 194–207.
31. Rockrohr, "Jesus' Sacrifice Death in an African Context," 194.
32. Ellipsis marks indicate a pause in the conversation.

saying the land god, but maybe he wants to say more. To whom is it given?

ATP: It is given to God.

Rockrohr: Oh, it is given to God?

ATP: Yes.

Rockrohr: To which god?

ATP: The Creator God.

Rockrohr: The Creator God. So the sacrifice they give to the land god is to the Creator God?

ATP: Yes, the land god takes the sacrifice to the Creator God.

Rockrohr: Okay, fine. And what is the reason for that sacrifice?

ATP: When God created the world he created these idols too. And then the idols, they kind of serve as mediators between us and God. And then before you can go and make sacrifice to send to God, God also created people that we call soothsayers. And sometimes if your house is having problems, like people are getting sick, or maybe you are facing some problem, you have to go to a soothsayer. A soothsayer will predict that the land god needs some sacrifice to be taken to God. So, the soothsayer will tell you everything and then you come to make the sacrifice to the land god. And the land god will take that to God for blessings. That is why sometimes you have to make the sacrifices, that is the reason.

Rockrohr: So, I understand that God gave these idols as a place to give sacrifices to Him? That is what he means, and also that it solves so many problems that the soothsayer may identify. Is that it?

ATP: Yes. And what he wants to add is that every human being is like a child, when you are born you cannot speak until such a time comes when you are able to walk and you are able to speak. So, besides that we don't know what the Lord God wants us to do. But we can only know that through the soothsayer. And so it has been a habit [?][33] since from the beginning, since from their grandparents. So they also find it to be a good thing to follow up to this day.

Rockrohr: Okay. Thank you. So when they make this sacrifice to the land god is there some special time? Or date?

ATP: Yes, when they get to the planting season they have to gather chickens and an animal to go and make sacrifice to the Lord [?] to make some vows. That he should bless them on their farms and protect their houses. And so after harvest then they will go back and say thank you with another animal and chickens again.[34]

Comment: Our Konkomba neighbor explains his belief that the Creator God has made all lesser gods and spirits. They all serve Him. These gods served as mediators to the Creator God, but it is the human soothsayer who has to give directions on how and why the sacrifices should be made. Expressed with various descriptions is the belief that the Creator God gives blessings, but He is not available for direct communication or offering. The Konkomba man offers the analogy that people are like children who cannot speak and need the soothsayer's help to communicate with the Creator God.

Excerpt 3:

Rockrohr: I wanted to just ask a further question, when they give the liver to the *kuulog*, do they put it on the bag or what?

ATP: They smash a little on the bag, and then they also eat.

Rockrohr: When they give that blood sacrifice and liver to the *kuulog*, who is it going to?

---

33. Unintelligible word.
34. Rockrohr, "Jesus' Sacrifice Death in an African Context," 195–96.

ATP: The *kuulog* also sends the sacrifice to the Creator God.

Rockrohr: The *kuulog* itself, is that a spirit there or what?

ATP: He says before they have *kuulog*, normally what they have to do is brew pito. And the people gather at your house that day, they will be dancing all night. And before the night breaks, the soothsayer will be there. After they kill the goat, they will take the skin from the goat [the bag is the skin from the goat]. They put some food inside. They take the bag into the bush. There are some spirits we call them *npawniim*, they will come and enter inside to enjoy the food that is being stored in that bag. So the soothsayer will come and quickly cover the entrance of that bag. And then they will be there crying inside the bag, "mwaa mwaa mwaa," and then you run with them to the house. And those will be the spirits helping you. Anytime you make sacrifice, those spirits take the sacrifice to the Creator God.

Rockrohr: So you never look in the bag again?

ATP: No. You never look inside. When you bring them home that is just all. They will fly out of the bag again. Each single time you want to seek something from them, maybe their protections or to find out something that is going wrong in the house, they have a cloth. They use some shaker. They have something called a shaker, a calabash thing. Normally they put stones inside, and it makes the sound, "cha cha cha." When you do that then all of a sudden they will come. Then they greet you and you greet them. They talk to you and also you talk to them. They tell you what is going on. These are the sacrifices you need to do, so that you will not get this kind of trouble, or this kind of bad thing will not happen to you.

Rockrohr: So the owner hears them talking?

ATP: Yes, the owner hears them clearly. Even the people outside hear them speak. They do not do it openly, unless always in a room. So they hang the cloth there [in the room] and then the *npawniim* enter there. . . . Those spirits speak different kind of languages. . . . If you do not speak Konkomba, but you speak Kusaal, then they speak to you in Kusaal. If Pastor _____ [name not printed] wants to come and talk to them, they would speak to him in Bimoba. They speak in different kinds of languages.[35]

Rockrohr: What are the reasons that you make sacrifices to *kuulog*?

ATP: Before one gets *kuulog*, maybe when you are in trouble, let's assume you are sick, or maybe you want to find money but you're not getting it or you want to find a wife and you're not getting a wife. Something like that. So you have to go to soothsayer or somebody who owns a *kuulog*. And he will tell you it is because you have not made sacrifice to *kuulog* that is why you are lacking all those things. So then you'll come back and you will brew your pito, as he said, find your animals as he also mentioned, and then you'll have your own *kuulog* for your protections and for your blessings.[36]

Comment: Again this type of sacrifice is taken to the Creator God. The spirits gathered in the goatskin bag audibly speak to the owner of the bag and they are capable of speaking in different languages. These spirits have a close relationship to the owner. They speak the owner's language and help solve problems in the owner's daily life.

Excerpt 4:

Rockrohr: How do you describe the high God? What is he like?

ATP: (*laughing*) It is only those who died, they know how he is. But none of them have come back to tell them how God looks like.

Rockrohr: Ok. Why do they know?

---

35. The reader should take note that the person indicated that the spirits of the *kuulog* are audibly heard by a number of people.
36. Rockrohr, "Jesus' Sacrifice Death in an African Context," 198–99.

ATP: They know this also from the soothsayer. Soothsayer tells you that those who die go to God. Then sometimes too they have a dream. You can get a dream at night, your father who died sometime ago. He will come in the night and be shouting. "This kind of thing . . . why don't you go and do it?" And because it was not clear to you, you will go to a soothsayer early in the morning, to predict to you what should be done.

Rockrohr: OK. So sometimes the dead people come and talk to you. That is an indication. . . . OK, What does he know to be the Lord God's relationship to people here on earth?

ATP: We are so related to God in the sense that he has created us all. And that he has given us the land to make farms and houses to live in. And the Lord God also wants that any time we eat we should also remember him, and the way to remember God is to make the sacrifice to the land god, so that the land god will take the sacrifice to the Creator God.

Rockrohr: Then he has also led to the next question, what do you believe is the Lord God relationship to other spirits?

ATP: Because the Lord God created all the spirits. He also feeds them. He created them plenty. And he created some for Bimobas, some for Kusasis, some for Konkombas, and some for every kind of human being on earth . . . to be feeding them. And for them, they often get angry. If you don't feed them, then they wait until it is about to rain, when the clouds form they will turn the rain into windy. And it will come and blow off your houses, push down your corn or whatever plant you have. That is their work, they will come and destroy all you have so that you also will suffer. So it always good to feed them and you will be free.

Rockrohr: Ok. Is there any sacrifice that can be made to the Lord God? If yes, what? If not, why?

ATP: There is no way you can do it. But you can do it through an idol.

Rockrohr: Does he have any reason why you cannot do it?

ATP: He does not know.

Rockrohr: Just everybody knows it. . . .

ATP: They all don't know it.

Rockrohr: And no soothsayer will tell you to make one direct?

ATP: Sometimes what a soothsayer does he tells you to go and make sacrifice to God. To Creator God, and it is not like any other ordinary type of sacrifice. But that one you come home and finds some beans cake, find some milk, some raw milk from a cow, and then maybe you can get a chicken or a Guinea fowl to slaughter and then roast it. And then gather all children to come together. And then you let the children enjoy the meat, and the milk, and the sugar, and the bean cake. So that the Lord God seeing you feeding the children will be happy to bless you.

Rockrohr: So you make some special meal for the children, and the Lord God takes this for His sacrifice?

ATP: Yes. The Lord God will take his sacrifice and will send you the blessings.

Rockrohr: So the house people eat it and the Lord God is happy?

ATP: It is not good only to let your house people alone to eat the food. After you slaughter the chicken and you roast it or cook it, then you stand outside and call. They have a special name for it, that call it "yaa-yaraa" meaning "food for everyone." Then when they all gather, you will serve the food for them. You say, "Take this because of God. Take this food because of God. Take this food because of God." And then whatever is remaining, that will be the milk and the bean cake. The you put that one down and they will all rush there pushing each other down eating it and so forth.

Rockrohr: That is all the questions I have. So I thank you very, very much. This was very interesting and helpful. I learned very much.[37]

Comments: The Creator God has made all things and is the provider for all good blessings. He seems not to be blamed for evil events; this is the work of the lesser spirits who need to be fed to stay pleased. The Creator God does not need to be fed, but rather feeds all beings. This last sacrifice directed to the Creator God by feeding the children and the neighbors perhaps indicates some knowledge that the Creator God is pleased by feeding children and neighbors. This "feeding" sacrifice was new information to the hosting pastor who is from a neighboring tribe and fairly well acquainted with Konkomba beliefs.

CONCLUDING REMARKS

The evidence of natural law is apparent in this brief glimpse into this man's belief. The Konkomba man believed in the existence of the Creator God. The Creator God is over all beings, spirits, humans, and animals. The Creator God is the provider for all things in life. Yet the Creator God is distant and various mediating spirits have to take offerings and sacrifices to Him. The spirits are not entirely trusted. The soothsayer guides the person to know what sacrifices are needed, but he also is not entirely trusted. The Creator God cares not only for humans and spirits, but also animals. He does not like animal life uselessly taken. The Creator God likes children and neighbors to be fed.[38]

The Konkomba man shared beliefs, practices, and experiences that might seem strange to the Western sensibilities. There is a temptation to disregard the man's words as "superstition." But one needs to listen long enough to carefully reflect and ask questions in a neighborly manner. The biblical teaching is that neighbor has access to natural law. Can the neighbor be respected enough to be taken seriously for the natural law that does exist in his beliefs?

---

37. Rockrohr, "Jesus' Sacrifice Death in an African Context," 203–5.
38. For examples of touch points for revealed Law and Gospel discussed later with the hosting ELCG pastor, see Rockrohr, "Jesus' Sacrifice Death in an African Context," 207–23.

Another approach that I have suggested at times to suspend Western "scientific doubts" when talking to my neighbor about his beliefs and experiences: Am I so absolutely experienced in all religious ways and knowledgeable in the history of mankind that I can discount what another person tells me he or she has seen and experienced? The biblical approach recognizes many possible spiritual experiences and powers, though not all are according to the will of the true God.

Theological discussions with the non-Christian neighbor about the Creator God and His will are times when the natural law of God can be acknowledged and revealed gifts of God shared. When the revealed gifts of God are shared, by God's grace the unbelieving neighbor might become a sister or brother in Christ.

> Oh, taste and see that the LORD is good! Blessed is the man who takes refuge in Him! (Psalm 34:8)

Natural Law
and Contemporary Issues

11

THE NATURAL LAW OF THE FAMILY

Ryan C. MacPherson

Nothing grabs a person's attention more suddenly or more seriously than death. Reactions to death reveal what people value most dearly. Personal experience attests to this truth. So does archaeology. Excavators of the ruins at Kourion, an ancient Greek city on the Mediterranean island of Cyprus, have discovered how the inhabitants responded to a devastating earthquake that struck in AD 365. Amid the ruins, they uncovered a fossilization of family love. As lead archeologist David Soren reports:

> Here we found a 25-year-old man and a 19-year-old woman, presumably husband and wife. To protect his wife from falling debris, the man had placed his leg over her pelvis and his arm over her shoulder. They were holding hands; she had a hairpin

in her hair. A large falling chunk of plaster had struck her skull, snapping her neck at right angles and killing her. The husband took the brunt of the falling blocks as he straddled his wife, and his skull was crushed. . . . Our young husband and wife were not only holding each other's hands; they were cradling an 18-month-old child in their arms. Both were touching the child's back, and the mother held the baby's face just under her chin.[1]

In the most dangerous moment of their lives, just twenty seconds before their impending deaths, the man and his wife knew what to do. No rehearsal had been possible. No rehearsal had been necessary. She drew her child to her breast. He wrapped his body around wife and child to protect them. Then, as suddenly as the tremor had begun, all was quiet. Sixteen and half centuries later, three skeletons remain in their dying embrace, preserved in the village of Episkopi at the Kourion Museum—testifying to the natural law of the family.

This essay offers, first, a definition of natural law and, second, a demonstration that a fundamental unit of the created order, as governed by natural law, consists of "one man and one woman united in marriage for life—and their children, whether begotten or adopted." This "natural family" is not merely a cultural tradition, nor is it reinvented by each individual according to his or her preference. Indeed, "society does not create and cannot redefine the natural family," but rather society "originate[s] from natural families serving one another."[2] Moreover, the natural family encompasses more than just the aforementioned individuals; it is an organic whole, linking a broad set of relationships and responsibilities among its own members and between itself and derivative institutions, such as civil government.

Precisely because society, by its very nature, consists of families—and because derivative institutions, by their very natures, are founded upon the family—a fiduciary reciprocity must be maintained for the sake of human flourishing. What harms the family ultimately will ruin society

1.   David Soren, "Death at Kourion," *Archaeology Odyssey* 6, no. 4 (July/Aug. 2003): 44–55, quoting p. 54. I learned of this dramatic discovery in a homily delivered by Dr. William B. Kessel, Trinity Chapel, Bethany Lutheran College, ca. 2008, and I thank Dr. Kessel for sharing his resources with me.

2.   The Hausvater Project, "Vision Statement," 2008, accessed September 28, 2010, www.hausvater.org/about.

and civil government, and vice versa; similarly, what strengthens the family ultimately will improve society and civil government. It is not that any of this happens without God, but rather that God has so ordained human nature that it must happen in this manner. Just as the law of gravity demands respect, so also injury within God's creation cannot be avoided unless the natural law of the family receives due attention. Indeed, God has so engraved the family into human nature that even the Church does not transcend, but rather rests upon and sanctifies, the natural family.

NATURAL LAW: THE CREATOR'S DESIGN FOR HUMAN NATURE

Natural law is not some mystical expertise available only to an elite class of philosophers. Nor is it something that common people cannot understand until a church hierarchy expounds it for them. "When [God] created man," explained the English jurist William Blackstone, "he laid down certain immutable laws of human nature . . . and gave him also the faculty of reason to discover the purport of those laws."[3] We cry when the family dog gets hit by a car, but we would have cried much harder if it had been our child, and upon reflection we find good reason to make such a distinction. We thus grasp natural law by a faculty higher than instinct or intuition, lower than religious faith, and more enduring than political coercion[4]: we *reason* concerning the divine design imprinted upon our human nature and the purposeful actions and interactions that constitute a fulfillment of that objective nature.[5]

Throughout history and across cultures, prophets of natural law have repeated a simple ethic in simple words. In Mesopotamia, 2100 years before Christ, the Code of Ur-Nammu forbade robbery, adultery, and

---

3. William Blackstone, *Commentaries on the Laws of England,* 4 vols. (Oxford: Clarendon, 1765–1769), 1:39.

4. David F. Forte, "The Natural Law Movement," in *Natural Law and Contemporary Public Policy* (Washington, DC: Georgetown University Press, 1998), 3–9.

5. For a schematization of natural law theory in comparison with other prevalent moral philosophies, past and present, see Ryan C. MacPherson, "Teaching Objective Morality to a Postmodern Audience," in *Here We Stand: A Confessional Christian Study of Worldviews,* ed. Curtis A. Jahn (Milwaukee: Northwestern, 2010), 127–75.

perjury.[6] In China, ca. 500 BC, Confucius advised, "What you do not like done to yourself, do not do to others."[7] In ancient Greece, the followers of Hippocrates vowed, "First, do no harm." In Judea, ca. AD 30, Christ taught, "As you wish that others would do to you, so do to them" (Luke 6:31). In sixteenth-century Saxony, Luther instructed, "We should fear and love God, so that we do no bodily harm to our neighbor, but help and befriend him in every need" (Small Catechism). In eighteenth-century Prussia, Immanuel Kant philosophized more esoterically, "Act so as to treat man, in your own person as well as in that of anyone else, always as an end, never merely as a means."[8] (Or, to phrase it in a more colloquial form: "I feel used. That just isn't right.") A common moral thread is stitched throughout the fabric of every society: children in all cultures learn to take turns, to share, and to say nice things about each other.

Every soul possesses the natural law; some of them happen to have explained it with clarity and precision. Thomas Aquinas (1225–1274), the great synthesizer of the pagan philosopher Aristotle (384–322 BC) with the Church Father St. Augustine (AD 354–430), defined natural morality as "the same for all, both as to rectitude and as to knowledge."[9] By "same . . . as to rectitude," he meant that the distinction between good and evil as it applies in one culture must also identically apply to all cultures. By "same . . . as to knowledge," he meant that just as people in one historical circumstance can know the difference between right and wrong, so also can people in other historical circumstances. That does not mean everyone can know it *perfectly* well, but simply that everyone can in principle know it *equally* well. Everyone can, for example, recognize at least the basic principles of ethics, such as the Golden Rule, which was quoted previously in its various cultural manifestations, or the Pauline Principle that it is immoral to "do evil that good may come" (Romans 3:8; cf. the secular colloquialism, "the ends don't justify the means").

---

6.   J. J. Finkelstein, "The Laws of Ur-Nammu," *Journal of Cuneiform Studies* 22, nos. 3–4 (1968–1969): 66–82.

7.   *The Analects of Confucius*, Book 15, http://ebooks.adelaide.edu.au/c/confucius/c748a/book15.html.

8.   Immanuel Kant, *Metaphysical Foundations of Morals* (1785), trans. Carl J. Friedrich, in *The Philosophy of Kant: Immanuel Kant's Moral and Political Writings*, ed. Carl J. Friedrich (New York: The Modern Library, 1993), 154–229, at 195.

9.   Thomas Aquinas, *Summa Theologica*, First Part of the Second Part, quest. 94, art. 4, http://www.newadvent.org/summa/2094.htm.

For Aristotle and Aquinas, natural law referred specifically to a set of responsibilities that one person owed to another; by the time of the American Revolution, however, the emphasis had shifted from *responsibilities* to *rights*.[10] Natural rights entitled each person to receive (or be protected from receiving) good (or harm) from others. At one level, the two conceptions differ only in phrasing, because *my responsibility* to preserve your life is *your right* to life that you claim against me. On another level, however, the concept of natural rights has proven to be more malleable than the concept of natural responsibilities, and that malleability has permitted people to drift considerably off course. Skewed by selfish inclinations, the human mind easily confuses an interest for an entitlement, a wish for a right. A philosophical sleight of hand leads from responsibilities through rights to privileges, sometimes ending at something that lacks even the goodness expected of a mere privilege. For example, contemporary opponents of the natural family clamor for the "rights" to sodomize their "lovers," to receive the trophy of children, and to have the public confer upon them the honor of "marriage"—all of this while defenders of tradition fail to speak adequately about the natural responsibilities that bind husbands and wives uniquely to one another, to their offspring, and to the society that their union and its fruit establish.

This essay seeks to articulate the natural law of the family particularly by appealing to human nature, together with its faculties of reason and conscience, to identify the set of relationships, responsibilities, and rights that naturally and uniquely cohere as the family. The notion of natural law employed here is broadly consistent with, even if not specifically identical to, similar expressions by St. Paul (Romans 1:20, 2:14–15), Thomas

---

10. James McClellan, *Liberty, Order, and Justice: An Introduction to the Constitutional Principles of American Government,* 3d ed. (Indianapolis: Liberty Fund, 2000), 126–30.

Aquinas,[11] Martin Luther,[12] Philip Melanchthon, Martin Chemnitz,[13] William Blackstone,[14] Thomas Jefferson,[15] Abraham Lincoln,[16] and Martin Luther King, Jr.[17] Some of these influential thinkers held widely divergent views on several matters of great importance, foremost among those being the nature and work of Jesus Christ. Nonetheless, their broadly shared consensus concerning natural law demonstrates the manner in which natural law generally transcends theological particulars.[18]

---

11.   Thomas Aquinas, *Summa Theologica*, First Part of the Second Part, quest. 90–108.

12.   Luther's "view of natural law did not differ substantially from that of St. Thomas Aquinas and other Roman Catholic theologians; however, he placed adherence to natural law more in the conscience than in the intellect." John Eidsmoe, "A Look at Law through Lutheran Lenses," in *Here We Stand: A Confessional Christian Study of Worldviews*, ed. Curtis A. Jahn (Milwaukee: Northwestern, 2010), 79–125, at 86. Natural law permeates the writings of Martin Luther and receives systematic treatment in "How Christians Should Regard Moses," trans. and ed. by E. Theodore Bachmann, *Luther's Works: Word and Sacrament I*, vol. 35 (Philadelphia: Muhlenberg, 1960), 161–74. More than other natural lawyers, Luther has emphasized the doctrine of vocation as a means for specifying the content of the natural law. Gifford Grobien, "A Lutheran Understanding of Natural Law in the Three Estates," *Concordia Theological Quarterly* 73 (2009): 211–29.

13.   Martin Chemnitz, "Promulgation of the Decalog," in *Loci Theologici*, trans. by J. A. O. Preus (St. Louis: Concordia, 1989), 2:352–55, containing at p. 355 an extended quotation from the *Loci* of Philip Melanchthon.

14.   Blackstone, *Commentaries*, 38–43.

15.   Thomas Jefferson, "Declaration of Independence," "A Bill for Establishing Religious Freedom," and "Notes on the State of Virginia," in *The Political Writings of Thomas Jefferson*, ed. by Merrill D. Peterson (n.p.: Thomas Jefferson Memorial Foundation, 1993), 25–29, 42–44 and 51–61, esp. 59–61.

16.   Abraham Lincoln, "A House Divided," June 16, 1858, www.americanrhetoric .com/speeches/abrahamlincolnhousedivided.htm; Harold Holzer, ed., *The Lincoln–Douglas Debates: The First Complete, Unexpurgated Text* (New York: Harper Perennial, 1994).

17.   Martin Luther King, Jr., "Letter from a Birmingham Jail," April 16, 1963, http:// www.africa.upenn.edu/Articles_Gen/Letter_Birmingham.html, accessed September 28, 2010.

18.   Indeed, even present-day agnostic philosopher Russ Shafer-Landau, in his book *Whatever Happened to Good and Evil?*, defends quite strongly one of natural law's central claims, namely, "Certain things are right, and others are wrong; some good, some evil; and we don't have the final say on what they are. There are moral standards not of our own making." Though rejecting theism, he at least acknowledges that the task of ethics is to "correctly describe the nature of the moral world." Russ Shafer-Landau, *Whatever Happened to Good and Evil?* (Oxford: Oxford University Press, 2004), 7, 90. In other words, *moral truth*—and, despite widespread skepticism in this postmodern age, yes, there is such a thing—*moral truth is embedded in nature itself*. Shafer-Landau says it evolved there on its own, whereas natural law theorists say God designed nature that way.

The Family: The Cradle of Human Nature

Human nature is irreducibly social. "No man is an island," wrote the seventeenth-century literary genius John Donne.[19] "It is not good that the man should be alone," spoke God in the most widely circulated creation narrative ever recorded (Genesis 2:18). Even in a culture so dedicated to personal autonomy as early twenty-first century America, frank recognition of the fundamental human need for interpersonal connectivity manifests itself in the popularity of Facebook, MySpace, and Twitter, or the surrogate lifestyles that viewers seek through reality television. People need people. And so it must be; we are all born that way.

A child comes into this world already in the context of a relationship with his or her mother. The mother, in turn, had (and perhaps still has) a relationship with the child's father. The biological facts of conception and birth correspond closely with the myriad ways in which a child remains in need of parental care after birth: physically, emotionally, intellectually, spiritually—no matter how one subdivides and categorizes human nature, it all amounts to a *total* dependence by the child upon the parents. "The new father takes on the protection of the new mother in her time of vulnerability and dependence. A happiness follows the trial of childbirth as the new mother nurses her baby."[20] Nature calls upon the two parents' distinctively male and female qualities for raising their offspring. "Both sexes are needed to raise the child, because the female is better designed for nurture and the male for protection and discipline; both are needed to teach the child, because every young one needs a model of his own sex as well as the other."[21]

We thus realize our full humanity in conjunction with others. In maturity, a man and woman discover the mystery of themselves by uniting in a potentially procreative manner. As mother and child co-experience gestation, parturition, and lactation, they continually rediscover who they are. As husband provides for and protects the more vulnerable members of his family, he, too, realizes his purpose in life. As father and mother share

---

19. John Donne, *Devotions upon Emergent Occasions* (1624), Meditation XVII, accessed September 28, 2010, http://www.ccel.org/ccel/donne/devotions.iv.iii.xvii.i.html.

20. Allan C. Carlson and Paul T. Mero, *The Natural Family: A Manifesto* (Dallas: Spence, 2007), 5.

21. J. Budziszewski, *What We Can't Not Know: A Guide* (Dallas: Spence, 2003), 36.

in childrearing responsibilities, they find out what they were designed for, even as they struggle to conform to that high standard. As children take cues from their progenitors to learn what it means to grow from a boy or a girl into a man or a woman, they prepare to complete the cycle, both by returning a favor to their parents in old age and by coupling with a suitable partner to bear the next generation. Just as two persons became one flesh in the beginning, so also each person has an individual identity that nonetheless cannot be removed from its social foundations, nor escape its social responsibilities.

HUMAN PERSONHOOD: FAMILIAL, NOT INDIVIDUAL OR STATIST

A compelling case could be made that human personhood is fundamentally familial, not individual or statist. Political philosophers in the modern West, by contrast, have generally erred toward one of two extremes: either individualism or else statism. As a result, a third option too often has been overlooked—namely, that the family is both the proper foundation of human society and the formative reality of human personhood.

Individualism, a tradition extrapolating the writings of John Locke (1632–1704), views each person as a social atom—complete in him- or herself, irreducibly fundamental, and thus constitutive of all social institutions. Accordingly, each person, *qua* individual, has an inalienable right to life, to liberty, and to property. Freely associating individuals may by social contract form corporations or even whole civil governments; they become bound by the authority of these institutions only insofar as they consent to surrender a degree of their personal autonomy in order to receive the expected benefits of the consensually formed organization. From such thinking arose the principle of popular sovereignty that animated the American Revolution.[22] A correlate commitment to equality requires that each individual has identical and interchangeable claims not

22. Edmund S. Morgan, *Inventing the People: The Rise of Popular Sovereignty in England and America* (New York: W. W. Norton and Company, 1988), esp. 143; Carl Becker, "The Natural Rights Philosophy," excerpted from *The Declaration of Independence: A Study in the History of Political Ideas,* in *What Did the Declaration Declare?*, ed. Joseph J. Ellis (Boston: Bedford/St. Martin's, 1999), 43–64.

only to those fundamental rights but also to basic social goods. When actual access to those goods is made contingent upon personal merit toward acquiring them, individualism spawns *laissez faire* capitalism in the economic sphere and libertarianism in the political sphere.[23] These ideals characterize a pervasive viewpoint in the political economy of the modern West.

An alternative perspective, apparently (though perhaps not very substantially) quite different than individualism, is statism. Karl Marx's (1818–1883) criticisms of capitalism have inspired much of this alternative perspective. In this tradition, the state, rather than the individual, becomes the fundamental unit of society, with the promise that the state will ensure equitable access by all individuals to scarce social goods. In contradistinction to the capitalist, the Marxist has removed the criterion of merit, dismissing it as propaganda by which the rich justify their hoarding of wealth from the poor. Even so, the Marxist retains a commitment to equality, and in fact promotes it more thoroughly, insisting not merely upon equal access to social goods, but also equal attainment.[24] The Marxist state, as distributor of goods, ensures *substantive* equality for all members of society, whereas the capitalist state, as adjudicator between competitors, ensures only *procedural* equality among those striving to improve their lives.[25]

The past two centuries have witnessed a series of debates—manifested by both political rhetoric and military might—between the individualist and statist models of human nature. Still, the two positions share much common ground, leading in recent decades to a mutual hostility toward the natural family. Both the libertarian and the statist regard all persons as equal individuals, *in principle* identical and interchangeable as to their rights and responsibilities. The statist goes two steps further: first, claiming all persons as equal (construed to mean identical and

23. The classic justification for *laissez faire* capitalism may be found in Adam Smith, *An Inquiry into the Nature and Causes of the Wealth of Nations*, 2 vols. (1776; rpt., Indianapolis: Liberty Fund, 1981).

24. Karl Marx and Frederick Engels, "Manifesto of the Communist Party," in *The Marx-Engels Reader*, ed. Robert C. Tucker, 2d ed. (New York: W. W. Norton, 1978), 469–500; Kelly James Clark and Anne Poortenga, *The Story of Ethics: Fulfilling Our Human Nature* (Upper Saddle River, NJ: Pearson, 2003), 81–85.

25. Historical examples in twentieth-century America include "affirmative action" with its pledge of "equality of result." Michael Les Benedict, *The Blessings of Liberty: A Concise History of the Constitution of the United* States, 2d ed. (Boston: Houghton Mifflin, 2006), 319–21.

interchangeable) *in practice*; and, second, attempting to materialize this claim by empowering the state to redistribute social goods until substantive equality is achieved and maintained. Although the libertarian stops short of—indeed, protests against—especially that latter step, the capitalist-statist consensus as to human equality already has denied one of the natural family's core reasons for existence: the just management of radical inequality inherent in human nature.

Human personhood, in fact, is neither strictly individual nor strictly collective. It is, rather, a mystery mediating between and transcending beyond those two false conceptions. The history of the word *person* (*persona* in Latin) reflects this mystery. The Church Fathers' efforts to express both the unity and multiplicity of God, in whose image all natural lawyers recognize humanity was created, solidified the now-familiar meaning of "person," a term previously denoting theatrical stage roles. At a loss to express, in extant theological terminology, the distinct and complementary roles of the Father, the Son, and the Holy Spirit while still affirming their equal natures as God, Tertullian (c. 160–220) became the first to apply the words *Trinity*, *persons*, and *substance* to the Godhead.[26] All of this relates directly to human nature and the nature of human families, for Scripture indicates that human fatherhood derives its divinely ordained station from the Fatherhood of God. Ephesians 3:14–15 states, "For this reason I bow my knees before the Father, from whom every family in heaven and on earth is named."

The Trinitarian analogy to human personhood also goes deeper. Special revelation (admittedly, the discussion has now gone beyond natural law) teaches that the relationships between the Father and the Son and between the Son and the Church provide models for understanding human relationships within the family. The Father-Son relation elucidates not merely the parent-child relation, but, more deeply, the husband-wife relation. The New Testament epistles consistently teach that wives are to respect and submit to their husbands (Ephesians 5:22–24; Colossians 3:18; Titus 2:3–5; 1 Peter 3:1–6). Such submission indicates that "the head of a wife is her husband" (1 Corinthians 11:3). Two qualifiers must immediately be added, however, lest the husband's headship be misconstrued. First, the same verse concludes by stating also that

---

26. Jonathan Hill, *The History of Christian Thought: The Fascinating Story of the Great Christian Thinkers and How They Helped Shape the World as We Know It Today* (Downers Grove, IL: InterVarsity, 2003), 37.

"the head of Christ is God." Thus, the Son's submission to the Father provides a model for the wife's submission to her husband. Such submission in no way suggests inferiority, for Christ possesses "the whole fullness of deity" (Colossians 2:9). Likewise, the wife shares fully in the humanity of her husband. Unlike the animals, Eve uniquely was "a helper fit for" Adam (Genesis 2:18). Second, Christ's headship of the Church—characterized by self-giving, self-sacrificing love—provides another model for understanding marital union. A head does not exercise dominion over the body for the body's detriment, but for its good. The head and the body have distinct and complementary roles; they are not identical or interchangeable. Nevertheless, they do not seek to be ranked one higher than the other, for they participate as cooperative members of a whole being (Ephesians 5:25–33).[27]

Contrary to the radical egalitarianism espoused—though in different ways—by both the capitalist and the statist, the natural lawyer of the family recognizes that individuals are not identical or interchangeable, particularly not in the family. A man is not a woman. A mother is not a child. A child is not his own father. Though equal partakers of humanity as to its substance, the family members are radically unequal as to their persons. They are neither identical nor interchangeable, but different, and intractably so. Their roles within the family *must* reflect such difference—not in the sense of *physical necessity* (as in, "water *must* boil at 212°F"), but rather in the sense of *moral obligation*. Although free will permits a person to act contrary to human nature—and contrary to the nature of the family—it does not permit such action to occur without adverse consequences. Free will also permits a driver to fill the gas tank with water instead of fuel, but the engine's design means that it will sputter, if it runs at all; similarly, for human nature and its design.

---

27. For further suggestions of understanding the family and the Church as analogues to the Holy Trinity, see Scott Hahn and Leon J. Suprenant, Jr., eds., *Catholic for a Reason: Scripture and the Mystery of the Family of God* (Steubenville, OH: Emmaus Road, 1998), 1–14.

THE NATURAL LAW OF THE FAMILY:
CONTEMPORARY APPLICATIONS

Rational analysis readily reveals that sexual intercourse between a man and a woman generally leads to babies[28]; that babies need caregivers; that a woman carrying her child within her womb is the best person suited for nourishing the child at her breasts after birth; and that the man whose union with her conceived that child has a responsibility toward her during the vulnerable times of pregnancy, childbirth, and infant nourishment—if not also longer. His responsibility toward her expands naturally to include a responsibility toward his child that she bears. From sexual union, therefore, emerge the natural duties of motherhood and fatherhood. The natural duty of spousal commitment correspondingly intensifies amid the awe and responsibility of procreation.[29] Just as a child thereby owes his or her existence to the parents, so also children have a natural duty to honor their fathers and their mothers. This, in brief, is the natural law of the family.

Any appropriate alternative must take the form of an effort to restore as best as possible the natural relationships among man, woman, and child. If a woman's husband dies prematurely, she understandably seeks a replacement. If a child suffers abuse by one or both parents, other people properly intervene to correct the situation and, if no correction is forthcoming, to place the child in the care of surrogates who will parent more adequately. If a woman becomes unfaithful to her husband, opening her womb to the potential offspring of a foreign man and exposing her body to whatever diseases this outsider may carry, then the husband may think

---

28. "Generally" does not here mean that the majority of instances of *coitus* result in pregnancy, for it is common knowledge that a woman is fertile for less than one week per month. Rather, "generally" indicates that over time pregnancy typically results from repeated instances of *coitus*. This sense of "generally" is in keeping with the natural design of the one-flesh union and consistent also with the prevailing medical standard that a clinical diagnosis of "infertility" applies when a couple does not conceive after twelve months of noncontraceptive intercourse.

29. Biological insights into the family include the discovery that the hormone oxytocin chemically bonds a man and woman to each other during intercourse and a woman to her child during lactation. The man and woman experience a greater cumulative hormone release when they regularly copulate with one another, rather than with multiple partners. Walt Larimore and Barb Larimore, *His Brain, Her Brain: How Divinely Designed Differences Can Strengthen Your Marriage* (Grand Rapids: Zondervan, 2007), 53.

it proper to dismiss her. On the other hand, his love also might win her back through forgiveness, thereby preserving not only his own bond with her, but also their joint connection to their current and future offspring.

At this point, opportunistic rationalizations begin to suggest a diversity of other possibilities. Now the game has new rules, involving projections into the future as to likely outcomes of possible actions—all speculated with a willingness to satisfy some persons' interests at the expense others', if only it can be shown that the interests of the "some" justifiably outweigh those of the "others."[30]

---

30. The classic statement of utilitarian ethics may be found in John Stuart Mill, *Utilitarianism* (1863). Utilitarian reasoning triumphed in the Progressive Era of the early twentieth century, when social reformers in both the United States and Europe abandoned the Western tradition of seeking timeless principles (such as natural law) and turned instead to contemporary conclusions derived from empirical science. Thus, what worked now (or could be expected to work in the future) took priority over what, in the abstract, had long been seen as good or just. Larry Schweikart and Michael Allen, *A Patriot's History of the United States: From Columbus's Great Discovery to the War on Terror* (New York: Sentinel, 2004), chs. 13–16. As society embraced moral relativism, the social order itself became diversified, as manifested, for example, in the declining rates of marriage and marital procreation and the increasing rates of divorce and extra-marital procreation during the mid century as well as the growing acceptance of same-sex coupling and childrearing by the turn of the century. Precisely because the ensuing social chaos makes long-range implications more difficult to project, the advantages of objective morality over its relativist competitors no longer seem so obvious. This moral confusion then lends further credence to the relativistic tenets that occasioned it, creating a self-validating cycle. Richard T. Gill, *Posterity Lost: Progress, Ideology, and the Decline of the American Family*, with a foreword by James Q. Wilson (London: Rowman and Littlefield, 1997), esp. 269.

   A substantial body of secular scholarship finds strong empirical support for the superiority of the natural family in raising children who develop into successful adults—whether measured in terms of educational attainment, career advancement, familial satisfaction, or avoidance of criminal and other dangerous behaviors. See Sara McLanaham and Gary Sandefur, *Growing Up with a Single Parent: What Hurts, What Helps* (Cambridge, MA: Harvard University Press, 1994); David Popenoe, *Life without Father: Compelling New Evidence that Fatherhood and Marriage Are Indispensable for the Good of Children and Society* (New York: The Free Press, 1996); Barbara Dafoe Whitehead, *The Divorce Culture: Rethinking Our Commitments to Marriage and Family* (New York: Vintage, 1996); David Popenoe, Jean Bethke Elshtain, and David Blankenhorn, eds., *Promises to Keep: Decline and Renewal of Marriage in America* (Lanham, MD: Rowman and Littlefield, 1996); Alan J. Hawkins, Lynn D. Wardle, and David Orgon Coolidge, eds., *Revitalizing the Institution of Marriage for the Twenty-first Century: An Agenda for Strengthening Marriage*, with a foreword by Linda J. Waite (Westport, CT: Praeger, 2002); and ongoing research posted by The National Marriage Project, http://www.virginia.edu/marriageproject (accessed September 28, 2010).

What if, for example, two men wish to be "married" and to adopt children? What if, indeed, they can be shown to be otherwise well qualified as parents—arguably better qualified than the father or mother in some dysfunctional natural family? What if a woman has found her husband to be unreliable, disinterested, and possibly destructive? Why should a socially conditioned allegiance to an ethical norm called "marriage" require her to remain in a situation that so obviously interferes with her pursuit of happiness? Indeed, does not the preservation of "traditional marriage" perpetuate the exploitation of women and children by guileful men? The liberal and the statist have each offered replies in keeping with the distinctive logics of their disparate philosophies. Despite their self-appraisals as political opponents, their reforms have merged into a common course leading away from the natural family and toward a post-family regime of sodomitical uncivilization.

For libertarians, it has proceeded in this way. First, the principle of personal autonomy broke away from its Enlightenment moorings. For example, the philosopher Immanuel Kant maintained that an individual's duty toward other rational beings grounded his liberty from their unnatural coercion of his will.[31] With duty depreciated and desire assuming its place, autonomy drifted from civility toward chaos. Next, a commitment to human equality led, first, to an equal exercise of personal choice by women as by men and, eventually, to a supra-equal exercise of choice by women. Here the events in American history run largely parallel to those in other nations. In 1920, the Nineteenth Amendment to the U.S. Constitution extended the privilege of voting to women. The 1964 Civil Rights Act mandated equal employment conditions and equal access to public accommodations not only for people of all races, religions, and national origins, but also for both sexes. With sexual distinctions now prohibited in the political and economic spheres, the family—from which and for which those spheres had come to exist—could not remain unaffected. In 1969, California became the first state to enact no-fault divorce legislation, with all other states doing so within the twenty years following. No-fault reform removed state mandates that

---

31. For Kant, autonomy had more to do with "I ought" than "I want," but contemporary medical ethics (perhaps the one area of postmodern life that still pays lip service to Kant) has construed personal autonomy in terms of individual desires. R. S. Downie and Jane McNaughton, *Bioethics and the Humanities: Attitudes and Perceptions* (Cavendish, UK: Routledge, 2007), 42–44.

a husband and wife remain married until just cause for their separation could be demonstrated. It also eradicated gender-specific standards as to post-marital responsibilities for supporting children and ex-spouses. The result, however, was not the promised equality, but rather a shifting of the welfare burden toward married men, a deteriorating socioeconomic status for divorced women and their virtually orphaned children, and, simultaneously, a superior political power for women regardless of their marital status.[32] In 1992, the Supreme Court enshrined the supremacy of a woman's personal choice into case law in *Planned Parenthood v. Casey*: "At the heart of liberty is the right to define one's own concept of existence, of meaning, of the universe, and of the mystery of human life."[33] No man—not the woman's husband nor (if different) the father—may choose between the life and death of their unborn child; she alone wields that power.

What first served to justify abortion on demand soon became the foundation for legalizing sodomy when the high court applied the *Casey* principle in *Lawrence v. Texas* (2003). The Massachusetts Supreme Judicial Court invoked both *Lawrence* and *Casey* when concluding, "Whether and whom to marry, how to express sexual intimacy, and whether and how to establish a family—these are among the most basic of every individual's liberty and due process rights."[34] From such premises, the conclusion necessarily followed: "We construe civil marriage to mean the voluntary union of two persons as spouses, to the exclusion of all others," regardless of whether the individuals be of the same or of opposite sexes.[35] Hence, the libertarian tradition extrapolated from the political philosophy of John Locke culminates in the legalization of same-sex "marriage."

Meanwhile, so does the socialist tradition drawn from the writings of Karl Marx. In part, statism parasitically achieves its goal precisely because individualism has attained sweeping political influence. Ironically, as

---

32. Lenore J. Weitzman, *The Divorce Revolution: The Unexpected Social and Economic Consequences for Women and Children in America* (New York: The Free Press, 1987); Stephen Baskerville, "Fathers into Felons: No-Fault Divorce Has Turned a Bastion of Private Life into a Colony of the State," *American Conservative*, May 2005, www.amconmag.com, accessed September 28, 2010; David G. Schramm, "Counting the Cost of Divorce: What Those Who Know Better Rarely Acknowledge," *The Family in America: A Journal of Public Policy* 23, no. 3 (2009): 55–64.

33. *Planned Parenthood v. Casey*, 505 U.S. 833, 851 (1992).

34. *Lawrence v. Texas*, 539 U.S. 1, 13 (2003), quoting the "mystery" doctrine of *Planned Parenthood v. Casey* and applying it to legitimatize consensual sodomy.

35. *Goodridge v. Dept. of Public of Health*, 440 Mass. 309, 329, 434 (2003).

autonomy has drifted from civility toward chaos, individualism occasioned a need for the regulatory state that the libertarian loathes. Moreover, the Marxist proclivity toward radical egalitarianism intensifies—even as it claims to socialize—the atomistic individualism espoused by the libertarian. For Marx, any hint of hierarchy—in the state, in the market, in the family—must yield to egalitarianism, the principle that individuals have equal value with one another as manifested by their identical and interchangeable roles. Therefore, if men vote, women should vote, too. When applied to a previously capitalist society, regulatory egalitarianism removes any competitive advantage for a corporation that offers wages sufficient for either a man or a woman to support a family alone; thus, the "family wage" reduces to an individualist's "living wage," and the state subsidizes equal educational opportunities for the men and women whom it socializes to expect an equal economic contribution from any potential spouse.

State-funded access to contraception and abortion reduces the biological distinctions between men and women, even as social reforms obliterate their political and economic distinctions. Marriage becomes an equal partnership between two persons who publicly have become identical and interchangeable. To ensure equal opportunity and equitable attainment of social goods, the state subsidizes breadwinning (unemployment benefits and job training), bread baking (food stamps), and childrearing (day care and schooling, from age six weeks through college). Bereft of its former functions (procreation, childrearing, and domestic economic productivity), marriage remains a convenient mechanism for sharing assets (including employment benefits, such as health insurance), transferring decision-making between adults, providing custodianship for children, and distributing accumulated wealth upon one's death—all without the formal legal requirements of forming a corporation, preparing a power of attorney, designating a legal guardian, or writing out a will.[36] The statist's commitment to egalitarianism necessitates, therefore, that persons who

---

36. Courts ruling in favor of same-sex "marriage" have defined the marital union exclusively in terms of economic and legal dimensions of marriage, with explicit denial that procreation and sexual complementarity intrinsically belong to marriage or rightfully claim unique recognition by the state vis-à-vis same-sex alternatives. *Goodridge v. Dept. of Public of Health,* 440 Mass. 309 (2003); *Varnum v. Brien,* 763 N.W.2d 862 (Iowa 2009).

are married must have the right to cease to be so, and those who are not married must have the right to become so.[37]

Same-sex "marriage" arrives as the jurisprudentially obvious counterpart to no-fault divorce: if any two people may cease to be married, simply because one or both so choose, then why shouldn't any two persons become married, as a mere exercise of preference? But just as with no-fault divorce, so also with same-sex "marriage"—its establishment and preservation require greater, not less, state regulation. To guarantee that some individuals can be married as husband and husband, or as wife and wife, requires that all members of society be coerced to recognize them as "married." The resulting bureaucracy encroaches not only upon the natural family, but also upon the personal liberties that the family once protected.[38] So we find, in the wake of those reforms championed by individualists and statists alike, a situation no better than the social ills they sought to correct, and by most measures, a situation that has become worse. To minds well-tuned to the natural law of the family, the explanation is obvious: "Egalitarian policies that simply ignore natural sexual differentiation as it relates to the well-being of the institution of the family may be as socially harmful as older inegalitarian policies that unjustly curtailed employment [or other] opportunities for women."[39]

The natural family, as a prepolitical institution from which society originates and in which human persons spontaneously take form, offers what political philosophers have sought, and failed, to find elsewhere. Nowhere but the natural family is human difference more starkly appar-

---

37. The preceding paragraphs offer but a rough outline as to how individualism and statism have both challenged the natural family during the period of modern industrialization and its postmodern aftermath. For further evidence, refer to the arguments advanced by, and the sources cited in Nancy Pearcey, *Total Truth: Liberating Christianity from Its Cultural Captivity*, with a foreword by Phillip E. Johnson (Wheaton, IL: Crossway, 2008), chap. 12; Carlson and Mero, *The Natural Family;* and, Andrew J. Cherlin, *The Marriage-Go-Round: The State of Marriage and the Family in America Today* (New York: Alfred A. Knopf, 2009).

38. See, for example, the list of statutory offenses in Canada associated with an unwillingness to accept and promote homosexuality. Hans C. Clausen, "The 'Privilege of Speech' in a 'Pleasantly Authoritarian Country': How Canada's Judiciary Allowed Laws Proscribing Discourse Critical of Homosexuality to Trump Free Speech and Religious Liberty," *Vanderbilt Journal of Transnational Law* 38 (2005): 443–504.

39. Christopher Wolfe, "Thomistic Natural Law and the American Natural Law Tradition," in *St. Thomas Aquinas and the Natural Law Tradition: Contemporary Perspectives*, ed. John Goyette, Mark S. Latkovic, and Richard S. Myers (Washington, DC: Catholic University of America Press, 2004), 197–228, at 210–11.

ent. Nowhere but the natural family is hierarchy more permanently embedded. And yet, nowhere but the natural family are the weak more securely protected, the hungry more efficiently fed, or the wealthy more compassionately directed to the needs of others. Nor can the individual, the corporation, or the state provide a better foundation for human flourishing, though each properly serves the family in unique ways. Natural law reveals these facts, as well as the failures of each person to conform to nature's divine imprint. Natural law also reveals the tragedy that results when derivative institutions seek to replace or suppress, rather than restore and supplement, the natural family.

CONCLUSION

When an earthquake struck Kourion in AD 365, a woman nurtured her child. Her husband sought to protect both her and the baby. None of them could have survived. The same quake wreaked havoc on the Alexandrian harbor to the south. To the northwest, tidal waves drove Mediterranean ships several miles inward of the Peloponnesian coast. The natural family knows no escape from death. Overcoming death requires divine intervention. This lesson, too, has been unearthed at Kourion:

> Lying near them was a small bronze ring, probably worn by the woman, inscribed with the first two letters of Jesus Christ's name in Greek, *chi* and *rho* (for Christos), plus the letters *alpha* and *omega*, signifying the beginning and the end.[40]

The young family likely knew how Christianity had first come to their island through the ministries of the converts who scattered after Stephen's martyrdom in Jerusalem, and through John as well as Paul, Barnabas, and Mark (Acts 11:19, 13:4, 15:39). It was Paul who later would write, "Husbands [should] love your wives, as Christ loved the church and gave Himself up for her . . . husbands should love their wives as their own bodies . . . let each one of you love his wife as himself" (Ephesians 5:25, 28, 33). To Titus, who served the church on the nearby island of Crete, Paul had written, "Older women . . . are to teach what is good, and so train the young women to love their husbands and children" (Titus 2:3–4). These exhortations fit the theological category called "sanctifica-

---

40. Soren, "Death at Kourion," 54.

tion," supplying concrete examples of what it means to be a new creation in Christ Jesus, one who strives to be holy even as Christ is holy.

This new creation, of course, is a restoration of the original creation: God's design for human nature, the source of natural law. To become fully human is to be redeemed by Christ's forgiving love and regenerated once more in God's holy image. The new life in Christ envisioned by the New Testament is, therefore, the highest expression of natural law. Even pagans retain a vestige of this truth, written in their hearts, discernible to a certain degree by human reason (Romans 2:14–15). That is why the excavation at Kourion speaks to a universal audience.

12

Natural Science, Natural Rights, and Natural Law:
Abortion in Historical Perspective

Korey D. Maas

The universal prohibition of homicide in the positive law, whether oral or written, of the world's societies is one of the most immediately obvious indications that such a proscription might in fact transcend these culturally conditioned legal codes and derive instead from a universal and implicitly recognized natural law. Similarly, though that which definitively constitutes homicide in positive law might be variously nuanced at different times and in different places, any acknowledgment of natural law's reality recognizes the prohibition of murder as one of its most fundamental tenets. The contemporary debate concerning abortion, as is well-known, quite rightly and almost entirely revolves around the question of whether elective abortion is to be deemed the moral and legal equivalent of homicide. Of course, positive law in much of the contemporary Western world does not so deem it. Moreover, and perhaps more significantly, such an equation was virtually unknown in the Western world before the rise of Christianity. That abortion was not only tolerated, but often advocated as an obvious good throughout Greco-Roman antiquity is a well-established fact;[1] indeed, this is one of the facts upon which the U.S. Supreme Court's decision in *Roe v. Wade* was predicated.[2] Equally well established, however, is that the ancient Greeks and Romans were the first to formulate coherently the very concept of natural law.[3] In this historical light, any argument that antipathy to abortion is itself a precept of natural law appears immediately to be undermined. The evident lack of anything close to a universal historical consensus on the morality of abortion—in stark contrast to incest, homicide, and even suicide, for example, which have met with condemnation across nearly all cultural boundaries—seems strongly to suggest that objections to the practice of abortion are not grounded in any moral knowledge that is natural to, and thereby accessible to, all rational individuals.

Yet another historical factor seems only to strengthen this view. As implied previously, consistent moral opposition to abortion in the West arose only in tandem with the rise of Christianity to public prominence. As a result, the abortion advocate might appear justified in positing that anti-abortion sentiment is peculiar to Christianity. Perhaps understandably, but in some respects unfortunately, Christian apologists have occasionally adopted this interpretation of events in attempts to demonstrate the superiority of a morality grounded in special revelation rather than natural reason.[4] Though this conclusion is not entirely indefensible, it is by no means unproblematic. To concede that one can recognize abortion as a moral evil only if one first presupposes Scripture's divine inspira-

---

1. See, e.g., John M. Riddle, *Contraception and Abortion from the Ancient World to the Renaissance* (Cambridge: Harvard University Press, 1992), and Konstantinos Kapparis, *Abortion in the Ancient World* (London: Duckworth Press, 2002), as well as Michael J. Gorman, *Abortion and the Early Church* (Downers Grove, IL: InterVarsity Press, 1982).

2. See *Roe v. Wade*, 410 U.S. (1973), at 130–32.

3. For a concise overview, see J. Rufus Fears, "Natural Law: The Legacy of Greece and Rome," in *Common Truths: New Perspectives on Natural Law*, ed. Edward B. McLean (Wilmington, DE: ISI Books, 2000), 19–56.

4. See, e.g., Benjamin Wiker, *Moral Darwinism: How We Became Hedonists* (Downers Grove, IL: InterVarsity, 2002), 100.

tion is to imply, intentionally or otherwise, that there are no common principles by which common laws—laws applicable to all, even in a pluralistic society—can be established, and that, by further implication, any legal prohibition of abortion would be no more than a coercive imposition of "Christian morality" upon those who do not share the Christian faith. This reduction of antipathy to abortion to an article of faith, as such relevant only to those sharing the faith, would, in effect, legitimize trite pro-abortion slogans such as "Keep your rosaries off my ovaries."

The facile equation of moral objections to abortion with a uniquely Christian or biblical worldview is not only self-defeating as a rhetorical or political strategy, however; it is also in many respects simply inaccurate. While it is indeed the case that opposition to abortion only became widespread after the public establishment of the Christian religion, it is not the case that the practice remained entirely unopposed even in the pre-Christian West. To cite only a few notable examples, abortion was discouraged by Rome's first Emperor, Caesar Augustus, and even punished by the similarly pagan emperors Septimus Severus and Antoninus Caracalla.[5] The Stoic philosopher Musonius Rufus, in particular, and the philosophical school of Stoicism more generally, objected to it.[6] Some first-century physicians, interpreting the Hippocratic Oath as forbidding all abortions, refused to perform them.[7] The satirist Juvenal could bluntly describe the abortionist as one "paid to murder mankind in the womb."[8] The Roman poet Ovid, not otherwise given to moralizing, could be so harsh as to declare that "Who unborn infants first to slay invented, Deserved thereby with death to be tormented."[9] Similarly, despite polemical attempts to portray opposition to abortion as deriving only from dogmatic Christian convictions, this assumption is not borne out even by contemporary evidence. Hence, not only do organizations such as Lutherans for Life exist, but also Democrats for Life, Feminists for Life,

---

5.   See Justinian, *Digest*, 47.11, for the rescripts of Septimus and Antoninus, and 48.8.8 for the Roman jurist Ulpian's interpretation of the *Lex Cornelia* of Augustus as prohibiting abortion.

6.   See Musonius Rufus, *Discourse 15*.

7.   John T. Noonan, Jr., "An Almost Absolute Value in History," in *The Morality of Abortion: Legal and Historical Perspectives*, ed. John T. Noonan, Jr. (Cambridge: Harvard University Press, 1970), 5.

8.   Juvenal, *Satires*, 6.596–7, quoting the translation of G. G. Ramsay in *Juvenal and Perseus* (Cambridge: Harvard University Press, 1957), 133.

9.   Ovid, *Elegies*, 2.14, quoting the translation of Christopher Marlowe in *The Works of Christopher Marlowe*, ed. A. H. Bullen (London: John C. Nimmo, 1885), 3:164.

the Pro-Life Alliance of Gays and Lesbians, and even the Atheist and Agnostic Pro-Life League.[10]

That such a disparate assortment of ideologies can reach a similar conclusion regarding the moral status of abortion not only demonstrates that peculiar theological assumptions are not the only grounds for decrying abortion; it illustrates concomitantly and quite clearly that they need not be. If traditional Christians, classical pagans, and modern atheists—though operating with wildly divergent first principles, and consequently holding vastly different worldviews—can alike conclude that something iniquitous inheres in voluntary abortion, there appears some legitimate basis for suggesting that this conclusion transcends narrow cultural, political, or theological categories. As noted previously, however, the fact that antipathy to abortion, despite being evident across geographical, chronological, and philosophical lines, has never enjoyed anything close to universal consensus might suggest that such agreement as does exist is no more than accidental. For if this antipathy were rooted in natural law, should it not be shared by all who possess a common nature? Should not a moral truth, if it is natural and universal, therefore be naturally and universally recognized?

Though such rhetorical questions appear eminently reasonable on their face, they betray a categorical mistake with regard to the very terms comprising the phrase "natural law." With respect to the term *law*, it bears reiterating the obvious: a moral law, in contrast to a physical law, is essentially prescriptive rather than descriptive; it asserts what *ought* to be the case rather than what *is* the case. For example, to declare that natural law (or even positive law) prohibits murder is, of course, not the equivalent of declaring that murder does not happen. More to the point, it does not even preclude the possibility that some individuals—or, indeed, even substantial populations—might find murder morally unobjectionable, at least in certain instances. Instead, it says only that such people ought to recognize murder as immoral. And this ought to be recognized because comprehension of such a law is part of the common nature of the uniquely rational and moral species *homo sapiens*. This is not to say that it is biologically innate or instinctual as is sometimes erroneously inferred. The proponent of natural law does not suggest that one is born with a conscious knowledge of certain ethical propositions any more than one

---

10. See lutheransforlife.org; www.democratsforlife.org; www.feministsforlife.org; www.plagal.org; and godlessprolifers.org (all accessed September 28, 2010).

is born with the innate understanding that a triangle is a three-sided figure, the sum of the angles of which is 180 degrees. But, analogous to mathematical knowledge, once the individual terms of certain moral statements are properly understood, one naturally recognizes the truth of such statements; their self-evident verity cannot be denied.

Unless, that is, one willfully and contrary to one's own nature suppresses this knowledge of what by nature is recognized as true. The force of the previously stated rhetorical questions is blunted by the fact that natural law proponents have never denied that otherwise rational people are indeed capable of suppressing such natural knowledge. This admission is made most familiarly, perhaps, in St. Paul's charge against those "who by their unrighteousness suppress the truth" and subsequently "exchanged natural relations for those that are contrary to nature" (Romans 1:18, 26). Paul's own status as a Christian should not, however, obscure the fact that neither his recognition of natural law, nor his understanding that knowledge of its truth can be suppressed, are convictions peculiar to Christianity. Already in the century before Christ, for example, the Roman orator Cicero acknowledged the same, describing natural law as "right reason, conformable to nature, universal, unchangeable, eternal," and saying that whoever "obeys it not, flies from himself, and does violence to the very nature of man."[11] Such sentiment is entirely commonplace in the natural law tradition. Thus, Origen of Alexandria argues similarly in the early third century that the reality and validity of the natural law can indeed be denied, but that one can do so only by doing violence to one's own nature.[12] Origen's own teacher, Clement of Alexandria, had not only asserted the same, but, significantly, had done so in the very context of explaining why the practice of voluntary abortion is a transgression of the natural law. Clement explains that life is to be lived in observation of this law common to all human beings, but that those who induce abortion "abort at the same time their own human feelings," that is, do violence to their own natures as rational and moral beings.[13]

---

11. Cicero, *On the Republic* [*On the Commonwealth*], 3.22, quoting the translation of Francis Barham in *The Political Works of Marcus Tullius Cicero* (London: Edmund Spettique, 1841), 1:270.

12. Origen of Alexandria, *Against Celsus*, 5.40.

13. Clement of Alexandria, *The Instructor*, 2.10, translating *The Ante-Nicene Fathers* [hereafter *ANF*], First Series, ed. Alexander Roberts and James Donaldson (Grand Rapids: Eerdmans, 1951), 2:262, where the Victorian translator refrained from

Clement's grounding of his condemnation of abortion in the natural law—rather than, for instance, in the special revelation of Scripture—was not at all unique among his contemporaries in early Christianity. Indeed, in the late antique milieu of cultural, religious, and philosophical pluralism in which the particular tenets of Christianity held little sway in the public realm (a context, it is worth noting, strikingly similar to that of the present day), it was almost entirely necessary. A culture hostile to Christianity was, and is, incredibly unlikely to assent to any truth claim predicated on peculiarly Christian presuppositions; thus, any hope to persuade virtually mandates an appeal to knowledge common, or at least commonly accessible, to all people regardless of cultural, religious, or philosophical commitments. Thus, it is the universality of the natural law, of right reason conforming to nature, to which the second-century apologist Tertullian also appeals in his address to Rome and its rulers. "Murder being once for all forbidden, we may not destroy even the fetus in the womb," he writes. "To hinder a birth is merely a speedier man-killing; nor does it matter whether you take away a life that is born, or destroy one that is coming to birth. That is a man which is going to be one; you have the fruit already in the seed."[14] Similarly, Athenagoras of Athens, writing to Emperor Marcus Aurelius, asserts uncompromisingly that those who "bring on abortion commit murder," and explains the Christian rejection of abortion by simply stating: "We are in all things always alike and the same, submitting ourselves to reason, and not ruling over it."[15]

The clear implication of such a position is not simply that there is something unchristian about the practice of abortion—an assertion that quite logically could be dismissed by the non-Christian audience in view—but that there is something inconsistent and irrational in this pagan practice, that to sanction such a deed one must, contrary to one's own nature, suppress one's own rationality. By nature, all people understand that murder is evil; but denying that abortion is murder is irrational and contradicts that understanding. This is the central and nearly universal claim of anti-abortion advocates from antiquity through to the present. What distinguishes the ancient and modern debates surrounding

---

rendering into English a substantial portion of Clement's commentary on unnatural sexuality.

14. Tertullian, *Apology*, 9, quoted in *ANF* 3:25.
15. Athenagoras, *The Embassy* [*A Plea for the Christians*], 35, in *ANF* 2:147.

the practice is only that the basis for deeming abortion utterly contrary to right reason in conformity with nature is far stronger today than it was even in antiquity.

Tertullian's assertion—"that is a man which is going to be one"—is, of course, entirely logical, as that which is conceived by two human parents cannot be other than human; it cannot, according to nature or reason, be a vegetable, a mineral, or nonhuman animal life. Such logic even in antiquity could not easily be ignored. It might be qualified, as it was in Roman law, for instance, with the assumption that the fetus is "human" only in the same sense that one might speak of a human heart or a human kidney; that is, the fetus is *pars viscerum mulieris*, part of the mother's body.[16] Even this assumption, however, leads also to conclusions irrational and unnatural, as one would then have necessarily to describe pregnant women as having, for example, two heads, two hearts, and four feet. Right reason in agreement with nature logically dictates, then, that the object of abortion shares a nature in common with the rest of humanity, and yet that it possesses an individual human nature, distinct from that of its mother or any other. Similarly, insofar as nature and reason dictate that life cannot result from that which is nonliving, the further conclusion that the fetus, from conception, is a *living* human being appears equally undeniable.

However rational these conclusions, though, it must also be noted that, given the limits of biological knowledge in antiquity, neither the claim that a fetus is human nor that it is living was capable of verification on strictly empirical or scientific grounds. Thus, even Aristotle, one of the most logically as well as empirically minded thinkers of antiquity, remained unconvinced that, before a certain point, the fetus was either human or alive. Yet even Aristotle, who desired not only to have abortion legal, but even in certain circumstances mandatory, could sanction it only "before sense and life have begun; what may or may not be lawfully done in these cases [of abortion] depends on the question of life."[17] His widely appropriated supposition elsewhere—that this line appears at forty days after conception for male children, and ninety days for female children—is, it goes without saying, entirely unsupported by

16. See Justinian, *Digest*, 35.2.9.1; 25.4.1.1.
17. Aristotle, *Politics*, 7.16, quoted in Benjamin Jowett's translation of *The Politics of Aristotle* (Oxford: Clarendon Press, 1885), 1:240.

any convincing evidence;[18] but equally obvious is that, despite having insufficient data with which to reason, his reasoning process is otherwise impeccable. In recognizing that the destruction *in utero* of any living human being must be deemed illicit, Aristotle, himself firmly convinced that "there really is, as every one to some extent divines, a natural justice and injustice that is binding on all men,"[19] was reasoning rightly in accordance with nature—or, at least, nature as best as it was then understood. That it is infinitely better understood today than it could be more than two millennia ago only amplifies the conviction that one can now only escape the facts of nature, and the reasonable moral conclusions in agreement with nature, by suppressing one's rational faculties and falling into blatant irrationality.

Indeed, one of the most extreme instances of such irrationality is evident, perhaps unsurprisingly, in the very document that repealed America's previous abortion legislation, Supreme Court Justice Harry Blackmun's majority opinion in *Roe v. Wade*. "We need not resolve the difficult question of when life begins," Blackmun wrote. "When those trained in the respective disciplines of medicine, philosophy, and theology are unable to arrive at any consensus, the judiciary . . . is not in a position to speculate as to the answer."[20] The disingenuous sleight of hand evident here is breathtaking. In asserting that "we need not resolve the difficult question of when life begins," Blackmun does not simply lament what he believes to be a lack of consensus on this question; he dismisses as irrelevant the very question that, from antiquity, has stood at the center of the controversy. The utter irrationality—and, consequently, not only amorality, but immorality—of such a position is vividly illustrated by analogy. A hunter sees movement in the brush; it may be a deer, or it may be a child. If he knows with certainty it is a deer, he pulls the trigger; if he knows with certainty it is a child, he holds his fire. If he does not know whether it is a deer or a child? The correct answer to this question is so self-evident as to need no explication.

What does warrant further comment is the fact that, in justifying his own admitted ignorance, Justice Blackmun offers both a red herring and a patent falsehood. The appeal to disagreement between various

18. Aristotle, *The History of Animals*, 7.3.
19. Aristotle, *On Rhetoric*, 1.13, quoted in W. Rhys Roberts' translation of *Aristotle: Rhetoric and Poetics* (New York: The Modern Library, 1954), 78.
20. *Roe v. Wade*, 410, U.S. (1973), at 159.

philosophers and theologians is entirely irrelevant and beside the point, because the question of when life begins is not a philosophical or theological question. It is a biological question, and *only* a biological question. It is the evidence of biology that reveals the falsehood in the assertion that even those trained in medicine have been unable to arrive at consensus. As noted previously, there was indeed a lack of scientific consensus in antiquity, and even through the Middle Ages and much of modernity (during which the Christian West nevertheless had the good sense to err on the side of caution); but since the nineteenth century, by which time scientific advances had made possible the discoveries of the nature of the male sperm, the female egg, and the cellular structure of life, there has been an absolutely overwhelming medical consensus.[21] Indeed, less than a decade after *Roe* was decided, the official Senate report on its own "Human Life Bill" could conclude emphatically, "Physicians, biologists, and other scientists agree that conception marks the beginning of the life of a human being—a being that is alive and is a member of the human species. There is overwhelming agreement on this point in countless medical, biological, and scientific writings."[22] The agreement is so overwhelming, in fact, that even prominent advocates not only of abortion, but even of infanticide, are forced to admit that "there is no doubt that from the first moments of its existence an embryo conceived from human sperm and egg is a human being."[23] As embryological research continues to advance, this conviction that there can be "no doubt" about the facts of nature becomes only more firmly established. In 1994, for instance, British researchers announced that they had devised a technique by which the eggs from aborted females could be retrieved, fertilized *in vitro*, implanted *in utero*, and carried to term.[24] Any who dare to ask the most obvious question—whether the biological mother of a living human being could herself have been anything other than a living human

---

21. See Frederick N. Dyer, *The Physicians' Crusade Against Abortion* (Sagamore Beach: Science History Publications, 2005) for details of the American Medical Association's prominent nineteenth-century role in revising legislation to agree with the consensus on the biological facts.
22. Report, Subcommittee on Separation of Powers to Senate Judiciary Committee S-158, 97th Congress, 1st Session, 1981, 7.
23. Peter Singer, *Practical Ethics*, 2nd ed. (Cambridge: Cambridge University Press, 1993), 86.
24. See William Tuohy, "Use of Fetus Eggs for Fertility Sparks Furor," *Los Angeles Times*, January 3, 1994, A1.

being—will be compelled by right reason in agreement with nature to answer negatively.

One is entitled to one's own opinion, it is said; but one is not entitled to one's own facts. The facts revealed by the natural sciences are unambiguously and undeniably on the side of the pro-life advocate. These facts thus explain the frequent and, at times, even hysterical objections from abortion proponents to the peaceful yet public display of sonograms, embryological models, and especially photographs of aborted fetuses, as these only complicate efforts to deny what one cannot not know. As even the pro-choice feminist Naomi Wolf could honestly ask, "How can we charge that it is vile and repulsive for pro-lifers to brandish vile and repulsive images if the images are real? To insist that truth is in poor taste is the very height of hypocrisy."[25] Indeed it is, and so the pro-choice movement since *Roe* has increasingly modified the framework in which its arguments are cast. Wolf herself reveals such a shift of emphasis in arguing that "women must be free to choose" abortions even in spite of "a recognition of the humanity of the fetus"; therefore, abortion advocates "need to contextualize the fight to defend abortion rights within a moral framework that admits that the death of a fetus is a real death."[26] Despite her startling honesty about the fact of prenatal life, Wolf can nevertheless assert that one "must" be free to choose abortion—because it is a "right."

That elective abortion is indeed a right was, of course, the conclusion of the U.S. Supreme Court in *Roe v. Wade* and many subsequent decisions. It is hardly surprising, then, especially in a society already saturated with rights-talk, that such phrases as "abortion rights," "a woman's right," and "the right to choose" are ubiquitous in pro-abortion rhetoric. And yet any attempt to sanction abortion on the basis of certain fundamental rights must inevitably fail upon a critical examination of the nature of rights. The implicit pro-choice assumption that a right to abortion was not the novel 1973 invention of the Supreme Court, but a natural and inalienable right simply recognized and defended by the Court, may well be a politically necessary assumption. For if the right to abortion were not a fundamental human right, possessed simply by virtue of being human, but instead merely a right arbitrarily granted by the State, then

---

25. Naomi Wolf, "Our Bodies, Our Souls," in *Religion in Legal Thought and Practice*, ed. Howard Lesnick (Cambridge: Cambridge University Press, 2010), 307.

26. Wolf, "Our Bodies, Our Souls," 308, 305.

there could be no principled objection to the State arbitrarily revoking this right.

Yet it is precisely this framing of the right to abortion as a natural right that also reveals its fundamental irrationality. Natural rights and natural law being correlative, any argument grounded in natural rights can, inevitably, serve only to confirm the position grounded in natural law. Because some rights are indeed possessed naturally, simply by virtue of one's possessing human nature, and because no rights at all can be exercised unless one is actually alive, then the most fundamental natural right is the right to life itself. Thus, the question immediately reverts to whether the fetus is a human possessing life; and this question already having been answered affirmatively and irrefutably, it must be concluded that even the fetus has a natural right to life that cannot be denied. The illogic to which the abortion proponent is therefore reduced is well illustrated by Hadley Arkes, who recounts having attended a vigil in support of abortion rights. Also present was a woman with her two-week-old daughter; when asked by Arkes why she was there, the woman replied that she wished to preserve for her newborn daughter the same right to abortion that she herself possessed. Arkes reasonably wonders what possibly could be the source of this right the woman hoped to preserve for her daughter. If truly a natural right, then it came into being at the moment her daughter came into being. But if her daughter possessed inalienable rights the moment she came into being these would include the primary right to life; thus, her mother could not have had the right to abortion that she believed she had. Arkes quite rightly concludes that a natural right to abortion would be a right that destroys itself by logically contradicting itself.[27]

But, as is also implicit in the case stated by Arkes, the logic of defending abortion as a natural right not only destroys itself; if pressed to its conclusion, it necessarily results in the destruction of all natural rights. To defend an individual right to terminate the life of another human being is nothing less than a defense of the old Roman *patria potestas* by another name—or another gender. This ancient and absolute "power of the father" encompassed within it the *ius vitae necisque*, or "right of life and death," by which not only abortion but also infanticide and even parricide were most frequently justified in antiquity. Simply by exercis-

---

27. Hadley Arkes, *Natural Rights and the Right to Choose* (Cambridge: Cambridge University Press, 2002), 179–80.

ing his "right" not to recognize his own offspring—or any member of his household—as a person, and thus also a possessor of inherent rights, the *paterfamilias* could have them put to death without need of explanation or fear of recrimination. It is only by embracing a shocking perversion of reason that the "right" by which the arbitrary deaths of wives, sisters, and daughters were once justified comes to be defended as "a woman's right."

What is more, it should be readily apparent that the violence that is done to human thought and human language in order to deny that a living human, simply by virtue of being human, is also necessarily a person, one recognized as having rights, is the very same by which was justified the actual and horrific violence more recently inflicted upon "human nonpersons" both in America's antebellum South and under Germany's Third Reich. That even relatively recent world history has evidenced such inhuman evils as chattel slavery and the Holocaust only demonstrates once again that even substantial populations, even over extended periods, are in fact capable of willfully suppressing knowledge of moral truths that cannot otherwise be unknown. Indeed, such evils are rightly described as inhuman precisely because, as Cicero knew, they could only be committed by one trying "to fly from himself," to deny his own nature as a human being.

The suppression of truth, however, does not eradicate it, as even modern psychology confirms. Events or truths too unwelcome or too traumatic to be confronted consciously may be suppressed or repressed; but they will not allow themselves to be erased or entirely ignored, and so reveal themselves in a variety of unconscious or subconscious ways.[28] Thus, an otherwise entirely rational individual—a Cornell educated cardiologist—confesses after an elective abortion: "I would do it again. But you know how in the Greek myths when you kill a relative you are pursued by furies? For months, it was as if baby furies were pursuing me."[29] Thus, similarly, in a presentation before a conference of fellow abortionists, one doctor and his nurse could describe the results of a survey taken among their current and former staff: some acknowledged their refusal to view the aborted fetus, while others admitted to being

28. For an insightful treatment of this issue with regard to the suppression of humanity's natural knowledge of God, see R. C. Sproul, *The Psychology of Atheism* (Grand Rapids: Bethany House, 1974), subsequently reprinted in various editions as *If There's a God, Why Are There Atheists?*

29. Quoted by Wolf, "Our Bodies, Our Souls," 305.

dismayed, disgusted, and saddened upon viewing; some offered that performing abortions must psychologically damage physicians, and others described dreams in which they found themselves vomiting up fetuses.[30]

That such vivid and disturbing effects are entirely commonplace is evidence of the tremendous difficulty of attempting to deny what is self-evident, to escape the verdict of natural law.[31] It is precisely this difficulty that recommends the natural law argument against abortion in attempts to reshape the conscience and, consequently, the positive laws of the modern Western world. Several recent studies, for example, have provided evidence that the percentage of Americans holding pro-life convictions has actually increased over the last decade.[32] That there has been over the same time no measurable increase in the number of those embracing the tenets of traditional Christianity suggests once again that the case against abortion is not and need not be grounded in such tenets, and, arguably, that bases other than the articles of a particular religion will ultimately prove more effective. One recently published study reveals, in fact, that religious conviction is very often the *result* of participation in the pro-life movement rather than the cause of it.[33] Though hardly unique, perhaps the most dramatic and well-known about-face of this sort is that of Bernard Nathanson, an original founder of the National Association for the Repeal of Abortion Laws (NARAL) and former director of what was then the largest abortion clinic in the world. Despite having performed abortions numbering in the thousands, and despite being at the time a convinced atheist, Nathanson would later note, "When ultrasound in the early 1970s confronted me with the sight of the embryo in the womb, I simply lost my faith in abortion on demand."[34]

Whether intentional or not, Nathanson's choice of the word *faith* could not have been more revealingly accurate. Contrary to the predominate rhetoric, it is the pro-choice rather than the pro-life argument that

---

30. Warren M. Hern and Billie Corrigan, "What About Us? Staff Reactions to D&E," *Advances in Planned Parenthood* 15 (1980): 3–8.

31. For the regularity of such effects, see, e.g., J. R. Ashton, "The Psychosocial Outcome of Induced Abortion," *British Journal of Obstetrics and Gynecology* 87 (1980): 1115–22.

32. See, e.g., William McGurn, "Gallup's Pro-Life America," *The Wall Street Journal*, June 1, 2010, A17; Jennifer Parker, "Gallup Poll Shows More 'Pro-Life' Backing; First-Time Majority Since 1995," *The Washington Times*, May 16, 2009, A1.

33. Ziad Munson, *The Making of Pro-Life Activists: How Social Movement Mobilization Works* (Chicago: University of Chicago Press, 2009).

34. Bernard Nathanson, *The Hand of God: A Journey from Death to Life by the Abortion Doctor Who Changed His Mind* (Washington, DC: Regnery Publishing, 1996), 140.

is predicated upon "blind faith" and guilty of rejecting both sound evidence and sound logic; the case for life, by contrast, remains, as it has for centuries, firmly grounded in right reason in agreement with nature—in natural science, natural rights, and natural law.

13

NATURAL LAW:
A Basis for Christian-Muslim Discourse?

Adam S. Francisco

INTRODUCTION

It is often presumed—and rightly so—that the law written on every human heart (Romans 2:14–15) provides a basis for Christian engagement in the secular realm. For one, it recognizes the existence of some common ground from which Christians can address moral issues in a pluralistic environment. It also provides a point of connection for evangelistic and apologetic efforts, for our innate sense of right and wrong and inability to consistently choose the former is a touchstone for articulating how at odds we are with the Author of the moral law.[1]

---

1. Robert Kolb, *Speaking the Gospel Today: A Theology for Evangelism* (St. Louis: Concordia, 1984), 42–43.

For all its promise, though, working from natural law has its share of difficulties. This is particularly the case in a culture predominated by the assumptions of naturalism, a view of (at least knowable) reality being comprised of nature and only nature.[2] Without a supernatural author behind moral law there can, upon analysis, be no real meaningful morality, only changing opinions guided by the shifting standards of culture.[3] This certainly impedes evangelism, too, for consciences informed by naturalism yet convicted of failing to do what is right may experience guilt, but it will be interpreted as, at best, an imposition of culturally conditioned morality.[4]

That is the problem when the presumption of the natural law meets a naturalistic worldview. The latter presupposes a certain ontology that *a priori* denies metaphysical realities necessary for the existence of real natural law. But what about non-Christians who, while they may not confess the triune nature of God, believe in an objective moral law and transcendent moral lawgiver? Can a Christian carry on discourse with, for example, a Jew or a Muslim on the basis of some shared understanding of natural law? David Novak, a prolific conservative Jewish scholar, recently argued that certainly, with some qualification, Jews and Christians can. In fact, he contends that they must work together cooperatively in the realm of ethics, though he insists that Christians (and Jews) must, if they are to remain united in their joint ethical pursuits, resist attempts to use such discourses as venues for proselytizing.[5] (The Christian might agree,

---

2.   See Phillip E. Johnson, "Darwinism as Dogma: The Establishment of Naturalism" and Nancy R. Pearcey, "Darwin Meets the Berenstain Bears: Evolution as a Total Worldview," in *Uncommon Dissent: Intellectuals Who Find Darwinism Unconvincing*, ed. William A. Dembski (Wilmington, DE: ISI Books, 2004), 23–40 and 53–73; Gary H. Locklair, "The Impact of Origin Paradigms on Culture," in *Christ and Culture in Dialogue*, ed. J. L. Menuge (St. Louis: Concordia, 1999), 220–38.

3.   See J. Budziszewski, *The Line through the Heart: Natural Law as Fact, Theory, and Sign of Contradiction* (Wilmington, DE: ISI Books, 2009), 79–95. However, also see the more rigorous critiques of those optimistic of discourse on the basis of natural law such as Carl F. H. Henry, "Natural Law and Nihilistic Culture," *First Things* (January 1995): 54–60; Daniel Heimbach, "Rethinking Natural Law: Is It Our Best Strategy for Engaging the Public Square?" *Liberty University Law Review* 2:3 (Spring 2008).

4.   For robust critiques of naturalism, see Stewart Goetz and Charles Taliaferro, *Naturalism* (Grand Rapids: Eerdmans, 2008) as well as Phillip E. Johnson, *Reason in the Balance: The Case against Naturalism in Science, Law & Education* (Downers Grove, IL: InterVarsity, 1995).

5.   David Novak, "Is Natural Law a Border Concept between Judaism and Christianity?" *Journal of Religious Ethics* 32:2 (2004): 249.

but would certainly look for opportunities and venues appropriate for evangelization.)

Interestingly, Novak also asks whether the same could be said of Islam and Muslims. He recognizes the difficulties presented by today's political climate, but he is optimistic about the possibility. There are progressive Muslim leaders, too, who would be quick to answer in the affirmative. For example, speaking of how Muslims might assimilate and contribute more in American society, Ingrid Mattson, president of the Islamic Society of North America (ISNA) and director of the MacDonald Center for the Study of Islam and Christian-Muslim Relations at Hartford Seminary, has argued that the "natural law tradition in Islam" needs to be recovered by Muslims for service in public moral discourse.[6] Russell Powell, a (Catholic) Christian and Associate Professor of Law at Seattle University School of Law, has gone so far as to argue that each tradition's understanding of natural law not only makes common moral pursuits such as social justice and human rights possible, but it could also promote reconciliation between the two faiths.[7] Alan Wisdom of the Institute on Religion & Democracy (IRD) is not so optimistic, but he has suggested that the motifs both religions hold in common may help illustrate "the 'natural law' or 'common grace' that is revealed to all, as Paul argues in Romans 1–2."[8]

This essay addresses the potential such an approach to Islam might hold. But before any assessment of the promise or perils can be achieved, the nature of Islam and, more specifically, natural law in Islam must be considered. Only then can the following question be addressed: Does natural law serve as an adequate basis from which Christians and Muslims can dialogue?

---

6. United States Institute of Peace, *Ijtihad: Reinterpreting Islamic Principles for the Twenty-first Century* (Washington DC, 2004), 8.

7. Russell Powell, "Toward Reconciliation in the Middle East: A Framework for Christian-Muslim Dialogue Using Natural Law Tradition," *Loyola University Chicago International Law Review* 2:1 (2004): 1–30.

8. Alan Wisdom, "Christian-Muslim Dialogue: A Guide for Churches," *Institute on Religion and Democracy* (May 2003), http://www.theird.org/Page.aspx?pid=1082 (accessed November 4, 2010).

THE NATURE OF ISLAM

To identify the nature of Islam is difficult, for it is and has been to some extent or another diversely interpreted and appropriated throughout its history. This is especially true with Muslims living in the West in the twenty-first century. If there is one way to characterize it, though, it would be to reject the tendency to view Islam as a religion.[9] It is more appropriately viewed as an ideology that, as ideologies do, purports to explain and seeks to inform (and ultimately legislate) every realm of human life. As the Muslim Student Association puts it, Islam is "the only true way of life. . . . The scope of this way of life is vast enough that it transcends the traditional notion of 'religion'. Islam includes submitting to Allah in the realm of politics, economics, law, etc."[10]

In a pluralistic environment one might expect Muslims to conceal or at least qualify this aspect of Islam. However, Muslim intellectuals are usually forthright about their totalizing vision for humanity. A leading Palestinian-American scholar in the previous century, Ismail al-Faruqi, for example, asserted that the principles of Islam and the subsequent culture it gave birth to "purports to speak for all humans and for all times."[11] More recently, Tariq Ramadan, one of the most influential yet controversial Western Muslim intellectuals, submitted that the principles advanced in the Qur'an as well as the example and assertions of Muhammad contained in biographies (*sira*) and collections of sayings and deeds of the so-called prophet (*hadith*) were "given for the universe . . . for all times and across all frontiers."[12]

It is in these sources that an ideology is advanced which is designed to be impressed upon human societies everywhere (using a variety of means) through a perpetual struggle (*jihad*) that will last until the Day of Judgment or up until the world confesses there is no god but Allah,

9. For more on the nature of ideology, see Kenneth Minogue, *Alien Powers: The Pure Theory of Ideology* (Wilmington, DE: ISI Books, 2008), 5–6.

10. "Compendium of Muslim Texts," MSA West, http://www.msawest.net/islam/ (accessed January 29, 2010).

11. Ismail al-Faruqi, "Islam and Culture and Civilization," in *Islam and Contemporary Society* (New York: Longman, 1982), 142.

12. Tariq Ramadan, *Western Muslims and the Future of Islam* (New York: Oxford University Press, 2004), 63. For focused analyses of the Qur'an and the life and example of Muhammad, see Robert Spencer, *The Complete Infidel's Guide to the Koran* (Washington DC: Regnery Press, 2009) and *The Truth of Muhammad: Founder of the World's Most Intolerant Religion* (Washington, DC: Regnery Press, 2007).

and Muhammad is his messenger.[13] This struggle can take a variety of forms. Historically, it has been conceived, almost completely, as offensive political and military action. Currently, it is being carried out in a variety of other ways. The most obvious one is terrorism. Some, however, have gone so far as to completely redefine jihad not as an outward struggle to advance the cause of Islam in society but as an internal struggle with one's own temptation.[14] Probably the most notable form of jihad in the West (that is occurring virtually unnoticed) is what has been referred to as civilizational jihad, which seeks to supplant the values of western society by presenting Islam as a legitimate and rational alternative.[15]

NATURAL LAW AND ISLAM

There is a rationale behind the efforts of Muslims to advance Islam in the West, and it is linked to the Islamic view of nature. To begin with, Muslims regard Islam as the religion of nature (*din al-fitrah*). In fact, the Qur'an "regards the whole universe as 'Muslim.' "[16] Everything in the heavens and earth, reads Qur'an 3:83, submits to its creator. That is, the design, order, and purpose of all of nature and creation are but a reflection of its submission to the laws of nature and, behind them, their author, Allah. While the universe and all its parts operate in accordance with these divinely written laws, there is one exception—humankind.

Unlike the rest of creation, humans have free will (albeit ultimately limited by God's will) and are therefore capable of disobedience. This is not to suggest the Qur'an teaches that humans have an inherently

---

13. Abu Dawud al-Sijistani, *Sunan Abu Dawud*, trans. Ahmad Hasan (Lahore: Ashraf Press, 1984), 2:702; Muhammad ibn Umar al-Waqidi, *Kitab al-Maghazi* (Oxford: Oxford University Press, 1966), 3:113.

14. David Cook has demonstrated this reformulation, when characterized as the essential nature of historical jihad, to be completely false and misleading. See his *Understanding Jihad* (Berkeley: University of California Press, 2005).

15. Mohamed Akram, "An Explanatory Memorandum on the General Strategic Goal for the Brotherhood in North America" (May 1991), http://www.investiga tiveproject.org/document/id/20 (accessed November 4, 2010). On jihad in America generally, see Steven Emerson, *Jihad Incorporated: A Guide to Militant Islam in US* (Amherst: Prometheus Books, 2006); Robert Spencer, *Stealth Jihad: How Radical Islam is Subverting American without Guns or Bombs* (Washington DC: Regnery Publishing, 2008).

16. Fazlur Rahman, *Major Themes of the Qur'an* (Chicago: University of Chicago Press, 2009), 65.

sinful disposition. Quite the contrary; Islam decries the biblical doctrine of original sin and advances a very different anthropology. The term usually associated with it is *fitrah*. Linguistically, it refers to the inborn natural disposition of things. As a theological anthropological concept, it refers to the inherent righteousness or, at the very least, morally neutral essence of human beings. What is more, though, is that *fitrah* also refers to the status of the natural human, who has yet to go through various circumstances in life (nationality, family, etc.) and be seduced away from Islam, as being a Muslim since and even before birth. Qur'an 7:172 says that even before the creation of Adam, all of humankind was in some way raised into existence, and a covenant was established between Allah and humankind whereupon all humankind, so that that they would be without excuse on the last day, testified that Allah was their Lord.

This passage "provides the best introduction to the Islamic under-standing of humans' relations with God [Allah]," writes Hartford Seminary's Yahya Michot. Allah "is the creator of everything . . . Whose decree none of His creatures is able to escape. We are God's [Allah's] slaves, totally subjugated . . . to God's [Allah's] creative will, decision, and power."[17] If the nature of human beings is understood this way—as those born in a state of submission and owned by Allah—then it is easy to see why or at least understand the rationale behind the drive in Islam to struggle, as Qur'an 9:33 puts it, to cause Islam to prevail over all other systems of belief. For if the whole universe is Muslim and humans have even made a covenant with Allah himself and yet they go their own way by constructing their own religious, political, and domestic institutions, this would represent the height of arrogance, disobedience, and rebellion, leading to universal chaos and ignorance.

The resulting ignorance from the rebellion of humankind is one of the reasons Allah enjoined Muslims to struggle and fight to advance the cause of Islam (Qur'an 2:216). It is also the reason, the Qur'an teaches, that Allah once raised up prophets—beginning with Adam through Abraham, Moses, David, Jesus, and terminating with Muhammad—so that people in former times might turn to Allah and his law. The words of the prophets in Islam are not necessarily viewed as special revelation though. Rather, the prophets told the people what they could know for

17. Yahya Michot, "The Image of God in Humanity from a Muslim Perspective," in *Abraham's Children: Jews, Christians, and Muslims in Conversation*, ed. Norman Solomon, Richard Harries, and Tim Winter (London: T & T Clark, 2006), 167–68.

themselves by reflecting upon nature. "The primary task of the prophets is to awaken man's conscience so that he can decipher the primordial writing on his heart more clearly and with greater conviction."[18] It is only because the "abundant revelation in nature has by itself mostly failed to elicit the appropriate response from human beings" that Allah sent prophets. But when Muhammad, the seal of the prophetic revelation, died in 632, the duty to "ensure that [Islam] is everywhere recognized" has now been passed onto the global Muslim community.[19]

The motif of Islam being the religion as well as the divinely created law of nature and, moreover, that it is available to those that search deep and hard enough, is quite prominent in the Qur'an. In fact, one of the greatest American Muslim scholars of the last century asserted that the Qur'an regards Allah's law as being "written upon man's heart."[20] Yet, scholars have shown that historically and even contemporaneously the prevalent view suggests "humans could not have an inner moral compass, or any 'law written on their hearts' (Romans 2:15), enabling them to live moral lives on the basis of their own unaided reason."[21] This has, in fact, led to a peculiar view that all "knowledge, any 'science' in Islam, as well as the initiative and the ways to practice it, must be derived from the Holy Qur'an, the Word of God, and from hadith, the reports of the sayings of the Prophet of Islam."[22]

There is logic to this too. It is, as one scholar explains, "because there is always the possibility that reason may lose sight of the limits imposed on her as an instrument of knowledge and mistake herself for both the chief subject and object, not only the sources of knowledge but also the procedures of knowing must be formulated on the ground of divine and prophetic authority. In other words, reason may not always be able to determine by herself whether she 'follows reason.' "[23] Reason and nature are not the most trustworthy sources of spiritual or ethical insight, for

---

18. Rahman, *Major Themes of the Qur'an*, 24.
19. Daniel A. Madigan, "Themes and Topics," in *The Cambridge Companion to the Qur'an*, ed. Jane Dammen McAuliffe (New York: Cambridge University Press, 2006), 84–85, 94.
20. Rahman, *Major Themes of the Qur'an*, 24.
21. Patricia Crone, *God's Rule: Government and Islam* (New York: Columbia University Press, 2004), 263–64.
22. Steffen A. J. Stelzer, "Ethics," in *The Cambridge Companion to Classical Islamic Theology*, ed. Tim Winter (New York: Cambridge University Press, 2008), 161.
23. Stelzer, "Ethics," 162.

they will always be potentially misused and misinterpreted by humans. Thus, the view that "there was no better way of speaking about God—and therefore no better theology—than quoting what God Himself says about Himself in the Qur'an" has largely prevailed in classical Muslim thought.[24]

But there has always been a rationalist school of Islamic thought, and it seems to be gaining ascendancy.[25] Contemporary Muslim scholars, particularly those working in or at least attempting to influence Islam in the West, are resurrecting what seems to be a new emphasis on reason and natural law. One such example is Ali Ezzati's unique book, *Islam and Natural Law*.[26] After a brief excursus on the origins of natural law theory in Greco-Roman thought, its appropriation by medieval Christian theologians, and eventual decline, neglect, and rejection in modern Western intellectual history, Ezzati concludes his first chapter on natural law in the West by drawing attention to its revival in the last quarter of the twentieth century. Then in subsequent chapters he details its place in Islam, as if to proffer it (Islamic ideology) as a viable alternative to the morass of Western relativistic pluralism.

Ezzati is clearly confident of the primacy of natural law in Islam. Islam teaches, he writes,

> its adherents that God [Allah] created nature and implanted therein its laws, orders and ends. It commanded man to discover these in order to enable him to enjoy nature as God [Allah] has entitled him to do. Islam suggests that God [Allah] has created everything in nature perfect. He has fashioned each creature and given it an essence, a structure that determines its life and from which it never deviates. He has placed every creature and all parts

---

24. Yahya Michot, "Revelation," in *Cambridge Companion to Classical Islamic Theology*, 190. See, for example, A. Kevin Reinhart, *Before Revelation: The Boundaries of Muslim Moral Thought* (Albany: SUNY Press, 1995), 70–75. Cf. with Robert R. Reilly's fascinating thesis entitled *The Closing of the Muslim Mind: How Intellectual Suicide Created the Modern Islamist Crisis* (Wilmington, DE: ISI Books, 2010).

25. For an historical study of the Rationalism or, as it is often called, *mu'tazilism*, in Islam, see Richard Martin, *Defenders of Reason in Islam: From Medieval School to Modern Symbol* (Oxford: Oneworld Publications, 1997).

26. Ali Ezzati, *Islam and Natural Law* (London: Islamic College for Advanced Studies Press, 2002). For a scholarly historical study of natural law in the Islamic tradition, see Anver M. Emon's "Natural Law and Natural Rights in Islamic Law," *Journal of Law and Religion* 20:2 (2004–2005): 351–95 and, more recently, *Islamic Natural Law Theories* (New York: Oxford University Press, 2010).

of nature within the general nexus of nature so that its birth, its whole life and its death all happen according to patterns which are themselves constituents of the divine will. To every creature He has ordained a career and objective to which its existence is forever subject. There is no gap or conflict in nature. No object or event in nature is an accident. Everything that is or happens does so because of predictable cause and with predictable consequences. That is why nature is real cosmos, not a chaos where events never take place with cause, or sometimes with and sometimes without cause.[27]

As such, Ezzati can describe Islam as both "natural" and "rational."[28] This, he argues, is the way it has been regarded throughout the classical age of Islam; any descriptions of it as being nonrational are misinterpretations (perhaps even willful misinterpretations) of history. In fact, Ezzati argues that if there is a major religious tradition hostile to reason and natural law, it would be Christianity since at least the time of the Reformation.[29]

To advance a principle or position on something as natural (that it corresponds to what one finds in nature) and rational (that it is internally coherent) implies that it is objective. And if something is objective it means that, at least in principle, rational persons reflecting on the world outside of themselves will draw similar (if not the same) conclusions. Ezzati makes this exact claim for Islam.

Basically, two different religions and ethical systems exist, he argues. One is the religion of nature, "*din al-fitrah* or *religio naturalis*, which any human being possesses by birth." The other is historical religion or the "religious traditions of history." By this Ezzati means those religions that have developed in and are a product of historical processes. They may be "outgrowths of *din al-fitrah*." Yet, in varying degrees they are "accumulations, figurations, interpretations or transformations of history," the product or inventions of "time, place, culture, leadership and other particular conditions." Christianity and the ethics that spring from it, and all other religions, fall within this category. They may have elements of truth within them insofar as they agree with natural religion, but they are still not commensurate with the natural religion. Islam, however, is, for in

---

27. Ezzati, *Islam and Natural Law*, 74–75.
28. Ezzati, *Islam and Natural Law*, 72.
29. Ezzati, *Islam and Natural Law*, 29ff., 186–87.

quintessentially circular logic, Ezzati states, "Islam calls this *din al-fitrah* or Ur-religion, 'Islam.'"[30]

Even more interesting are the claims Ezzati makes for the objectivity of Islamic law and ethics. Both are the heart of Islam. The former may be more fundamental than the latter, but the two are inseparable and comprise the essential makeup and character of Islam.[31] Ultimately, the source of Islamic law (*shari'ah*) is the Qur'an and the multitude of traditions related to Muhammad (contained in biographies and orally transmitted anecdotes), but analogical reasoning and the consensus of the Muslim community also play a determinative role for issues not explicitly addressed in the foundational texts.[32] And even though drawn from texts written in a particular language at a certain point in history, Islamic law (and ethics) is still regarded as comprehensive and universal. It is designed as legislation for all people and for every aspect of their individual and collective behavior—from domestic to international relations and everything in between—for it is seen not as the law of human beings, but Allah's law for humanity. And just as the theology of Islam is proffered not only in texts but also in nature, the same could be said for Islamic law. There is, Ezzati maintains, perfect harmony between Islamic law and reason and the ethical principles it finds in nature.[33] In light of this, Ezzati expects that human beings who think rationally about nature and its laws will draw the same conclusions of traditional Islamic law and ethics.

This is the overall thrust of Ezzati's book (and contemporary Islamic Rationalism), but his ambitious volume serves even a larger purpose. He advances a clandestine apologetic for Islam within it. His central argument is that the West is mired in ethical relativism, which is largely because the Western mind is no longer anchored in any sort of metaphysic. While Christianity once provided one, Western society has distanced itself from its historical intellectual roots and, conversely, Christianity has distanced itself from rationality and nature. In Ezzati's estimation, the only way to

---

30. Ezzati, *Islam and Natural Law*, 62.
31. See A. Kevin Reinhart, "Islamic Law as Islamic Ethics," *Journal of Religious Ethics* 11:2 (1983): 186–203.
32. For an introduction to the theory of Islamic law, see Mohammad Hashim Kamali, *Shari'a Law: An Introduction* (Oxford: Oneworld Publications, 2008), and for an historical overview, see Knut S. Vikør, *Between God and the Sultan: A History of Islamic Law* (New York: Oxford University Press, 2005).
33. Ezzati, *Islam and Natural Law*, 88–89.

resolve the resulting relativism on the one hand and irrationalism on the other is through Islamic Rationalism. Not only can Islamic Rationalism help one navigate the secular realm,[34] employing reason and studying nature the way even a non-Muslim would, but Muslims can rest assured that its rational pursuits will yield the result of Islam.

CHRISTIAN-MUSLIM DISCOURSE

The presumption that natural law provides a basis for Christian discourse with others in the domain of ethics is reasonable. This is particularly true when it comes to discourse with those who hold nature and its laws as the work of a creator. Thus, it must be maintained that there is always the possibility for Christians to engage in reasoned discourse with Muslims. Such discourse may even be fruitful, if not necessary, in the secular realm, as David Novak has argued, to combat the ethical relativism legitimized by the ideology of secularism.[35]

But one must be realistic. Islam is an ideology, and ideologies ultimately do not allow for rational neutrality. Any shared ethical principles derived from reflection upon nature will, in the end, be interpreted by a Muslim in light of Islamic law. Or at least the expectation is that the findings of reason will conform to the principles proffered in the Qur'an and traditions of Muhammad. One should also be aware of the way any sort of conceived consensus between Christians and Muslims is used to advance the cause of Islam. The Qur'an endorses such an approach.[36] In fact, Christians in particular are singled out as being the closest potential friends of Muslims, but only because they are potential converts.[37]

---

34. On this theme, see Abdullah Ahmed an-Na'im, *Islam and the Secular State: Negotiating the Future of Shari'a* (Cambridge: Harvard University Press, 2008).

35. Novak, "Is Natural Law a Border Concept between Judaism and Christianity?" 252. One should, however, be aware of the fact that it is a fairly standard polemic to blame Christianity and its distinction between the sacred and secular realm for the rise of secularism. See, for example, Syed Muhammad Naquib al-Attas, *Islam, Secularism and the Philosophy of the Future* (New York: Mansell, 1985), esp. 13–46; Sayyid Qutb, *Islam: The Religion of the Future* (Riyadh: International Islamic Federation of Student Organizations, 1984), esp. 34–60.

36. See, for example, Qur'an 3:64–73.

37. See, for example, Qur'an 5:82–83.

One conspicuous example of the awkward results of Christian-Muslim discourse was the Common Word initiative.[38] It began in the fall of 2007 when 138 influential Muslims came together in Jordan under the auspices of the Royal Aal al-Bayt Institute for Islamic Thought and produced a document entitled "A Common Word between Us and You." Afterward, this document was sent to the pope, patriarchs, archbishops, presidents, and general secretaries of Christian church bodies everywhere. It asserted that for the purpose of peace Christians and Muslims, who collectively make up over half of the world's population, must work together, for "our common future is at stake." And in view of this it concluded by urging Christians to, on the basis of the common ethical motifs they share with Muslims, work with Muslims "in righteousness and good work . . . and live in sincere peace, harmony and mutual goodwill."[39]

The response from Christians was overwhelming. The University of Yale's Center for Faith and Culture, for example, immediately drafted "Loving God and Neighbor Together: A Christian Response to *A Common Word between Us and You*," and published it, affixed with the signatures of three hundred prominent Christian scholars and clergy, in the *New York Times* on November 18, 2007.[40] In their desire to extend a hand of friendship to the Muslim world, the respondents ultimately, but presumably unwittingly, acknowledged the legitimacy of Islam. Even a cursory read of the response from the Yale Center for Faith and Culture made it clear that the authors (and signatories) presumed nature's creator to be both the God of Islam and Christianity,[41] named Muhammad as a prophet, and made other desperate concessions (such as implicating contemporary Christians in the medieval Crusades and apologizing for excesses in the war on terror, as if it were a new crusade instigated and led by Christians). The letter from Yale wasn't anomalous either, for since

---

38. See http://www.acommonword.com and Miroslav Volf, Ghazi bin Muhammad, and Melissa Yarrington, eds., *A Common Word: Muslims and Christians on Loving God and Neighbor Together* (Grand Rapids: Eerdmans, 2010).

39. "A Common Word between Us and You," http://www.acommonword.com/index.php?lang=en&page=option1 (accessed November 4, 2010).

40. "Loving God and Neighbor Together: A Christian Response to *A Common Word between Us and You*," http://www.yale.edu/faith/acw/acw.htm (accessed November 4, 2010).

41. On this, see Timothy George, *Is the Father of Jesus the God of Muhammad?* (Grand Rapids: Zondervan, 2002).

the fall of 2007 there have been innumerable appeasements made by Christian leaders from every tradition.[42]

Despite the dubious nature of common initiatives advanced under the guise of Christian-Muslim dialogue, there is still room for discourse. Only such discourse, if it is truly to be natural law discourse, will not be Christian-Muslim discourse. It will be discourse between humans reflecting on the innate knowledge of right and wrong as well as moral principles reflected in nature. There will always be trouble, however, when such findings are absorbed or appropriated into a previously existing set of beliefs such as Islamic law. Islam cannot help itself, though, for it is ideological and legal in nature, whereas Christianity is chiefly concerned with the status of the human before God, and, while there may be ethics peculiar to Christians, Christianity is largely comfortable with secular law being interpreted and implemented by any just legislator.

So while Christians strive to "live peaceably with all" (Romans 12:18), including Muslims, we would be wise to proceed cautiously in joining with Islam in a common cause in any regard. In fact, a cursory examination of Islam and its final view of Christianity reveals that, under certain circumstances, Muslims are enjoined to fight Christians until they willingly embrace Islam or compulsorily submit to Islamic governance and law (Qur'an 9:29). Being aware of this and a host of other issues is essential for any serious discourse with people who describe themselves as Muslim.

Still, it is equally necessary that Christians avail themselves to Muslims, as difficult as it may seem, for the sake of the Gospel; for though their assumptions may tell them differently, Muslims stand before God by nature sinful and unclean and, like us, in desperate need of a Savior. Since Islam has no Savior, a strong proclamation of Law and Gospel is the Christian's best dialogue and evangelistic tool. The Holy Spirit still works through the Word to convict sinners of their sin and bring them to repentance and saving faith.

---

42. For analyses and critiques of the Common Word initiative, which unsurprisingly get no media attention, see Jochen Katz, "A Common Word between Us and You: Evaluating the Muslim Open Letter," http://www.answering-islam.org/Letters /common_word.htm (accessed February 20, 2010); Sam Solomon and E. al-Maqdisi, *A Common Word: The Undermining of the Church* (Charlottesville: Advancing Native Missions, 2009).

14

ACCORDING TO NATURE, *ADIAPHORA*, AND ORDINATION

Albert B. Collver III

INTRODUCTION AND BRIEF OVERVIEW

In an age in which natural law has become suspect, can it still be of help in addressing theological questions? Christians, in an attempt to challenge a postmodern world where nearly everything is considered relative, have attempted to engage in discussions, particularly in the public square, on the basis of natural law. The battles of the late twentieth century in America over the public display of the Ten Commandments were at least as much battles over natural law as they were freedom of (from) religion.[1]

---

1. On June 28, 2005, the United States Supreme Court ruled 5–4 that the Ten Commandments could not be displayed in court buildings or on government property.

To further complicate matters, when people speak of natural law, the referent is not always apparent. What is natural law?[2] Does natural law refer to morals, ethics, natural rights, legal theory, or the orders of creation? In some cases, it refers to all of the above. Martin Luther certainly thought positive or legislated law and natural law should be connected. In fact, he thought legislated law needed to be based on natural law and love, in order to "hit upon a decision that is pleasing to God."[3] How far we have come since then!

In a sense, natural law as an intellectual and philosophical movement in Western thought has come full circle from its development in ancient Greek philosophy. Did natural law originate in Greek thought?[4] No. As Philip Melanchthon wrote in his 1521 edition of *Loci Communes*, "A natural law is a common judgment to which all men alike assent, and therefore one which God has inscribed upon the soul of each man."[5] This common judgment inscribed on the heart by God—which all men, more or less, share—is the reason natural law developed in Greek philosophy. Because the Greeks had this common judgment inscribed upon their hearts by God, even though they did not recognize the one true God,

Jane Roh, "Supreme Court Bars Commandments From Courthouses," *Fox News*, June 28, 2005, http://www.foxnews.com/story/0,2933,160781,00.html.

2.   Otto Alfred Piper, "What Is Natural Law?," *Theology Today* 2, no. 4 (1946): 459. "It is obvious that no fruitful discussion is possible as long as we have no clear view of 'natural law' and its relation to the ethical absolutes by which our conduct is guided."

3.   Martin Luther, "Temporal Authority: To What Extent It Should be Obeyed," 1523. "But when you ignore love and natural law you will never hit upon the solution that pleases God, though you may have devoured all the lawbooks and jurists. Instead, the more you depend on them, the further they will lead you astray. A good and just decision must not and cannot be pronounced out of books, but must come from a free mind, as though there were no books. Such a free decision is given, however, by love and by natural law, with which all reason is filled; out of the books come extravagant and untenable judgments" (AE 45:128).

4.   Richard V. Pierard, "Natural Law or God's Law? A Historian's Perspective," *Ex Auditu* 11 (1995): 133. "However, it must be emphasized that the origins of natural law thinking are actually secular. The Greeks wrestled with the idea of law as inherent in the nature of universe which in turn provided the moral basis for human laws. Behind all human laws they saw an eternal and unchangeable law that was valid for all peoples and times. This transcendental or metaphysical law was the ethical foundation for and gave life to human or 'positive' law. The task of the philosopher was to find the best laws and the best state that could make this moral basis binding."

5.   Philip Melanchthon, *The Loci Communes of Philip Melanchthon, 1521*, trans. Charles Leander Hill (Boston: Meador, 1944), 112.

natural law developed in Western thought in response to the problems Greeks noticed in their legislated law.

These Greek men of reason were searching for a universal law, a universal truth to rescue them from the capriciousness of law enacted both by gods and kings and from the plethora of customs found in each land. The best the Greeks devised was something resembling the Ten Commandments and what Cicero and later Jewish and early Christian writers called natural law.[6] In continuity with the Greek thought, Cicero coined the phrase "natural law" in reference to the Stoic philosopher Zeno.[7] Philo seems to be the first person to coin or at least widely use the term νόμος φύσεως (natural law) in Greek.[8] From there, natural law continues its development through the Early Church, Aquinas, the Reformation, the Enlightenment, and so on until the present.

Those who operate with a developmental or evolutionary approach to the history of ideas argue that the idea of natural law originated with the Greeks and underwent various modifications and developments until the present time. In a postmodern age, such an approach certainly contributes to the notion that natural law is relative, not universal, and not divine.[9] Between the Reformation and the Enlightenment, natural law shifted from the ethical/moral realm into the physical realm as the laws of nature. The natural knowledge of God had been seen as knowing God through reason as expressed in natural law and in the laws of nature. Eventually, to know God was to know nature—almost a rebirth of paganism on a philosophically sophisticated level. There was a shift from the prescriptive to the descriptive; in that process, God was lost. Werner Elert sees this emphasis on the natural knowledge of God, natural law, and

---

6.   Gerhard Kittel, ed., *Theological Dictionary of the New Testament*, trans. Geoffrey William Bromiley, vol. 9 (Grand Rapids: Eerdmans, 1974), 265, footnote 151.

7.   Cicero, *De Natura Decorum* I, 14, 36. "Zeno autem, ut iam ad vestros Balbe veniam, naturalem legem divinam esse censet." Marcus Tullius Cicero, *M. Tvlli Ciceronis Scripta qvae manservnt omnia 45. De natura deorum*, ed. Otto Plasberg (Lipsiae: Teubner, 1917).

8.   Kittel, *Theological Dictionary of the New Testament*, 9:266. "As a current term in common use we first find *lex naturae* or *lex naturalis* in Cic. and the equivalent νόμος φύσεως in Philo."

9.   Pierard, "Natural Law or God's Law? A Historian's Perspective," 143. "Many sociologists and anthropologists are still committed to cultural relativism, and insist that one cannot transfer the moral ideas of a given culture to another one. They make a valid point, and the modern proponent of a natural moral law must not fall into the error of taking for eternal and universal what in fact is temporary and culturally conditioned."

the laws of nature resulting in the teachings of Nietzsche and the death of Christianity in Europe.[10] The Reformed theologian Otto Piper would agree with Elert's observation with one exception. Otto Piper identifies the cause of this as deriving from Luther's theology on natural law,[11] whereas Elert sees it as caused not by Luther but rather by Melanchthon, affecting some of the orthodox theologians, and ultimately manifesting itself after the Enlightenment. A distortion of natural law from the Lutheran tradition lends itself toward reductionism and relativism, while the Calvinist view of natural law leads toward an absolutist position of a Christian kingdom on earth.[12] From the perspective of Roman Catholic

---

10. Werner Elert, *The Structure of Lutheranism: The Theology and Philosophy of Life of Lutheranism especially in the Sixteenth and Seventeenth Centuries*, trans. Walter A. Hansen, Concordia Classics (St. Louis: Concordia, 2003), 57–58. "The development of 'natural theology' is the march of history from Luther's primal experience (*Urerlebnis*) up to the Enlightenment. It ended with the ominous error that Christian faith in God and 'natural knowledge of God' are essentially identical. For the naive apologists, for many a dogmatician, even for many a politician who wanted to 'preserve religion for the people,' this was a comfort and a satisfaction. For the church Philistine, as Tholuck addressed him, it was reason for no longer knowing of an anguished conscience. But then came Ludwig Feuerbach. Then came Karl Marx and Nietzsche. They showed that the knowledge of 'natural' man arrives at a totally different result. And when it came to the great test of the revelation of God's goodness, faithfulness, and mercy on land, at sea, and in the air—which Zöckler and many others taught—the result was decidedly negative. Was it surprising that the generation of the war and the collapse declared the Christian belief in God to be a delusion because it had been refuted by the terrors and the fate that had been experienced? If that generation had heard Luther instead of the theology of the nineteenth century and the preaching that lives on such theology—it would have understood him and his primal dread (*Urgrauen*)."

11. Piper, "What Is Natural Law?" 469. "History has shown that the Lutheran view may lead to a complete dissociation of social and political exigencies from Christian goals." Piper regards Calvin's view of natural law preferable to Luther's. Of course, the problem with Calvin's view is that it necessarily leads to the creation of a Christian kingdom on earth, not entirely unlike Islam.

12. Pierard, "Natural Law or God's Law? A Historian's Perspective," 143. "The problem as I perceive it is the avoidance of the two extremes of relativism and absolutism. I do not regard the alternative offered by the more extreme Calvinist, either an appeal to some vague 'orders of creation' or to the imposition of 'kingdom rule' in a theonomic or Christian Reconstructionist fashion, as very attractive. They would see the function of the natural law as the formulation of norms that should be imposed, virtually if not actually, in a theocratic sense. On the other hand, the situationists, who deny that there can be any universal norms since human conduct is always conditioned by circumstances, do not offer us an option that is any more appealing."

thought, both Lutheran and Calvinist views on natural law are derivative and incomplete in comparison with Thomas Aquinas.[13]

As a result, natural law is a neglected stepsister of sorts in theology. An entire class of intelligentsia including secularists, jurists, scientists, and theologians both liberal and conservative has had little use for natural law in the twentieth- and early twenty-first centuries. Part of the challenge in speaking about natural law on the contemporary scene is the accumulation of two and a half millennia of natural law theory.[14] What natural law meant to the Stoic is not the same as what it meant to Augustine or Aquinas or to us today. Noah Fehl's quotation of Jean Paul Richterm that every war brings about a new theory on natural law is in part true, in that events such as war tend to make people reconsider what is just and right. Major wars such as the Thirty Years' War and War World II all brought about new consideration and theories about natural law.[15]

Two points should be kept in mind. First, the discussion about various theories on natural law is not a denial of natural law, nor is it a denial that natural law is not applicable to all human beings. The fact that there are so many theories about natural law in some measure suggests that natural law exists. It also is not surprising that people have reconsidered the nature of natural law, its scope, and how to best express it as the *Zeitgeist* changed and after events that shook humankind's faith in its own civility

---

13. Noah E. Fehl, "An Essay on Natural Law," *Anglican Theological Review* 39, no. 4 (1957): 318. "With respect to comprehensiveness of concept and specificity of norms the theory of Thomas Aquinas is the only complete natural law formulated in Western thought, and in this respect it is significantly different from all classical theories."

14. Fehl, "An Essay on Natural Law," 332. "The historical character of human thought explains the ambiguity we have encountered in the term nature and in the phrase 'natural law.' 'Every fair and every war' wrote Jean Paul Richter, 'brings forth a new natural law.' We are not to conclude that the fact of difference invalidates all formulations of natural law or the concept of natural law itself. We must, however, raise the question of what the meaning of absolute norms can be outside the context of the horizon against which they were formulated."

15. After the Thirty Years' War there was an attempt to distance natural law from religion and from locating its source in God. The source of natural law was reason; in some ways, this was a move back toward the position of the Stoics. Considering that the Thirty Years' War had been fought over disputes over theology and religious ideas, it is not surprising that some would seek to redefine natural law apart from religion and theology. After World War II, another reexamination of natural law took place, especially in Germany, where some had used natural law and the orders of creation to justify the Nazi regime and the inhumanities it perpetuated.

(such as war and other events of inhumanity). The various formulations about natural law do not invalidate the concept of natural law.

Second, there has been a shift in the formulators about natural law. In ancient Greece, the primary formulator of natural law was the philosopher. With Philo and on through the Christian Church, the primary formulator was the theologian who used philosophy as a tool. In both of these cases, the philosopher and the theologian saw natural law as prescriptive. After the Enlightenment, there was a shift in understanding natural law as descriptive. Therefore, the formulators of natural law shifted toward scientists, political theorists, and in the twentieth century, to psychologists and sociologists with an emphasis on the individual.[16]

As the Greeks, especially the Stoics, demonstrated, the concept of natural law can be expressed outside of and apart from a Judeo/Christian background. The Greek philosophers concluded natural law must exist, because it was not reasonable for so many customs and contradictory laws (not to mention unjust laws) to exist. The Greeks came to such a conclusion (unrealized by them) first and foremost because God wrote the law on the heart of man. In the early twenty-first century with the reign of relativism and individualism, societal thinking is not much different than it was in ancient Greece. The irony is that the ancient Greek philosophers seem to be wiser in terms of natural law than postmodern/post-Christian twenty-first century Western society.

There is a need to discuss and teach natural law both in a postmodern culture and in the Church today. If Greek philosophers could make use of natural law arguments in their society, there is no reason Christians living in the twenty-first century cannot. For instance, in a recent blog post from the Archdiocese of Washington titled, "Natural Law Is Not New and Is Needed Now,"[17] the author describes how a Florida appeals court ruled that having two mothers or two fathers was equivalent to having a mother and a father. The author writes, "But once again it is

---

16. Fehl, "An Essay on Natural Law," 319. "Modern theory is concerned primarily with the rights of the individual and the political regime is justified only on the grounds that it protects and supports these rights. Secondly, the source of natural law is found in the reason but in the sentiments of the passions of men. Thus, sociology and psychology rather than philosophy provide the source and shape of modern natural law. Man in the state of nature is a passionate individualist."

17. Charles Pope, "Natural Law Is Not New and Is Needed Now," Archdiocese of Washington, September 26, 2010, http://blog.adw.org/2010/09/natural-law-is-not-new-and-is-needed-now/ (accessed November 4, 2010).

troubling how disregarded natural law is today in favor of ideological views. I must repeat, even before Scripture is opened, it is clear that the human body does not lie. A man is not for a man, a woman is not for a woman. Rather, the man is for the woman and the woman is for the man. Scripture surely confirms what natural law discloses." The ideology of the Florida Court of Appeals attempts to overcome what is natural to the physical, biological nature of male and female bodies. Of course, wishing or declaring something to be doesn't make it so. Even Plato, when he commented on the practices of the Spartans, recognized homosexual intercourse was against nature. He writes, "If one were to follow the ordinance of nature . . . declaring it right for a male not to engage in intercourse with a young man just as he has sexual pleasure with a female, a witness is brought forward from the nature of wild beasts, and pointing out that a male does not touch a male for such purposes because this is against nature."[18] The argument is so simple that even a child can understand it: if the animals don't behave that way, a person ought not either. If the ancient Greek philosophers recognized that such behavior was unnatural and they argued as such in the public sphere, even against the customs and laws of other peoples such as the Spartans, surely the Church, which has a much better foundation than Greek philosophy, can do so too.

There is a need to teach natural law in the Church. In many recent discussions about natural law, the focus tends toward engaging the public square. Natural law discussions ought to happen in the public square and be used for apologetic purposes, but recent discussions in the Church and newspaper headlines about the Church indicate that the Church itself is weak on the teaching of natural law.[19] Many mainline Christian churches

---

18. Plato, Laws 8.836c. "γάρ τις ἀκολουθῶν τῇ φύσει θήσει . . . λέγων ὡς ὀρθῶς εἶχεν τὸ τῶν ἀρρένων καὶ νέων μὴ κοινωνεῖν καθάπερ θηλειῶν πρὸς μεῖξιν ἀφροδισίων, μάρτυρα παραγόμενος τὴν τῶν θηρίων φύσιν καὶ δεικνὺς πρὸς τὰ τοιαῦτα οὐχ ἁπτόμενον ἄρρενα ἄρρενος διὰ τὸ μὴ φύσει τοῦτο εἶναι." Plato, Platonis opera, ed. John Burnet, Scriptorum classicorum bibliotheca Oxoniensis (Oxonii [Oxford, England]: E typographeo Clarendoniano, 1900), http://www.perseus.tufts.edu/hopper/text?doc=Perseus:text:1999.01.0165:book%3D8:section%3D836c (accessed October 7, 2010).

19. For example, recent headlines read: "PCUSA, Anglicans, Virginia Episcopalians Affirm Homosexual Ordination"; "PCUSA General Assembly Votes to Allow Homosexual Ordination"; "How the ELCA Left the Great Tradition for Liberal Protestantism"; "United Methodist Bishop Takes Pro-Choice Stand"; "Late-Term Abortionist, 'Faithful Lutheran' Martyr Like MLK?"; "Presbyterian Church Committee: Allow Same-sex Marriage," and so on.

in the United States now endorse and approve of a number of practices that were once forbidden not only by natural law, but also by the Ten Commandments: same-sex marriage, the ordination of women, the ordination of homosexuals, elective abortion, and fetal stem cell research.[20] The Church, congregations, and parishioners need to be better instructed on natural law.

The remainder of this essay explores how natural law arguments can assist the Church in forming better theological arguments. The next section of the essay turns to the Stoics for a brief review of how the phrases "in accord with nature" and "against nature" were used. In this examination, the topic of *adiaphora* is discussed. The final part of the essay applies these arguments to the debate about women clergy and ordination of practicing homosexuals.

THE STOICS AND ACCORDING TO NATURE

According to Epictetus, a Stoic philosopher who lived in the second half of the first century AD, a person needed a mind that was in accord with nature.[21] This was important to the Greeks because law/custom (νόμος) was antithetical to nature (φύσις).[22] Plato provides one of the earliest examples of this antinomy in *Protagoras* written around 380 BC. Plato writes, "Hippias, the wise, spoke, 'O men,' he said, 'Those who are present, I consider you to be both kinsmen and friends, and fellow-citizens—by nature, not by law. For like is kin to like by nature. But the

---

20.   Natural law and the Ten Commandments are not at odds nor do they teach something different. The point here is that the Ten Commandments are revealed in the Scripture as the revelation of God. The Church has in its possession both the natural law and the will of God as revealed in the Holy Scriptures.

21.   Epicetus Diss. III.9. 17. Τίνος οὖν ἔχω χρείαν; —Τοῦ σοὶ μὴ παρόντος: τοῦ εὐσταθεῖν, τοῦ κατὰ φύσιν ἔχειν τὴν διάνοιαν, τοῦ μὴ ταράττεσθαι. ("Therefore what do I need? What you do not have: to be stable, to have a mind in accord with nature, to not be in turmoil.") Epictetus and Heinrich Schenkl, *Epicteti Dissertationes ab Arriano digestae; ad fidem codicis bodleiani iterum recensuit Henricus Schenkl; accedunt fragmenta, Euchiridion ex recensione Schweighaeuseri, gnomologiorum Epicteteorum reliquiae, indices.*, Bibliotheca scriptorvm graecorvm et romanorvm Tevbneriana (Lipsiae: in aedibus B. G. Teubneri, 1916), 262.

22.   Henry George Liddell, Henry Stuart Jones, and Roderick McKenzie, *A Greek-English Lexicon: with a Supplement 1968* (Oxford: Clarendon Press, 1925), 1965. "φύσις . . . opp. νόμῳ (by convention)."

law, being the tyrant of man, many times constrains us against nature.' "[23] Plato expressed an idea that was further developed by the neo-Platonists, that like was attracted to like. In the passage cited from Plato, the men were alike and drawn together by their natures (which were similar); a decree of law could not put people together in such a way. In fact, "laws" often put people together in ways against their natures. The gods, rulers, authorities, and people legislated and made laws and customs that were not necessarily reasonable, rational, or logical.[24] In fact, many times the laws were not reasonable, rational, or logical. The only alternative was to consider nature (φύσις) to provide stability and consistency beyond the laws and customs of a given god, people, or nation. Polytheism is incompatible with natural law.[25] There cannot be a universal law if multiple gods are making rulings. This is why some Greek philosophers rejected the "gods" in favor of the logical conclusion of monotheism or relegated the gods outside the realm of morality.[26] This is entirely consistent with natural law because polytheism is "against nature." In some ways, nature

---

23. Plato, *Protagoras* 337c-d. " Ἱππίας ὁ σοφὸς εἶπεν, ὦ ἄνδρες, ἔφη, οἱ παρόντες, ἡγοῦμαι ἐγὼ ὑμᾶς συγγενεῖς τε καὶ οἰκείους καὶ πολίτας ἅπαντας εἶναι—φύσει, οὐ νόμῳ· τὸ γὰρ ὅμοιον τῷ ὁμοίῳ φύσει συγγενές ἐστιν, ὁ δὲ νόμος, τύραννος ὢν τῶν ἀνθρώπων, πολλὰ παρὰ τὴν φύσιν βιάζεται." Plato, *Platonis opera*.

24. Piper, "What Is Natural Law?," 460. "It should be noted that this idea of 'natural laws' first developed in Greece in reaction to a movement in which the divine origin of the existing laws was generally denied. The new idea did not reinstate the gods, however, it rather barred them definitely from the sphere of legislation. They were considered as superfluous for establishing objective principles of general validity. Socrates and his followers agreed with the Sophists that there were no God-given laws. They only tried to curb the unlimited subjectivism of the Sophists by pointing to certain objective rules which could serve as guiding principles of human legislation and which with more or less clarity had been used by the ancient legislators."

25. This is perhaps the reason why the concept of natural law seems most prominent in societies subscribing to monotheism—Jewish, Christian, Islamic.

26. Zeno of Citeus, the great Stoic philosopher who greatly developed the concept of "natural law" in Greek thought, taught there was one god. It seems that he was really a panentheist, holding that there was one god who was ubiquitous throughout nature. In his explanation of the ubiquity of god, he spoke of Zeus as the powers of nature and Poseidon as god in the water. This almost appears to be a form of modalism, describing the one god throughout nature in terms of its form expressed in Greek mythology. Alfred Chilton Pearson, *The Fragments of Zeno & Cleanthes with Introduction & Explanatory Notes. An Essay Which Obtained the Hare Prize in the Year 1889* (London: C. J. Clay & Sons, 1891), 13. "It remains to consider Zeno's attitude towards the popular religion. Although, in the strict sense, he teaches that there is but one God, yet he admits that there is a certain amount of truth in polytheism, as implying a recognition of the ubiquity of the divine

(φύσις) had the tendency to become a sort of god in itself.[27] For the Stoics, natural law was identified with reason, a view that combined the thoughts of Plato and Aristotle.[28]

For the Stoic, what was according to nature (φύσις) could essentially be equated with reason or common sense. In fact, Zeno of Citeus argues that adultery is against nature (παρὰ φύσιν) by the ideas held in common (διὰ τὸ κοινωνικόν).[29] Because law/custom (νόμος) and nature (φύσις) are opposites, the "ideas held in common" (διὰ τὸ κοινωνικόν) refer to something different than the habitual use or customs. Basically, people held the common idea that adultery was wrong because it went against nature, that is, it specifically went against the nature of marriage. Whether it is "legal" or "lawful" to adulterate another man's wife isn't the issue; it simply is wickedness (κακά) because it is against nature (παρὰ φύσιν). "Ethics, which are the crowning point of the stoic system, come next in order. The aim and object of life is to live in agreement with nature, which is, in other words, to live according to virtue: for this is the goal to which nature conducts us."[30]

Yet the ethics developed from the ideas held in common ("common sense"), the ideas which were according to nature, were incapable of establishing an absolute standard for good (ἀγαθά) and wickedness (κακά).

---

presence. The manifestation of God in the powers of nature is symbolised by Zeus, Hera and Poseidon, who represent the aether, the air, and the water respectively."

27. Piper, "What Is Natural Law?," 460. "The Stoic concept of the law of nature seems at first sight to restore the divine prerogatives since this school identified the divine with nature."

28. Piper, "What Is Natural Law?," 460. "Plato taught that the knowledge of these natural or unwritten laws was based upon man's innate, intuitive knowledge of justice, that all human legislation was some kind of approximation to this idea, and that the true laws could be inferred deductively from it. Aristotle chose a different approach. He held that the natural principles of legislation could be discovered in the very nature of social relations and be learned from the observation of the facts. The Stoics combined these two views."

29. Hans Friedrich August von Arnim, *Stoicorum Veterum Fragmenta: Zeno et Zenonis Discipvli*, vol. 1 (Tuebneri: Stutgardiae In aedibus B.G., 1964), 58. ἐκκλίνουσι τὸ μοιχεύειν οἱ τὰ τοῦ Κιτιέως Ζήνωνος φιλοσοφοῦντες . . . διὰ τὸ κοινωνικόν· καὶ <γὰρ> παρὰ φύσιν εἶναι τῷ λογικῷ ζώῳ νοθεύειν τὴν ὑπὸ τῶν νόμων ἑτέρῳ προκαταληφθεῖσαν γυναῖκα καὶ φθείρειν τὸν ἄλλου ἀνθρώπου οἶκον. ("Those who pursue the philosophy of Zeno of Citeus avoid engaging in adultery on account of ideas that are commonly held. For [they say that] it is even against nature for the creature of reason to engage in adulterating a woman who is still legally married, and to engage in ruining the home of another man.")

30. Pearson, *The Fragments of Zeno & Cleanthes*, 13.

This same Zeno of Citeus, who taught that adultery was against nature, euthanized himself by strangulation in 264 BC after he fell and broke a finger in his old age. Suicide apparently was not against nature (παρὰ φύσιν), at least in that particular situation. This helps to demonstrate the limitations of arriving at natural law on the basis of reason. Human reason has been corrupted by the fall. Reason is distorted and can come to a wrong conclusion, for example, that suicide is in accord with nature.

APPLICATION TO *ADIAPHORA* AND ORDINATION

In philosophical thought (especially among the Stoics), *adiaphora* (ἀδιάφορα "indifferent things") was the term developed to describe something that was κατὰ φύσιν (*kata physin*, "according to nature"), but not παρὰ φύσιν (*para physin*, "against nature"). Both "natural law" and the "orders of creation" fit into this understanding, for the male being created before the female is κατὰ φύσιν (*kata physin*, "according to nature") and as such, "male" and "female," while equal in terms of humanness and importance, do have different roles and responsibilities. *Adiaphora* are in between what is "good" and "bad" and between what is "according to nature" and "against nature." Things considered to be *adiaphora* cannot be "against nature," lest they would be bad. The Stoic understanding of what is "in accord with nature" and what is "against nature" is understood in ethical/moral terms, not in physical terms. Therefore, the Stoic could understand "death" as an *adiaphoron* because it is neither good nor bad.[31] Some authors have argued that St. Paul adopted the Stoic view and regarded "death" an *adiaphoron* in Christ Jesus.[32] Once again, the limitations of natural law according to reason, apart from the revelation that death is the result of sin and rebellion against God, become apparent.

---

31. Epictetus, *Discourses* 2.19.13. "Of things some are good, some are bad, and others are indifferent. The good then are the virtues and the things which partake of the virtues: the bad are the vices, and the things which partake of them; and the indifferent are the things which lie between the virtues and the vices, wealth, health, life, death, pleasure, pain." Translation from Epictetus, *The Discourses of Epictetus, with the Enchiridion and Fragments*, trans. George Long (London: G. Bell & Sons, 1890).

32. James L. Jaquette, "Life and Death, Adiaphora, and Paul's Rhetorical Strategies," *Novum Testamentum* 38, no. 1 (January 1, 1996): 30–54.

In terms of natural law, homosexuality cannot be regarded as an *adiaphoron* because homosexual relations are "against the natures" of the sexes, although proponents of normalizing homosexuality argue that it is not against nature to use the sexual organs in a manner different than the Creator's original intention.[33] In the late twentieth and early twenty-first centuries, some people within historic Christian denominations have argued that homosexuality is an *adiaphoron*.[34] Often those who argue that homosexuality is "not against nature" and is an *adiaphoron* do so in part on the basis that sexual mores vary from age to age and place to place.[35] Such an argument that sexual mores vary is, by definition, against natural law. Until relatively recently, this traditional "natural law" common sense generally was accepted by most people. In these last days, when the human race lives with a seared conscience (1 Timothy 4:2), the basic orders of creation are challenged and overturned as people attempt to remake creation in their own fallen image.

In 1 Corinthians 11:8 and 1 Timothy 2:12–13, St. Paul argues against women preaching and teaching on the basis of the order of creation—namely, that the Lord created Adam before Eve. Since most exegetes today interpret Paul's injunction about women wearing head coverings in worship (see 1 Corinthians 11:5–6) as culturally conditioned and an *adiaphoron*, some have attempted to use that argument to displace the prohibition against women teaching found in 1 Timothy. If head coverings are culturally conditioned, an *adiaphoron*, then so must the prohibition against women teaching. Some have explained these verses as relating to

---

33. Timothy W. Bartel, "Adiaphora: The Achilles Heel of the Windsor Report," *Anglican Theological Review* 89, no. 3 (June 1, 2007): 413. "Of course, it has often been objected that homosexuality is morally wrong because it is 'unnatural,' or contrary to nature, in some morally relevant sense. But this line of objection is easily refuted if it contends that homosexual activity is immoral simply because it uses the sexual organs for a purpose different to any which God originally intended for them. . . . Nor can homosexual activity be deemed 'against nature' because the exclusive or predominant sexual orientation of all human beings is toward those of the opposite sex, and therefore homosexual activity is a willful, perverse choice to override that orientation."

34. Bartel, "Adiaphora: The Achilles Heel of the Windsor Report," 414. "What is settled is that the morality of homosexuality is *adiaphora*."

35. Bartel, "Adiaphora: The Achilles Heel of the Windsor Report," 413–414. "Apart from the fact that sexual behavior and sexual norms differ widely from society from society, it is also a fact that many human beings are attracted to those of the same sex as strongly, and as unalterably, as many are attracted to those of the opposite sex."

the lives of believers in "their homes within the society of that age." The apparent conclusion is that these passages only apply to family life and/or the people of that time.

The apparent contradiction in St. Paul is really no contradiction. Paul's admonition for women to wear head coverings in worship is the cultural expression of the order of creation reality that there are differences between men and women. How various cultures express that recognition can change. But the root cause that originates these various cultural expressions of the reality does not change.[36] St. Paul's argument, in fact, is much broader and applies to "women" in general and not simply "wives." Again arguing from the "orders of creation" and what is κατὰ φύσιν (*kata physin*, "according to nature"), men and women "according to nature" from the beginning of the human race until now, pair off, marry, and have children.

The ordinary expectation not only in Paul's time but also ours is for men and women to marry. Married couples, according to the natural order of things, produce children. If this were not the case, the human race would not continue on the earth. Paul describes the natural order of things—how things normally proceed between a man and woman. According to nature (κατὰ φύσιν, *kata physin*), men and women marry and have children. According to nature (κατὰ φύσιν, *kata physin*), in the sense that St. Paul understands "authority," a woman is always under the authority of a man. She is either under the authority of her father or her husband. Once again, Paul treats the "exceptions," widows, divorcees, orphans, single women, as such—exceptions—and not strictly speaking "according to the natural order of things" or according to how the Lord created the world and intended men and women to operate.

St. Paul's arguments regarding the role of women in the Church appeal to the natural law. What is κατὰ φύσιν (*kata physin*, "according to nature") does not change throughout the age of the human race. It

---

36. Benjamin L. Merkle, "Paul's Arguments from Creation in 1 Corinthians 11:8–9 and 1 Timothy 2:13–14: An Apparent Inconsistency Answered," *Journal of the Evangelical Theological Society* 49, no. 3 (2006): 529. "The direct application of his reasoning is to show that creation affirms gender and role distinctions between men and women—and in the Corinthian context that distinction needed to be upheld through head coverings. Therefore, Paul's argument from creation to show that men and women are distinct cannot be culturally relegated. The application of that principle (i.e., head coverings), however, can change with culture. In contrast, the argument from creation in 1 Timothy 2 applies directly to Paul's prohibition and therefore is transcultural."

extends through time and across cultures. Granted, what we have understood as being "according to nature" can be influenced by the times in which we live and by our culture, but what is truly "according to nature" does not change. Thus, "according to nature" male humans will never give birth, for only female humans, according to the way they are naturally designed, can become pregnant and give birth. Having received dominion over the earth—even in the sense that such dominion remains after the fall into sin—allows human beings to do some things that are παρὰ φύσιν (*para physin*—"against nature"). Yet, our ability to do things "against nature" does not mitigate or alter what is "according to nature."

The recognition that St. Paul's argument regarding the ordination of women flows from an understanding of what is κατὰ φύσιν (*kata physin*, "according to nature") and παρὰ φύσιν (*para physin*, "against nature") may help us understand other consequences to the ordination of women. The violation of the created order with the ordination of women corresponds with another violation—the ordination of practicing homosexuals. In the majority of the church bodies that have ordained women, there is pressure to ordain practicing homosexuals as ministers of the Gospel. The very same hermeneutical arguments used to support the ordination of women are also applied to the ordination of practicing homosexuals. Many churches have succumbed to the pressure to ordain practicing homosexuals and, in the process, have departed from the faith. If the ordination of women brings judgment, the ordination of practicing homosexuals brings condemnation (1 Corinthians 11:29–32).

Connected with *adiaphora* is the *satis est* ("it is enough") from the Augsburg Confession, Article VII 2, which states "it is not necessary to have absolute uniformity in all matters." Some have attempted to relegate woman's ordination, among other practices, as a matter in which uniformity is not needed. This is a quotation from the Latin text of the Augsburg Confession, Article VII. In the immediate context, the Roman Church was demanding "uniformity" in liturgical and ritualistic practices. To this, AC VII in both Latin and German, confesses "it is enough (*satis est*) for the true unity of the Christian church that there the gospel is preached harmoniously" (*einträchtiglich*, "with one accord"). The Latin text of the AC VII defines the minimum, while the German text defines the maximum.[37] The Church is not able to preach the Gospel

---

37. Hermann Sasse, *We Confess the Church*, trans. Norman Nagel (St. Louis: Concordia, 1986), 67. "The great 'It is enough' (*satis est*) is clearly directed against Rome.

with one accord when there is a dispute over the means by which the Gospel is delivered (AC V, the "Preaching Office"/"The Office of the Holy Ministry"). The Gospel of Jesus Christ is proclaimed by means of the Office of the Holy Ministry. The "means" used to deliver the Gospel can be in accord with the Gospel or against the Gospel. The ordination of women, in fact, is against the Gospel. It goes against the very heart of the how the Gospel is delivered and, therefore, is not an *adiaphoron*.

Adiaphora can never be contrary to nature.[38] The concept of *adiaphora* grew out of Stoicism's discussion about natural law (what is in accord with nature and what is against nature). An *adiaphoron* was something that was neither good nor bad, but could not be contrary to virtue; hence, it could not be contrary to nature. This recognition can help us formulate better theological arguments, discussions, and presentations when discussing controverted matters. Lutherans are most accustomed to speaking about *adiaphora,* as the Formula of Concord, Solid Declaration, Article X describe it, as matters "which are neither commanded nor forbidden by the Word of God."[39] What FC SD X describes does not disagree with the statement that *adiaphora* cannot be against nature, or the nature of the thing being discussed. Often the phrase "neither commanded nor forbidden" is taken in a reductionistic sense. *Argumentum absurdum*: the Scriptures do not mention automobiles, computers, or cell phones, so we can use these items anyway we see fit. A more pertinent example is the claim that Jesus said nothing about homosexuality. On its face this appears true, since the word *homosexual* did not even exist until

---

For the unity of the church Rome required more than unity in the faith; it required the acceptance of human traditions and ceremonies. *Satis est* does not then postulate a minimum of agreement, a consensus, which we achieve in the course of our discussions, but a maximum: '. . . that [with one accord, *einträchtiglich*] the Gospel be preached *in conformity with a pure understanding of it* and that the sacraments be administered in accordance with the divine Word' [italics Dr. Sasse's]. Not the agreement in doctrine—the Roman church has a consensus in doctrine, the Baptists also have one; every church has some sort of consensus, even if it is a consensus in agreeing that doctrine is not important—but only the consensus in the *pure* doctrine and in the right administration of the sacraments is the consensus demanded in the Augsburg Confession. That is the 'great unanimity' (*magnus consensus*) with which the first article of the Augsburg Confession begins, a consensus not made by men but given by God, the consensus in the right faith, which only the Holy Spirit creates."

38. Pearson, *The Fragments of Zeno & Cleanthes*, 15. "A virtuous action can never be contrary to nature."

39. FC SD X, "welche in Gottes Wort weder geboten noch verboten sind" and "quae Verbo Dei neque mandatae neque prohibitae sunt."

the eighteenth century.[40] Yet Jesus did teach about and uphold the Sixth Commandment.[41] Similar examples can be drawn from other controverted issues in the Church such as woman's ordination, contemporary worship ("guitars are not mentioned in the Bible"), homosexual marriage, and other issues.

One idea that we can reappropriate from the Stoics in our discussions about natural law and *adiaphora*, especially within the Church, is what is "in accord with nature" and "what is against nature." Here, the realm of "nature" extends beyond the ethical or the physical. For example, a man and man as a "married" couple goes against the nature of marriage. The ordination of female clergy goes against the "nature" of the Office of the Holy Ministry and against "ordination," in part, because it is against the very order of creation. Likewise, homosexuality is against the way creation has been ordered, and the ordination of practicing homosexuals also goes against nature. There are other examples and applications as well.[42] The same reductionistic argumentation that allows for the ordination of women corresponds to the ordination of practicing homosexuals. Recent Church history has shown there are very few exceptions.

Being female is not sinful. Both women and men were created in the image of God, and both women and men were redeemed by Christ. However, a female who enters into the Office of the Holy Ministry is in a state of sin, for she has acted against nature by violating the order of creation and the institution and mandate of Jesus, who puts men He has chosen into the office. In contrast, a practicing homosexual is in a state of unrepentant sin. Homosexual practice is in violation against nature; putting practicing homosexuals into the Office of the Holy Ministry goes against the nature of that office. Neither can be considered an *adiaphoron*

---

40. Karl Maria Kertbeny coined the term "homosexuelle" in 1869 as a replacement for the term "Sodomite." "Karl-Maria Kertbeny—Wikipedia, the free encyclopedia," http://en.wikipedia.org/wiki/Karl-Maria_Kertbeny (accessed October 7, 2010).

41. Ironically, while some pro-homosexual ordination writers acknowledge that Jesus taught against divorce and adultery, they suggest that a committed, non-promiscuous homosexual relationship stays within the moral teaching of Jesus.

42. In recent times, the Church has struggled with cooperation in externals and what are the boundaries. A simple approach: cooperation in externals cannot be against natural law in the point of cooperation. For instance, if the cooperation in externals involves the adoption of children, the said cooperation cannot work together in an area that is against natural law, such as the adoption of children by homosexual couples, which in itself is against nature.

because both are against the nature of ordination and the Office of the Holy Ministry.

In a similar way, just because a church is able to "ordain" a woman does not mean such an action is approved by the Gospel or mandated by Christ's institution of the holy ministry as it is established in Matthew 28 and in John 20. Sinful human beings who still retain some measure of dominion over the earth are able to do all sorts of things that are "against nature"—physically, morally, and spiritually. Human beings are able to violate the natural order of things by creating human/mouse chimerae,[43] engaging in homosexual acts, ordaining women, and so on. Such usurping of the natural order illustrates that unnatural acts can be described as "humanity displaces God and elevates itself as the sole source of all value."[44] Ultimately, it is the violation of the First Commandment, the murder of God, and the replacement of God with man. Nothing that is adiaphorous can be against the nature of the Lord's Holy Law or His life-giving Gospel.

CONCLUSION

The Church's confession of natural law to both Church and world has been too weak. Vices and moral corruption that even pagan philosophers could identify via natural law, the mainstream Protestant church has difficulty in identifying as sin. There are not two laws—one for Christians and one for pagans.[45] There is one law established by the Lord, that is known in part (though that knowledge is now distorted by sin) because it

---

43. "Mouse with Human Brain May Live | LiveScience," February 17, 2005, http://www.livescience.com/technology/technovel_mouse_050217.html. "Now, Stanford University has given famed researcher Irving Weissman permission to create a mouse-human hybrid. The intent is to inject human brain cells into the brains of developing mice to see what happens. The National Academy of Sciences will unveil guidelines on chimera and stem cell research this spring."

44. Gregory Morgan Swer, "'Nature,' Physis, and the Holy," *Journal for the Study of Religion, Nature and Culture* 2, no. 2 (2006): 238.

45. Dietrich Bonhoeffer, "The Concrete Commandment and the Divine Mandates," in *Ethics*, vol. 6, Dietrich Bonhoeffer Works (Minneapolis: Fortress Press, 1996), 339. "The church does not have a twofold word, the one general, rational, and grounded in natural law and the other Christian—that is, it does not have one word for unbelievers and the another for believers." Actually, the Lord does speak with two words: the Word of Law and the Word of the Gospel. The Lord does not have two laws, one for believers and one for unbelievers.

is written upon the heart of man. That law also has been revealed clearly and infallibly in the Holy Scriptures. If the Church cannot proclaim and teach the law to the Church, how can she stand in the public square to bear witness to the truth before the world? If the Church reduces the Law and becomes Antinomian, the Church cannot proclaim the Gospel that rescues us from sin and death, for people do not know they are in need of rescue and salvation. Yet people do know on the basis of natural law that things are not right and that they need help, causing them to seek it in various places. No doubt evangelism would be improved if the Church clearly proclaimed the Law of God and the Gospel that delivers us from the Law's condemnation. Of course, one without the other does not help. A Law reductionism leads to a Gospel reductionism. The development of natural law in the history of ideas has come full circle and, in some sense, today is similar to the time of the ancient Greek philosophers. The cultural climate of the day gives us great opportunity to provide not only guidance and leadership in moral and ethical issues, but also to proclaim the truth of Law and Gospel to a world seeking answers. Now is the time for us to boldly confess to the Church and to the world.

15

A Way Forward?

Continuing Conversations on Natural Law

Matthew E. Cochran

The Rise and Fall of Natural Law

The classical Christian tradition has always held a place for the idea of natural law. From Paul's assertion of a law written on the heart, through Augustine and Aquinas, to Luther, other Reformers, and beyond, Christians have always recognized that God's moral law is both right and known by all people. God's moral law is known whether or not people have had access to Scriptures, prophets, or other forms of special revelation. Modernism, however, with its search for an utterly belief-neutral and universal methodology for acquiring knowledge, was not kind to this idea. For example, Dutch philosopher Hugo Grotius (1583–1645) suggested that natural law would maintain a kind of authority even if God did not exist.[1] Others took Grotius to mean that natural law could be independent of any divine authority.[2] Scottish philosopher David Hume (1711–76) had an even more destructive influence on natural law theory. In addition to his skepticism concerning the ability to discern anything about God from nature, Hume also wrote that one could not deduce a genuine morality from nature—to discern an *ought* from an *is*.[3]

As many elites sought to distance God first from natural law and then from nature, and as epistemology was influenced by Rationalism and empiricism, the idea of natural moral law gradually faded from view. The scientific method could discover no such law; therefore, it did not exist. Further, modernism's eventual failure to achieve certainty and common agreement on many issues led many to believe that nothing is certain; therefore, there is nothing on which to agree—especially morality.

Accordingly, many people describe our era as *postmodern*. They assert that no common or objective morality exists, or if it does, there is no neutral or objective means of knowing it—only individuals and societies constructing morality for themselves. But this, too, has proven problematic. Human beings were created for moral objectivity; that we cannot stop condemning one another and rationalizing our actions prove this.[4] The relativist who creates his own morality judges people who "force" their morality on others. The nihilist who denies the existence of meaning looks down on those who do not embrace the harsh truth as he does. Even those who deny an objective moral standard invariably act as though such a standard exists and that everyone else ought to know it. In such a climate, it is certain that many postmodern dogmatisms will not long survive.

If postmodernism has made morality so subjective that meaningful conversations on the subject are difficult, then a law written on the heart—known to all and right for all—would have obvious utility. Rather than trying to impose an entire moral system from the outside, one could

---

1.   Hugo Grotius, *Prolegomena to the Law of War and Peace,* trans. Francis W. Kelsey, (Indianapolis: Bobbs-Merrill, 1957), para. 11.

2.   Although it is unlikely that Grotius himself would have accepted this.

3.   David Hume, *A Treatise of Human Nature,* ed. L. A. Selby-Bigge (Oxford: Clarendon, 1896), 3.1.1, 469.

4.   A fact that Paul points out in Romans 2.

appeal to the basics that are already there. As Luther writes, "Were it not naturally written in the heart, one would have to teach and preach the law for a long time before it became the concern of conscience. The heart must also find and feel the law in itself."[5] Objective moral standards are necessary for humans to determine how they ought to act among one another; the Enlightenment has not produced anything as satisfactory. For this very reason, there has been a resurgence of interest in natural law theories, not only among Roman Catholics whose tradition never abandoned natural law, but also among a growing number of evangelicals.

Nevertheless, natural law theory has hardly remained unscathed. With God out of the picture, natural law theory becomes confused with mere naturalism. The narrow epistemology of Hume and other Enlightenment thinkers makes it difficult to discern and justify moral precepts. Additionally, the natural knowledge of God and natural law have been obscured and darkened by man's fall into sin. In light of such challenges, is it possible to rehabilitate natural law theory and make it useful once more? This essay will argue that a natural law theory, connected to God through divine revelation but whose basic principles are nevertheless intuitively known by all people, can indeed serve as common moral ground, even with secularists. This essay does not propose to offer the final word on how to resolve apparent difficulties with reappropriating a natural law theory. However, it will suggest that reviving our long-dormant conversation about natural law might help prove if such a project has potential.

Mere Naturalism

First, a problem. Christians are not the only ones seeking out a form of natural law. Because of its history, "natural law" often brings to mind a purely naturalistic concept. What is more, some see advantages in building a purely secular ethic in light of the same circumstances accompanying a Christian reappraisal of natural law. One recent example is *evolutionary psychology*, which seeks to derive morality from a universal human nature using a Darwinian hypothesis. Moral precepts are said to have evolved in situations benefitting ancient humans' chances of propagating

---

5.   Quoted in Paul Althaus, *The Ethics of Martin Luther*, trans. Robert C. Schulz (Philadelphia: Fortress, 1972), 28.

their genes, thus supporting the survival of the species. For example, caring for offspring became a moral precept because it increased parents' chances of reproducing themselves and passing on their genetic material.

Using this hypothesis, it seems reasonable that we would naturally love our children. It even seems "right" that we would do so. Of course, even if one were to accept evolution, such an account of human nature is dubious. J. Budziszewski suggests that evolutionary psychology does not discover anything. It makes an observation about human behavior, and then attempts to provide an evolutionary scenario for how such behavior became programmed in our minds.[6] At best, evolutionary psychology offers hypothetical (and typically unverifiable) explanations for aspects of a universal human nature. It has little to offer in terms of access to that nature.

Of course, Hume's *is-ought* critique remains another concern for evolutionary psychology. That a behavior might advantage reproduction (or at least was allegedly advantageous at some point in prehistory) does not mean that it is moral—that it ought to be conformed to. Genes do not help us distinguish between right and wrong. To leap from a state of nature to good and evil requires an inference. Social Darwinism, which sought to base morality on the notion of survival of the fittest, had a rather infamous and short-lived turn at the helm of moral philosophy. A more popular attempt to bridge the *is-ought* gap has been utilitarianism, which seeks to maximize pleasure and minimize suffering in the world. Many suggest that utilitarianism provides the only real moral principle common to humanity. As Robert Wright describes in *The Moral Animal*,

> Belief in the goodness of happiness and the badness of suffering isn't just a basic part of moral discourse that we all share. Increasingly it seems to be the only basic part that we all share. . . . It is the common denominator for discussion, the only premise everyone stands on. It's just about all we have left.[7]

The way Wright's utilitarian argument is constructed parallels notions of natural law. For example, Wright quotes John Stuart Mill (1806–73) in describing pleasure good/pain bad as a moral first principle. A first principle needs no proof because nearly everyone already acts as though

---

6.   J. Budziszewski, *The Line through the Heart* (Wilmington, DE: ISI Books, 2009), 84.
7.   Robert Wright, *The Moral Animal* (New York: Vintage Books, 1994), 334.

it were true.[8] While the form of utilitarianism is strikingly similar to that of many natural law theories, its content leaves much to be desired. Pure physical pain is not bad in itself. When one places a hand on a hot stove, the real problem is not that it hurts, but that one's flesh is burning. Pain merely indicates that something is going wrong with a part of the body. In fact, the inability to feel pain is a dangerous problem rather than a fortuitous circumstance. Budziszewski notes that much of the Western philosophical tradition has held that pleasure is likewise not an end in itself, but a by-product of seeking other goals.[9] Pleasure and pain can be connected to good and evil, but utilitarianism fudges the connection. Even if pleasure and pain are directly connected to good and evil, they are not a source but an indication.

Naturalistic ethicists offer a moral system whereby most people get what they want by helping others, but have no response to those who believe they can get what they want without playing along. Even when common human nature is brought to the table, there can be no moral condemnation of individual choice. For example, the best Wright can manage is the weak suggestion that wrongdoers are incorrect about their own self-interest.[10] When it comes to heinous crimes such as murder or rape, humans seek something more substantive than "he was misinformed about his own happiness" or "he miscalculated the pleasure he would receive with respect to the pain he would cause." In Los Angeles, for example, a doctor raped an anesthetized patient. Utilitarianism might suggest that, if the rapist enjoyed himself and the patient felt no pain, such an act might have been a moral good.[11] Even if the patient's indignation and mental anguish were considered as pain, the doctor's crime would have been more a case of his carelessness and indiscretion than a grave moral misdeed. Most people would find this conclusion unacceptable. For a utilitarian, an analysis of the greater implications for pleasure and pain might *follow* such a judgment, but it need never *precede* such a judgment.

---

8.   Wright, *The Moral Animal*, 333–34.
9.   Budziszewski, *The Line through the Heart,* 86.
10.   Wright, *The Moral Animal*, 335.
11.   Gregory Koukl, "Minimalist Ethic—Too Minimal," *Stand to Reason*, http://www
    .str.org/site/News2?page=NewsArticle&id=5448, para. 14 (accessed November
    4, 2010).

The problem with such a naturalistic conception of natural law is that it purports a different understanding of "law." The laws of nature are the rules according to which nature behaves; they are descriptive rather than prescriptive. However, laws with a genuinely moral dimension involve the will. The will takes no part in our conformance to the law of gravity or whether we feel pleasure or pain. Yet, our will inheres in our conformance to the Ten Commandments—if indeed we do conform. That "if" is the key to the issue. Except for miracles, matter will always obey the laws of physics; when a miracle occurs, matter still has no say—it merely obeys different rules. Before the fall, man could choose good or evil; today, even fallen man may choose better and worse courses of action despite genuinely good choices being beyond his grasp. It is choice—the exercise of the will—that can be condemned as immoral. Moral law indicates an authority that we *ought* to obey rather than a rule that simply *is* followed—an authority who is concerned with those affected by our actions and with whose will our own actions are meant to align.

God and Natural Law

The failure of a naturalistic alternative to classic natural law and the role of authority in moral law show why God must be brought back into the picture. Godless natural law has been tried and it has failed. While the Enlightenment's approach to natural law suggested that binding norms were independent of belief, contemporary natural law scholars are concluding that belief is necessary. In *The Changing Face of Natural Law*, William Mattison considers two respected Roman Catholic scholars, Russell Hittinger and Jean Porter, who have recently sought to develop an understanding of natural law more in line with that of Thomas Aquinas. According to Mattison, both Hittinger and Porter agree that natural law does not and cannot provide some kind of "free-floating" moral norms independent of any kind of authority. Though they hold natural law to be right and known to all, they also acknowledge the necessity of belief in order to "identify and justify" its precepts.[12] Each of these scholars notes that prior to the Enlightenment, thinkers boldly used Scripture and the-

---

12.   William C. Mattison III, "The Changing Face of Natural Law: The Necessity of Belief for Natural Law Norm Specification," *Journal of the Society of Christian Ethics* 27 (Spring–Summer 2007): 251.

ology to formulate a theory of natural law.[13] In addition to Hittinger and Porter, one could also add Budziszewski, who likewise argues for the essential role of God and revelation in natural law.[14]

While seemingly counterintuitive, religious belief acquired through divine revelation helps to determine what we know naturally. It also serves as a necessary component of any plausible natural law theory. True, the sometimes profound variations between different cultural moral systems, and likewise their historical development, present argumentative challenges to natural law. Nevertheless, one must remember that the moral precepts written on the heart do not comprise a complete moral system, but rather a starting point. Likewise, conclusions drawn from the God-given ability to reason morally have no guarantee of being identical in all circumstances. Porter argues that despite a broad common basis, how that basis is expressed may vary either by mere circumstance or by sinful corruption.[15]

Cultural differences result in different sets of rules. Additionally, we must consider man's fall into sin. Sin darkens man's knowledge of God and of God's law. We try to suppress and avoid God's law. Both of these factors will result in variation; it is only natural that personal or cultural beliefs about God and the world will deeply influence such variation. Consequently, standing between the law written on the heart and any theory that attempts to describe it is the art of interpretation. For Christians, the Holy Scriptures, which are inspired by the Author of natural law, are the infallible norm for clarifying the distortions wrought by sinful man. Even with the Scriptures, Christians sometimes arrive at different conclusions about them. Undoubtedly, people without such a norm also will arrive at different conclusions. Theories of natural law cannot ultimately be belief-neutral.

If natural law depends on belief, however, how does it provide common ground with those who do not share our faith? In his essay, "Rethinking Natural Law," Daniel Heimbach questions the utility of the natural law tradition for restoring moral standards in an increasingly decadent culture. While he recognizes two streams of thought within the history of natural law—that which depends on divine authority ("supernaturalistic") and that which does not ("naturalistic")—he only criticizes

---

13. Mattison, "The Changing Face of Natural Law," 252–53.

14. Budziszewski, *The Line through the Heart*, 41–59.

15. Jean Porter, *Nature as Reason* (Grand Rapids: Eerdmans, 2005), 14–15.

the naturalistic variety. As noted above, this variety has little to no value. Yet Heimbach seems to assume that the alternative—a supernaturalistic natural law theory—has no value either. He writes, "In a post-Christian, postmodern context, restoring moral foundations sustaining civil happiness will not come from relying on natural law on terms denying the supernatural, but rather from appealing to the supernatural origin whose laws permeate nature."[16] Here Heimbach appeals to God, not to natural law given by God. Nevertheless, Heimbach lists Budziszewski, whose view of natural law is in no wise naturalistic, among contemporary natural law authors. But what of the alternative approach? Can a supernaturalistic version of natural law serve as common ground with the nonbeliever? We should not dismiss the possibility.

Common Ground?

In seeking to establish moral common ground with those who do not share our beliefs, natural law *theory* must be distinguished from natural law *fact*. Regardless of the theory, God assures us in His Word that He has written His law on the hearts of all mankind.[17] One need not subscribe to any particular natural law theory or even have a theory to have basic moral knowledge. Talking about the fact of natural law is invariably an attempt to theorize, but it remains *about* the fact.[18] As C. S. Lewis observed, different cultures may permit one or many wives, but every culture recognizes that a man cannot simply take any woman he wants whenever he wants.[19] Regardless of the path of cultural development, every culture recognizes marriage between a man and a woman, even if there are variances to the number of spouses permitted. The same is true for other laws. The Decalogue summarizes enduring moral principles that exist, even if suppressed, denied, or obscured. These principles will always influence, to some degree, every moral system. The law written on the heart is consistent, even though man's heart, corrupted by sin, is not.

---

16. Daniel Heimbach, "Rethinking Natural Law: Is It Our Best Strategy for Engaging the Public Square?" http://www.phc.edu/journalfiles/heimbach on natural law .pdf, 8 (accessed September 29, 2010).

17. Romans 2:15.

18. Budziszewski, *The Line through the Heart*, 2–3.

19. C. S. Lewis, *Mere Christianity* (San Francisco: HarperCollins, 2001), 6.

This means that while the law written on our heart may be suppressed, it may not be erased. However misinterpreted, misused and disobeyed, it is always present and active. Consider, for example, a man who is confronted over an adulterous affair. He may deny having done anything wrong, but even his denial indicates that he knows adultery is wrong. He may, for example, claim that while he and his wife are not technically divorced, they have grown so far apart that they might as well be. Such an excuse acknowledges the wrong of violating marriage in such a way, while denying the reality that he is actually married. Another man may claim that he and his wife have an "understanding" about this sort of thing—that while he is allowed to see other women from time to time, he always returns to his wife. Such an excuse also acknowledges the wrong of violating marriage, but it denies that his adulterous affairs are really violations because he has his wife's permission.

The same can be seen in the case of abortion. Most people understand that intentionally killing an innocent human being is wrong. We see this even in arguments defending abortion: People typically deny that the fetus is human, alive, or innocent (i.e., the fetus "invaded" the woman's body), or suggest that abortion is unintentional (i.e., "she had no choice").[20] While people deny their own sin, they do so in a way that acknowledges sin's existence. Then they excuse themselves of it. This suggests that natural law remains common ground, although we may need to modify our understanding of "common." Budziszewski points out that because of our sinful evasions, we cannot define natural law as "what everyone concedes" or "what no one denies" because such things do not exist.[21] Our common ground does not always reveal itself in common assent, but we cannot afford to act as though lack of assent is therefore a lack of common ground. As sinners, we are not always honest even with ourselves, let alone with others. Any practical use of natural law will therefore involve revealing latent moral knowledge, which people may not realize they possess. Such a task is not always easy, but it can be profitable when other approaches to moral persuasion have failed to gain traction.

Consider, for example, the issue of premarital sex—an issue that Mattison uses to illustrate the necessity of belief for the application of

20. Budziszewski, *The Line through the Heart*, 18–19.
21. Budziszewski, *The Line through the Heart*, 5.

natural law.[22] It indeed serves as a good example of latent knowledge, given that the Christian tradition has considered the wrong of extramarital sex to be a part of the natural law. Yet this does not seem self-evident in today's culture. Mattison explores the difficulty in moving beyond a basic and more or less universal imperative that we ought not "sexually instrumentalize others." He notes that one cannot bridge the gap between this and the Christian rule of "no sex outside of marriage" without appealing to other less universal claims such as procreation or spousal unity being an essential purpose of sex. Without denying Mattison's conclusion that belief is necessary to generate moral norms, one can at least go further than Mattison before bringing new beliefs into the picture. One need not introduce new beliefs when existing ones will do. If the natural law is the ultimate source of personal and cultural moral codes, then it should be possible to connect the dots from those moral systems back to the original law written on the heart. The question then becomes what particular beliefs about sexual morality a person is likely to have.

As I have argued elsewhere, while it seems our culture has no sexual morality worth speaking of, an observant person will notice quite a few common precepts.[23] For example, a number of behaviors are nearly universally condemned as wrong, regardless of whether those behaviors carry a legal penalty. Examples include rape, "unsafe" sex, and sexual infidelity. That rape is wrong should be obvious. As for unsafe sex, many public education systems teach children to use techniques and devices to avoid disease and pregnancy. Those who do not are condemned as irresponsible. Sexual infidelity may be commonplace, but it is also looked down upon and frequently dissolves relationships. In fact, those whose partners are sexually unfaithful often feel victimized by the infidelity.

This list of precepts (along with others like them) demonstrates a pattern. People believe that sex should be given and received rather than simply taken—that mere taking falls short of what sex ought to be. Protection against disease and avoidance of illegitimacy indicates that sex should involve the mutual good of those involved, including children that may result from a sexual union. Views against sexual infidelity show that commitment, permanence, and exclusivity are still morally relevant. Combined, these moral precepts suggest that sex should be given within

---

22. Mattison, "The Changing Face of Natural Law," 267–68.
23. What follows is an abbreviated summary of my argument in *As Though It Were Actually True* (Eugene, OR: Resource, 2009), 191–94.

a permanent commitment of goodwill between a man and a woman. In short, they indicate that sex belongs exclusively within traditional marriage. A person may deny any of the preliminary moral beliefs with which the argument began. In fact, few people will remember all of those moral beliefs at any given time; they are forgotten when convenient.[24] Nevertheless, few would be willing to deny most of them. Who wants to be vilified as the person condoning extra-marital promiscuity? Here the contemporary natural lawyer needs divine revelation—God's Word in the Scriptures—to illuminate the situation so that the law in the heart becomes more apparent.

In addition to providing common ground with nonbelievers, engaging the faculty of moral reasoning can help teach the law to Christians as well. The law written in the Bible—the Ten Commandments, or Jesus' summary of them as the law of love—can be just as easily obscured and bent as those written on the heart—a fact that becomes increasingly clear as mainline denominations fall further away from biblical teaching. In the example of premarital sex, it seems as though those within the Church are not much more chaste than those without. Of course, the Sixth Commandment says that adultery is wrong, but many do not consider that this commandment also forbids fornication. One could point out other passages such as Jesus' condemnation of lust in the Sermon on the Mount, Paul's comment on homosexuality in Romans, or the frequent warnings against fornication in the epistles. Nevertheless, when some Bible translations call fornication "sexual immorality,"[25] few consider the gravity and the breadth of what this commandment forbids. Christian or not, the more witnesses that can be brought to bear, the harder it will be for an individual to hide from knowledge of sin, and the more natural Christian moral standards will appear.

The Broadening of Epistemology

However well one is able to work with beliefs that already exist, the eventual need for a supernatural grounding of the natural law has already been established. While the fact of natural law may be useful for a natural

---

24. Such "forgetfulness" is how behaviors such as serial monogamy become common in the first place.

25. This merely invites the suggestion that "*my* behavior is not sexually immoral."

lawyer to persuade an individual on a given moral question, a theory that might be adopted by a broader philosophical community requires more sophisticated justification. The Enlightenment's failed narrow epistemology and the practical necessity of broadening it leave its legacy of naturalism vulnerable, but do not themselves overthrow it. The question of a respectable basis for broadening epistemology remains—a way to move beyond requiring the kind of impossible belief-neutrality demanded by the Enlightenment without the postmodern abandonment of objectivity. A renewed interest in apologetics is one facet of this; many Christian scholars have redirected philosophy into supporting the objective claims of Christianity.[26] Another facet is the fact that a basic knowledge of God has been written on the heart along with the moral law.[27]

As Sennett and Groothuis suggest, a modern revival in natural theology may also help us broaden our epistemology.[28] They describe this new approach as a "modest" natural theology. Rather than attempting to absolutely *prove* the existence of God—which seems increasingly unlikely for any metaphysical theory—Sennett and Groothuis seek to provide plausible arguments. These arguments provide theistic beliefs with a measure of "epistemic pedigree."[29] That is to say, they refute the popular conceit of the Enlightenment that no rational thinking person could possibly believe in God or accept Christianity. Of course, humility in natural theology is essential not just for good philosophy, but for good theology as well. Lutherans are well aware of the dangers of natural theology. The temptation to hold onto an elegant theory that "only" violates a few Scripture verses is a strong one that must nevertheless be resisted. Furthermore, though law is the primary concern of this essay, Lutherans must continue to argue that natural law cannot possibly teach the Gospel. Natural theology cannot be as a substitute or even a parallel to the Bible. Its purpose is as a source of resonance in the nonbeliever with revealed Christianity—a way to make man's sinful hatred for God less intellectually credible.

Though Sennett and Groothuis's volume contains a wide variety of reevaluated arguments for theism in light of this new situation, Paul

---

26. James F. Sennett and Douglas Groothuis (eds.), *In Defense of Natural Theology* (Downers Grove, IL: InterVarsity, 2005), 10–11.
27. Romans 1:20.
28. Sennett and Groothuis, *In Defense of Natural Theology*, 15–16.
29. Sennett and Groothuis, *In Defense of Natural Theology*, 16.

Copan's version of the moral argument for God's existence is most relevant in this context.[30] He begins by critiquing David Hume's approach to morality on many of the grounds mentioned in this essay, such as the inability of skepticism to serve as a foundation and the unsustainable reduction of morality to common feelings. Copan then proceeds to argue for an account of morality that is much closer to our actual moral experience—that there are moral first principles that one intuitively knows to be objectively true. The inability of naturalistic explanations to account for this objective moral truth has already been noted, but Copan goes on to argue that a theistic explanation is a far better fit to what is known. Not only is a supremely good God a natural explanation for objective goodness in creation, but "a personal Creator, who made human persons in his image, serves as the ontological basis for the existence of objective moral values, moral obligation, human dignity and rights."[31] Copan argues that these moral facts cannot simply float about disconnected from any kind of personhood. If moral facts are objectively true for all human persons, then the most likely explanation is a personal being whom humans are intended and obligated to reflect. A good natural law theory does need to be supernaturally grounded. If natural law is indeed our actual experience, then this fact cuts both ways. The theory of natural law may depend on belief in God, but the fact of natural law itself points to God.

Such approaches cannot convince by rational argument that Jesus Christ is Lord, for this is impossible. Neither are they meant to prove that God exists, for this is unnecessary—humans already know that He does, whether we admit it or not. The great strength in these approaches is in removing our excuses for doubting God and His law. Nevertheless, simply removing excuses is not enough. There remains the matter of man's motivation to make excuses in the first place. Honestly examining the law written on our hearts cannot help but reveal that we have utterly failed to live up to it. In such a situation, the existence of a just God is almost the worst news imaginable. The only worse news is that no God exists at all. As Budziszewski points out, if no one gave the law, then nobody exists who can give us the forgiveness we need after breaking it.[32] This dilemma has the same solution it has always had. We are assured of

---

30. Paul Copan, "Hume and the Moral Argument," in *In Defense of Natural Theology*, 200–225.
31. Copan, "Hume and the Moral Argument," 224.
32. Budziszewski, *The Line through the Heart*, 36.

the forgiveness won for us on the cross, apart from our own ability to conform to the law. When salvation comes through faith in Christ rather than works of the law, one is freed from his chief reason to be dishonest about the laws written on his heart. Though much can be discerned from the natural law even without reliance on Christian doctrine, it can only go so far without the revealed Gospel. We cannot refrain from telling the whole story. We may have a great deal of common ground with the nonbeliever, but it does eventually come to an end. Our confidence in proclaiming the truth must not end with our common ground.

THE CONVERSATIONS CONTINUE

Despite its historical difficulties, the natural law can have both an immediate and potential utility. The former can be found in its present reality in the hearts of each man and woman. Moral common ground already exists; by learning about its nature, we can learn to use it effectively in our conversations. Rather than presentations of merely personal moralities with no common understanding, these conversations may begin to bear the possibility of persuasion on moral matters. The potential utility is in the theory itself becoming a more explicit part of common ethical thought. There remains much work to be done before this becomes a reality, particularly on the epistemological front.

Without a solid means of discerning between true and false intuition, moral intuition will drown in a sea of illegitimate appeals to authority. Likewise, the necessity of certain metaphysical beliefs remains a challenge in a secular society. While postmodernism has created possibilities for discussing natural law more openly, postmodernism simultaneously makes every truth claim simply a matter of personal opinion. Complete neutrality in evaluating ideas is impossible, but objectivity cannot be discarded along with it. A scorched earth policy should not be used. Whether the idea of natural law will reclaim a prominent role in the field of ethics is up for debate. Even in the best of circumstances, Christians must not confuse natural law with a panacea for the world's problems, or natural law theory with God's Word. Because of the difficulty in recognizing our transgressions of the moral law, as long as we are sinners, we will be tempted to do so. It is impossible to resolve this human conflict before Judgment Day.

Nevertheless, although natural law cannot solve all our problems, it is still worthy of our attention. In our morally confused society, natural law has potential for resolving that confusion for the simple reason that it exists. No matter how corrupt people are or become, they are still confronted with the *ought*. One cannot understand human nature without understanding this fact. If it is indeed a worthy goal to help those caught up in the current moral conundrum, then we cannot afford to neglect natural law. A struggle exists in the hearts of all mankind. God's law calls us to be holy, yet we are anything but. The natural law can help expose our plight. God's law, revealed in nature and recorded in the infallible Scriptures, still curbs and exposes our sin and points out our need for a Savior. To explain why we struggle and why we transgress what God has commanded, we would do well to begin with what is already known. Only then we can point to God's solution to our struggle and transgression of His law: the person and work of His Son, Jesus Christ.

GLOSSARY

Antinomianism. From Greek for "against the law." Antinomians maintain that a Christian is free from all moral law and that the Gospel causes knowledge of sin and repentance.

Book of Concord. Contains the confessional writings, or symbolical books, of the Evangelical Lutheran Church, including the three Ecumenical Creeds (Apostles', Nicene, Athanasian); the unaltered Augsburg Confession and its Apology; Luther's Small and Large Catechisms; the Smalcald Articles; the Treatise on the Power and Primacy of the Pope; and the Formula of Concord. The German edition appeared officially June 25, 1580, fifty years after the presentation of the Augsburg Confession; the Latin edition appeared 1584.

cause. A Greek philosophical term used in scholastic theology, also used during the period of Lutheran orthodoxy. A system of cause and effect describes how the world changes and remains the same. Tangible matter is the passive, *material cause* that an agent or subject (*efficient cause*) shapes through the structure of his thought (*formal cause*) toward a specific goal (*final cause*). For example, when speaking of the operation of the Holy Spirit through Scripture to create faith, the *material cause* is Scripture: human words written down. Yet those words do not come from human agents but are the inspired Word of God (*formal cause*) flowing from the Holy Spirit (*efficient cause*) in order to create faith and new life in a Christian (*final cause*).

Decalogue. The fundamental moral law in the form of ten sentences (Greek: *deka logoi*, Exodus 34:28). When God created people, He wrote the law into their hearts. Paul maintains that the Gentiles, who have not the Decalogue, carry out its precepts by nature and thereby show that the works of the law are written in their hearts (Romans 2:14–15). Luther said that the Ten Commandments do not concern Gentiles and Christians, but only Jews (AE 135:161–74). The Bible neither numbers the Commandments nor determines their respective position. The Evangelical Lutheran and the Roman Catholic Churches draw the second from Exodus 20:7, the third from Exodus 20:8–11, and make Exodus 20:17a the ninth and Exodus 20:17b the tenth. The respective Reformed, Orthodox Christian, and Jewish numbering of the commandments differs from the Lutheran and the Roman Catholic numbering.

deontology. From Greek *deon* ("duty") and *logos* ("study of"). Ethics of duty rather than right or goodness.

existentialism. A philosophical position popularized by Søren Kierkegaard (1813–1855) and others, including the more contemporary Jean-Paul Sartre (1905–1980; an irrationalist). Theologians associated with existentialism include Rudolf Bultmann (1884–1976; Lutheran), Karl Barth (1886–1968; Reformed), Bernard Lonergan (1904–1984; Roman Catholic), and Karl Rahner (1904–1984; Roman Catholic). Contrary to the Aristotelian view, which holds that objects of thought have an essence that can be known through rational processes of reflection or inquiry, existentialists generally insist that in the case of man no such essence is prior in time to the actual existence of human consciousness. Among several themes, existentialists emphasize man's freedom and his responsibility for his nature and all his choices; the anxiety (*angst*) that man faces when he recognizes that he is responsible for the consequences of his decisions; and man as himself being the source of value. Existentialists say that once one realizes and courageously accepts the fact that human freedom necessarily gives rise to anxiety, which affects all one's knowledge and volition, one is an authentic person. Authenticity is an important existentialist theme.

Gnosticism. From Greek, *gnosis*, "knowledge." This religious movement has its roots in pre-Christian times, though it flowered during the second and third century AD and has experienced a modern revival after discoveries at Nag Hammadi, Egypt. Gnosticism draws on many ancient traditions and often emphasizes occult lore, magic words, and secret names. In contrast to the rational insight of the classical mind, the basic theme of Gnosticism is redemption from the material world (matter considered evil; ordered cosmos has a malevolent purpose) and escape into a world of freedom, thus achieving the liberty implied in human spirit. The soul, escaping from matter, is to be reunited with the *pleroma*, or fullness, of God.

idealism. System of philosophy that ascribes existence to ideas or thought perceptions rather than to material objects; that is, the essence of the world as a whole and of its various parts does not consist in phenomena that can be perceived with senses, but in "ideas" of external perceptions. The metaphysical idealism of Plato ("extreme realism") holds that forms (ideals that people discover in the process of thought, such as "equality," "circularity," etc.) exist eternally and unchangingly. For Aristotle, ideas rely on grounding in the eternal thought of the Unmoved Mover. Idealism suggests that reality belongs to the idea rather than to the phenomenon. The degree of reality attributed to any phenomenal form is to be measured on the scale in which it embodies the original idea. Enlightenment- and romantic-era idealism is marked by Kant's concept of the rather inapproachable idea of a "thing in itself" (*ding an sich*), and Hegel's understanding of history and being as a thesis encountering conflict in its antithesis and moving on to greater being as a synthesis of that event. Modern psychological idealism tries to answer the question: Do things exist in themselves (realism), or do only the ideas we have of them exist? It holds that there is no reality independent of consciousness. A person cannot be sure of the reality of a tree, but only of his personal perception, mental picture, or idea of a tree.

ius divinum. Latin for "divine right." God's right and authority over man; His principles, laws, or orders for man, which are unalterable. Often seen in the form *iure/jure divino*, "according to divine right."

ius gentium. Latin for "law of nations." Originally, law governing aliens subject to Rome as well as their relations with Roman citizens. Today, this term is sometimes used to refer to public, international law, or sometimes appears as a synonym for natural law.

ius humanum. Latin for "human right." Humanly arranged laws or rights, which can be altered. Often seen in the form *iure/jure humano*, "according to human right."

Law and Gospel. "The Law is properly a divine doctrine in which God's righteous, unchangeable will is revealed. It shows what the quality of a person should be in his nature, thoughts, words, and works, in order that he may be pleasing and acceptable to God. It also threatens its transgressors with God's wrath and temporal and eternal punishments. For, as Luther writes against the . . . [Antinomians], 'Everything that reproves sin is and belongs to the Law: its particular office is to rebuke sin and to lead to the knowledge of sins' (Romans 3:20; 7:7).' Because unbelief is the root and wellspring of ‹all sins that must be rebuked and reproved›, the Law rebukes unbelief also" (FC SD V 17).

"The Gospel is properly the kind of teaching that shows what a person who has not kept the Law (and therefore is condemned by it) is to believe. It teaches that Christ has paid for and made satisfaction for all sins [Romans 5:9]. Christ has gained and acquired for an individual—without any of his own merit—forgiveness of sins, righteousness that avails before God, and eternal life [Romans 5:10]" (FC Ep V 5).

Law and Gospel do not differ if Law is taken in a broad sense, as in Isaiah 2:3, or if Gospel is taken in a broad sense, as in Mark 1:1. They do not contradict each other. Both are God's Word; both are in the Old Testament and New Testament; both are to be applied to people everywhere, including Christians. Differences: (a) The Law was written into man's heart: the Gospel is not known by nature, but was revealed through Jesus and the Word of God. (b) The Law contains commandments of what we are to do and not to do and how we are to be; the Gospel reveals what God has done and still does for our salvation. (c) The Law promises eternal life conditionally; the Gospel promises it freely. (d) The Law demands perfect fulfillment and pronounces curses and threats if there is no perfect fulfillment; the Gospel has only promises and comforting assurances. (e) The purpose of the Law is to serve as a curb, mirror, and guide (see also FC VI); the purpose of the Gospel is to forgive sins and give heaven and salvation as a free gift. Law and Gospel are both operative in conversion. The very nature of justification excludes the Law and leaves the Gospel as the only means whereby God justifies the sinner. The incentive power of the Gospel and the criteria of the Law are operative in sanctification.

Luther Renaissance. During the nineteenth century, pietism, Rationalism, and German nationalism contributed toward broader interest in earlier forms of Lutheranism, including the works of Martin Luther. The reawakening of confessional Lutheranism in various forms and the ensuing controversies helped to develop a body of literature on doctrinal and historical themes dealing with Luther. In the twentieth century, a more academic "back-to-Luther" movement, sparked partly by Karl Holl, tried to discern the motives of Luther's coworkers and successors. In particular, the Ludensian School strongly emphasized Luther's theology as the legitimate renewal of New Testament thinking; it stressed that Philip Melanchthon and the theologians of the Orthodox Lutheran period did not always grasp the depth of Luther's thought. The Luther Renaissance also played a part in European and American neo-orthodoxy.

natural law. From Latin, *lex naturalis*. A term used in various senses and more or less synonymous with "natural justice" (*ius naturae, ius naturale*), the "law of nations" (*ius gentium*), and "natural rights." Following Aristotle, early Greek Stoics further developed the concept of natural law, asserting that behind all changing laws of man is the rational, changeless law of nature. Because human reason reflects this rationality, man can know not only what is, but also what ought to be. The content of natural law, they believed, is deducible from those rules of conduct that are similar among widely separated peoples. Roman jurists further developed the concept of natural law. Early Latin Church Fathers identified the natural law concept with the primitive natural revelation of God in man's heart, the innate knowledge of right and wrong, and regarded it as evidence of the truth of Romans 2:14–15. This concept was further developed, but not fundamentally modified, by medieval thinkers. The best-known of these is Thomas Aquinas, who divided all law into four classes: (1) eternal law (existing only in the mind of God); (2) divine law (part of eternal law and directly revealed to men); (3) natural law (discernible by human reason and the knowledge of which has been moving from the imperfect to the perfect); (4) human law (implementation of natural law within the changing situations of life).

The Protestant Reformation generally accepted the patristic view of natural law. Martin Luther and Philip Melanchthon followed Augustine of Hippo in regarding the Decalogue as the directly revealed codification of natural law. But the Renaissance, especially in its humanistic aspects, deemphasized the divine and overemphasized the purely rational character of natural law. As a result, in the age of reason the concept of natural law was pressed into service as the ideological basis of "natural rights," the "social contract," constitutional government based on the consent of the governed, and the right of revolution, of which the most typical and politically effective expressions of this view are the American Declaration of Independence and the French Declaration of the Rights of Man and of the Citizen. Early nineteenth-century individualistic, liberal, democratic thought and action were largely the fruits of this concept. The concept of natural law has been heavily critiqued, especially from two quarters: (1) the historical school of jurisprudence regards law as nothing more than a product of historical development; (2) positive social scientists regard law as nothing more than a result of personal and social relationships. Writers who profess to have rediscovered the spiritual and teleological character of the universe support the concept of natural law. In Lutheran theology, natural law is a remnant of the knowledge with which man was created. Because man's awareness of natural law was obscured by sin, God gave man the Decalogue and elaborated on it in the Bible. According to the *sola scriptura* principle (Scripture is the highest authority), the law from within (subjective morality) must be interpreted in light of the law from without (objective morality), specifically God's revealed Word, the Bible.

nominalism. From Latin, *nomina*, "names." Philosophers associated with nominalism include Peter Abelard (1079–1142) and William of Ockham (1288–1348). As opposed to realism and idealism, nominalism holds that only individual objects have real existence, while "universals" (general or abstract ideas) are but names. For example, the idea of a tree does not really exist in itself; only individual trees exist.

orders of creation. Teaching that emphasizes God's structuring areas of human interaction such as the family, the church, the state, and so on. Several twentieth-century European Protestant leaders, including Karl Barth (1886–1968; Reformed) and Dietrich Bonhoeffer (1906–1945; Lutheran), inferred that along with natural law, the teaching about orders of creation led to the nazification of Germany. In fact, the "German Christian" movement, which supported the claims of Adolf Hilter and his followers, had misappropriated the orders of creation teaching by advocating unswerving support of a hypothetically pure, Aryan race.

realism. Realism is the theory that general abstract ideas have real existence, independent of individual objects. For example, the idea of a circle exists apart from round things.

Scholasticism. Western philosophical system developed by philosopher-theologians at cathedral schools and the new universities, ca. AD 1100–1500. Scholastics used dialectics and speculation in discussing and trying to comprehend, harmonize, and prove doctrines rationally; reasoning came to be patterned largely after that of Aristotle. Scholasticism fought for recognition in the twelfth century; it reached its zenith in the thirteenth century, and declined in the fourteenth and fifteenth centuries. Lutheran Scholastics such as Melanchthon, Chemnitz, and Gerhard sought to systematize Luther's insights using Scholastic categories and approaches. Among Roman Catholics, Scholasticism experienced revivals in the nineteenth and twentieth centuries.

teleology. Greek for "doctrine, theory, or science of the end." Branch of philosophy represented by Plato (428–348 BC), Aristotle (384–322 BC), Anselm of Canterbury (ca. 1033–1109), Thomas Aquinas (1225–1274) and others that studied evidences of design or goal-directed activity (Aristotle's "final cause") in nature. Virtue ethics is inherently teleological; some atheist philosophers who deny design in nature also appeal to teleology.

utilitarianism. Theory elaborated by Jeremy Bentham (1748–1832), John Stuart Mill (1806–1873), and others to which the morality of conduct is determined by its ability to promote the greatest happiness—the attainment of pleasure and the avoidance of pain—of the greatest number of people. Utilitarian themes are present already in the work of Greek philosopher Epicurus (341–270 BC).

via antiqua. Latin for the "old way." Philosophical schools after John Duns Scotus (ca. 1265–1308; followers are called Scotists) or Thomas Aquinas (1225–1274; followers are called Thomists).

via moderna. Latin for the "modern way." Philosophical school formed by followers of William of Ockham (ca. 1288–ca. 1348) in opposition to *via antiqua*. Followers are called Occamists or Nominalists.

STUDY QUESTIONS

ESSAY 1 ✾ CARL E. BRAATEN (PP. 3–15)

1. In the Introduction, the author suggests that Lutheran theologians use something from God to practice their discipline (p. 3). What is it?

2. What relationship "still continues to be a central issue of Christian belief and moral practice" (p. 4)? See also John 1:17 and 2 Corinthians 3:6.

3. Were Christians the first group to recognize that some sort of common, natural law exists among all people?

4. The author lists important historical and political documents informed by various concepts of natural law (p. 5). Can you think of other examples?

5. Where does Paul say that God's law was initially written? See Romans 2:25. What is God's plan to restore His law in our hearts? See Hebrews 10:12–17.

ESSAY 2 ✾ GIFFORD A. GROBIEN (PP. 17–38)

1. In the first section (pp. 18–20), the author notes that, beginning with Hugo Grotius, thinking about natural law changed. What—or *who*—was missing?

1. In the Golden Rule (Matthew 7:12 and Luke 6:31), does Jesus reduce, maintain, or expand our obligation to love others? Explain.
2. The Ten Commandments have been interpreted as summaries of the natural law. What makes actions like murder or stealing "unnatural"?
3. How does Paul account for the fact that people, who have God's law written in their hearts, do not live according to it? See Romans 1:21.
4. Should people trust in their obedience to the law? If not, in whom should they trust? See Romans 3:21–22.

Essay 3 ※ Thomas D. Pearson (pp. 39–63)

1. Scholars disagree on Luther's views about natural law. Why might Luther's views be important for Lutherans today?
2. The author suggests that Luther regarded natural law as "the basic instincts of human beings" (p. 42) What may be some examples of those instincts?
3. Luther tended to accuse, qualify, and scold (p. 49). Should we take that into account when trying to interpret him?
4. Paul wrote that we should "stand firm" in our Christian freedom (see Galatians 5:1–15). What in this passage shows that Paul did not mean "anything goes"?
5. Justified by God's grace through faith in Christ, faith works through love (Galatians 5:6). Give some examples of this in the life of a believer.

Essay 4 ※ Roland Ziegler (pp. 65–78)

1. The author notes the primary use of the law in the first paragraph (p. 66). What is this primary use according to Romans 3:20?

2. Romans 2:14–15 is the background for natural law in the Lutheran Confessions. Describe the feelings and actions of people when their conscience is accused.
3. Using footnote 10 (p. 68), how might Luther have responded to the suggestion that Christians are obligated to observe *all* Old Testament laws?
4. Ap XXIII uses natural law to argue against forcing ministers to remain single. Would a natural law argument help in the same-sex marriage debate? Why or why not?
5. We cannot justify ourselves before God by our obedience. However, what has God done for us in Christ? See Galatians 4:4–5.

Essay 5 ❋ Armin Wenz (pp. 79–95)

1. Lutheran scholars frequently equate natural law with the "orders of creation," whereby God creates and preserves earthly life. What might make such an approach attractive today?
2. How does the author suggest that God's creative and saving work is tied together in the Decalogue (p. 80; see Exodus 20)?
3. In Mark 10:4–6, Jesus goes back to the biblical account of the creation of male and female to talk about marriage. What does Jesus' approach suggest?
4. Paul warns that in the last days false teachers will argue against marriage and the enjoyment of certain foods (1 Timothy 4:1–5). How are such teachings "unnatural"?
5. How is God's good creation "sanctified" for holy use by believers (1 Timothy 4:5)?

Essay 6 ❋ Jacob Corzine (pp. 99–115)

1. Many people have left their home countries in order to practice their religious beliefs freely. Others, like Stahl, have chosen to remain. What are the pluses and minuses of each?

2. The author presents *philosophical* and *historical* influences on Stahl's life and work. What other influences affect the way a Christian approaches the world?
3. The author suggests that Stahl always view individuals as "a person within a larger community" (p. 107). Would many people share Stahl's view today?
4. One of the purposes of government is to bear the sword of God's punishment (Romans 13:4). Provide some examples of this.
5. "Sword" is also used to describe the power of God's Word (see Ephesians 6:17; Hebrews 4:12). How is this sword rightly used?

Essay 7 ❋ John T. Pless (pp. 117–134)

1. Some contemporary Lutheran scholars are attempting a retrieval of natural law due to moral concerns. What moral issues are particularly troubling today?
2. For Elert, law is both our security in the fallen creation and God's retribution for our sins. How could this be applied to a discussion about traditional marriage?
3. Paul uses the word *law* in several ways. What kind of law does he describe in Romans 7:14–24?
4. Like Paul, believers find themselves in conflict as they serve two "laws." What are these two laws (Romans 7:25)?
5. Who will rescue Paul—and you—from "this body of death" (Romans 7:24–25)?

Essay 8 ❋ Robert C. Baker (pp. 135–156)

1. The author mentions that there are at least two "schools" among confessional Lutherans (p. 136). What are they? How do their teachings differ?

2. How does Paul treat incompatible teaching, which results in division, within the Church (see 1 Corinthians 1:10–17)?

3. Among a list of immoral deeds (Romans 1:18–32), Paul mentions the chief sin of unbelief. Why is this important to remember when discussing human sexuality?

4. What claims do Luke, Peter, and Paul make about Scripture (Luke 24:27; Acts 4:12; 2 Timothy 3:15–17; 2 Peter 1:21)?

5. What claims about Scripture—and Jesus' connection to Scripture—are made in St. John's Gospel (3:16; 10:35; 14:6, 26; 17:3; 20:31)?

Essay 9 ❋ Marianne Howard Yoder and J. Larry Yoder, STS (pp. 157–177)

1. Natural law theory has been to determine whether or not human laws are just. Besides civil rights issues, what other issues might benefit from such an approach?

2. Today, *normative* moral statements (what we should or shouldn't do) are reduced to *descriptive* statements about behavior or social customs. List some examples.

3. In a discussion with a colleague, the second author quoted the marriage rite (service). In what ways do our worship rites reflect—and reinforce—what we believe?

4. Christians are "crucified with Christ": they die to sin and live in repentant faith in Christ (Galatians 2:19b–20). What makes that dying so difficult?

5. Using Romans 3:23, what is the bad news of our condition before God without His grace in Jesus Christ? What is God's good—even great!—news?

ESSAY 10 ✳ CARL E. ROCKROHR (PP. 179–197)

1. God extends His providential care to believers and unbelievers (Matthew 5:45). How does this inform Christians about treating their neighbor?

2. Jesus summarized the law as loving God and loving one's neighbor (Luke 10:25–37). How do we see love being fulfilled through the Good Samaritan's actions?

3. Christians are to obey and support legitimate government (Matthew 22:15–22). What are disciples to do when the Gospel is suppressed (Acts 5:27–32)?

4. Paul summarizes the Decalogue's second table in Romans 13:9: "You shall love your neighbor as yourself." Rephrase Paul's summary using your own words.

5. The author suspended "Western 'scientific doubts'" (p. 197) when speaking to his non-Christian neighbor. What other approaches are helpful when sharing the Gospel?

ESSAY 11 ✳ RYAN C. MACPHERSON (PP. 201–219)

1. Traditionally, society was understood as having *originated* from the family. Why do people today assume the reverse—that society *creates* or *defines*—families?

2. Citing a number of examples (pp. 203–4), the author suggests that basic moral principles have always been assumed. Can you think of other examples?

3. The author claims that human beings flourish best in (presumably loving) families—not simply as individuals or as citizens. Do you agree? Why or why not?

4. Describe the relationships between Christ and His Church and a husband and his wife (Ephesians 5:22–33).

5. In Christ, male and female are being renewed in God's image (see Genesis 1:27; Ephesians 4:23; Colossians 1:15; 3:10). Apply this to the Christian family today.

Essay 12 ❋ Korey D. Maas (pp. 221–234)

1. Some people argue that because civil laws reflect Christian values, they should be rejected. List three laws promoting values share by Christians and non-Christians alike.
2. The author distinguishes moral law, which *prescribes* behavior, from physical law, which *describes* behavior (p. 224). Provide some examples of *prescriptive* law.
3. Jesus condemns not only murder but also the sinful inclination to harming someone else (see Matthew 5:22; 15:19). Why is this insight important for Christians?
4. Jesus says that the devil comes to "steal and kill and destroy" (John 10:10). In contrast, what does Jesus comes to do for us?
5. How did Jesus, the Good Shepherd, show His great love for us? What is our God-graced response toward our neighbor (John 3:16; 10:11; 1 John 3:16)?

Essay 13 ❋ Adam S. Francisco (pp. 235–247)

1. The author notes difficulties in arguing for natural law with those having a naturalistic (non-spiritual) worldview (p. 236). What are some of those difficulties?
2. The author suggests that Western Muslims tend to view Islam as more of an ideology than a religion. Do you think that most non-Muslim Westerners share this view?
3. The author finds a link between the Muslim desire to see Islam advance and the Islamic view of nature. Does this remark surprise you? Why or why not?

4. Paul provides concrete examples of living a personal life of love and service toward our neighbor (Romans 12:9–21). List some of those examples.

5. What does God desire for us to do for all people? What does God desire for all people concerning His Son, Jesus Christ (see 1 Timothy 2:1–6)?

Essay 14 ✳ Albert B. Collver III (pp. 249–266)

1. Although the concept was older, Cicero (who refers to Zeno) and Philo were among the first to use the term "natural law." Why might knowing this history be important?

2. The author suggests that classical natural law theory assumes that God is primarily known through human reason. Would most people today agree with that view?

3. The author suggests that the variety of natural law theories tends to support the argument that natural law exists (p. 253). Would you agree? Why or why not?

4. Luther wrote, "I believe that I cannot by my own reason or strength believe in Jesus Christ, my Lord, or come to Him." What was Luther denying about human reason in this quote from his Small Catechism?

5. Luther continues: "But the Holy Spirit has called me by the Gospel, enlightened me with His gifts, sanctified and kept me in the truth faith." For Luther, who calls us to faith in Christ? What means does He use to do so?

Essay 15 ✳ Matthew E. Cochran (pp. 267–281)

1. In addition to Hugo Grotius, the author points to David Hume as having negatively influenced natural law theory. What famous claim was made by Hume (p. 268)?

2. The author notes that despite postmodernism's denial of objective morality, people tend to act as if objective morality exists. What are some examples of this?

3. Naturalistic (non-spiritual) law can be distinguished from natural law, which keeps God in the picture. Do you suppose people today would be open to such a view of law?

4. While believing, through the gift of faith (Ephesians 2:8–9), that Jesus Christ is Lord, what should be the attitude of Christians (Philippians 2:5–11)?

5. How might Paul's witness to the Epicureans and Stoics (who taught a natural theory) serve as an example of Christians witness using commonly-held ideas (see Acts 17:16–34)?

Index of Scripture

Index of the
Lutheran Confessions